IBM® WebSphere® System Administration

ON DEMAND COMPUTING BOOKS

On Demand Computing
Fellenstein

Autonomic Computing
Murch

Grid Computing
Joseph and Fellenstein

Business Intelligence for the Enterprise
Biere

DB2 BOOKS

DB2 Express: Application Development and Deployment
Yip, Cheung, Gartner, Liu, and O'Connell

DB2 Universal Database v8.1 Certification Exam 703 Study Guide
Sanders

The Official Introduction to DB2 for z/OS
Sloan

High Availability Guide to DB2
Eaton and Cialini

DB2 Universal Database v8.1 Certification Exams 701 and 706 Study Guide
Sanders

Integrated Solutions with DB2
Cutlip and Medicke

DB2 Universal Database v8.1 Certification Exam 700 Study Guide
Sanders

DB2 for Solaris: The Official Guide
Bauch and Wilding

DB2 Universal Database v8 Handbook for Windows, UNIX, and Linux
Gunning

Advanced DBA Certification Guide and Reference for DB2 Universal Database v8 for Linux, UNIX, and Windows
Snow and Phan

DB2 Universal Database v8 Application Development Certification Guide, Second Edition
Martineau, Sanyal, Gashyna, and Kyprianou

DB2 Universal Database v8 for Linux, UNIX, and Windows Database Administration Certification Guide, Fifth Edition
Baklarz and Wong

DB2 SQL Procedural Language for Linux, UNIX, and Windows
Yip, Bradstock, Curtis, Gao, Janmohamed, Liu, and McArthur

DB2 Universal Database for OS/390 Version 7.1 Certification Guide
Lawson and Yevich

DB2 Version 8: The Official Guide
Zikopoulos, Baklarz, deRoos, and Melnyk

DB2 UDB for OS/390: An Introduction to DB2 OS/390
Sloan and Hernandez

MORE BOOKS FROM IBM PRESS

The Inventor's Guide to Trademarks and Patents
Fellenstein

WebSphere and Lotus: Implementing Collaboration Solutions
Lamb and Laskey

IBM WebSphere: Deployment and Advanced Configuration
Barcia, Hines, Alcott, and Botzum

IBM WebSphere System Administration
Williamson, Chan, Cundiff, Lauzon, and Mitchell

Developing Quality Technical Information, Second Edition
Hargis, Carey, Hernandez, Hughes, Longo, Rouiller, and Wilde

Enterprise Messaging Using JMS and IBM WebSphere
Yusuf

Enterprise Java Programming with IBM WebSphere, Second Edition
Brown, Craig, Hester, Pitt, Stinehour, Weitzel, Amsden, Jakab, and Berg

IBM® WebSphere® System Administration

Leigh Williamson   Shawn Lauzon
Lavena Chan   Christopher C. Mitchell
Roger Cundiff

PRENTICE HALL
Professional Technical Reference
Upper Saddle River, New Jersey 07458
www.phptr.com

Editorial/production supervision: *MetroVoice Publishing Services*
Cover design: *IBM Corporation*
Publisher: *Jeffrey Pepper*
Editorial assistant: *Linda Ramagnano*
Marketing manager: *Robin O'Brien*
IBM Consulting Editor: *Tara Woodman*

 Published by Pearson Education, Inc.
PRENTICE HALL PTR Publishing as Prentice Hall Professional Technical Reference
Upper Saddle River, NJ 07458

Prentice Hall PTR offers excellent discounts on this book when ordered in quantity for bulk purchases or special sales. For more information, please contact: U.S. Corporate and Government Sales, 1-800-382-3419, corpsales@pearsontechgroup.com. For sales outside of the U.S., please contact: International Sales, 1-317-581-3793, international@pearsontechgroup.com.

Printed in the United States of America

First Printing

ISBN   0-13-144604-5

Pearson Education LTD.
Pearson Education Australia PTY, Limited
Pearson Education Singapore, Pte. Ltd.
Pearson Education North Asia Ltd.
Pearson Education Canada, Ltd.
Pearson Educación de Mexico, S.A. de C.V.
Pearson Education — Japan
Pearson Education Malaysia, Pte. Ltd.

Contents _____

Foreword   xi

Preface   xv

About the Authors   xvii

Acknowledgments   xix

CHAPTER 1   Introduction to WebSphere Administration   1

WebSphere Application Server Structure   2
     The Base Application Server Package   2
     The Network Deployment Package   3
Comparison of the Administration in Versions 4 and 5   5
Overview of Administration Tools for Version 5   6
     Command-Line Tools   7
     Administrative Console   7
     Scripting Tool   9
     Java Programming API   10

CHAPTER 2   Administrative Concepts and Architecture   13

Base Application Server Administration   13
     Anatomy of a Server   14
     Configuration   16

Run-time Control   17
Application Deployment   17
Administrative Security   18
Network Deployment Administration   18
Cell Structure   19
Administrative Agents   20
Distributed Administration Services   21
WebSphere Version 5 Configuration Repository   26
Directory Structure   26
Configuration Files, Content, and Structure   29

CHAPTER 3   **Administrative Commands**   **33**

Server Management Commands   34
Starting Servers   34
Stopping Servers   35
Server Status   36
Network Deployment Commands   36
Federation   37
Defederation   39
CleanupNode [Troubleshooting, Network Deployment Only]   40
SyncNode [Troubleshooting]   40
Backup/Restore Commands   41
Backing Up Your Configuration   41
Restoring Your Configuration   42
Other Commands   42
EAR Expander   42
Creating Additional WebSphere Instances   43
Using Ant to Automate WebSphere Commands   45

CHAPTER 4   **WebSphere Administrative Console**   **49**

Administrative Console Environment   49
Administrative Console Overview   49
Accessing the Administrative Console   56
Administrative Console Settings   57
Common Tasks   62

Administrative Console Task Reference   69

   Manage Servers   69

   Manage Applications   74

   Manage Resources   75

   Manage Security   77

   Manage Other Environment Elements   78

   Manage Systems Administration   80

Problem Determination Using the Administrative Console   82

   Status Tray   83

   Troubleshooting Tasks   84

CHAPTER 5   **Administrative Scripting**   **87**

Wsadmin Scripting Environment   87

   Wsadmin Overview   87

   Invoking Wsadmin Tool   89

   Properties   92

   Managing Configuration with Wsadmin   97

   Managing Applications with Wsadmin   111

   Managing Live Run-time Components with Wsadmin   121

Task Reference   129

   Manage Servers   130

   Manage Applications   157

   Manage Resources   168

   Manage Security   182

   Manage Other Environment Elements   199

   Manage System Administration   211

   Troubleshooting   217

Online Interactive Help   221

Problem Determination Using Wsadmin   225

   Wsadmin Trace Log   225

   Run-Time Log   225

   Configuration Validation   226

Common Admin Scenarios Using Wsadmin   226

   Scenario 1—Install and Start an Application on a New Server   226

   Scenario 2—Install and Start an Application on a New Cluster   229

CHAPTER 6   **Administration Programming Interfaces**   **235**

JMX   235
    Introduction to JMX   235
    JMX in WebSphere   236
Operational Management   238
    The AdminClient Interface   238
    Accessing MBeans   239
    Using MBeans   241
    Using Event Notifications   242
Configuration Management   244
    Configuration Objects   244
    The Configuration Service Interfaces   245
    Identifying Configuration Objects   247
    Locating Configuration Objects   248
    Using Configuration Objects   249
Application Management   256
    Application Preparation   256
    Managing Applications   263
    Using the ConfigService for Deployment Options   269
Building and Running an Administrative Client Program   269
Sample Tasks   270
Where to Find Additional Information   270

APPENDIX A   **Administrative Integration on z/OS**   **273**

Process Model Integration   273
Operations Model Integration   276
    Control Process JCL (BBO5ACR)   280
    Servant Process JCL   280
    STOP BBOS001   281
Workload Management Model Integration   281
Security Model Integration   283
    Global Security   283
    SSL   284
    SAF Key Ring   287
    ICSF   288
    Local OS   289
    zSAS   289

APPENDIX B   **WebSphere Version 5 Run Time MBeans   291**

Overall List of JMX MBean Types in WebSphere Version 5   291
Individual MBean Documentation   295

APPENDIX C   **WebSphere Version 5 Configuration**
                Models   297

Overview of Configuration Models   297
Configuration Model Tables   299

APPENDIX 4   **CD-ROM Contents   307**

Installing the Trial Version of WebSphere from the CD-ROM   308

              Index   313

Foreword

T his book was written by a team of experts that I've known for several years now and have only come to respect more and more. Leigh, Lavena, Roger, Shawn and Chris represent *the* driving force behind the WebSphere management system. The contribution of time and effort that they've put into this book is evidence of the dedication and confidence they have in what we're trying to accomplish with the WebSphere Application Server. The clarity and completeness of this book is an exquisite example of the precision and thoroughness they bring to their work. The resounding and enthusiastic acceptance we've gotten from customers of WebSphere, and especially its management system in Version 5, are a testament to their skill and leadership within our industry.

The Java Application Server industry is coalescing. The principles of application integration middleware and more specifically the use of component based technologies for implementing applications is beyond its infancy. Using an application server has become a critical success factor for production application development. Component based programming enables program modularity, composition and re-use. Application serving separates application business logic concerns from the concerns of the underlying information technology. Both of these attributes net increased programmer productivity. More importantly, they enable businesses to exploit information systems to benefit their business needs in a more timely fashion. Enterprises no longer spend time questioning whether they *should* use middleware—it's just accepted that middleware application servers yield tremendous benefits to business application developers and the businesses that run those applications.

However, application serving is about more than just developing applications to use component architectures. It is about creating a hosting environment for deployment and execution in which those applications and the resources they depend on can be managed to optimize the economy of those applications. The best managed hosting environments maximize the efficient utilization of computing resources and total systems throughput—minimizing the cost of the hosting environment at the same time as maximizing the productivity benefit to the business. The management system is essential to enabling those benefits. The degree to which the system can be controlled deterministically has a profound impact on the degree to which these positive economic results can be achieved under different circumstances. The degree to which this flexibility is encapsulated in well formed and intuitive concepts determines the degree to which these results can be achieved easily and reliably in any given circumstance.

With Version 5 of WebSphere we embarked on a significant re-architecture and re-engineering of the WebSphere management infrastructure. The decision to do so was painful. The prior management infrastructure was proving to be unscalable, unextensible, inconsistent across editions, and more fragile than we wanted for a mission-critical product. On the other hand, tearing into the management system at that level meant ripping up core elements of the application server itself. It meant investing in a massive undertaking, and taking on a significant risk. The team engaged in an intense debate over different approaches, factored in a tremendous number of new concepts and technologies that had to be integrated, and worked through huge technical challenges to find a balance between preserving release-to-release compatibility vs. enabling the value of other approaches as we transitioned from the old to the new. The team invested enormous hours and made tremendous personal sacrifices. The result is the stable, scalable, extensible and durable base for managing WebSphere that we see in the product now—one that continues to demonstrate those traits as we've moved through Versions 5.0, 5.1, 6.0 Technology for Developers and as we develop the next release of WebSphere. Not only has the WebSphere management system proved valuable to the foundation product, but this same management system is the foundation of the entire WebSphere Platform solution suite—including WebSphere Business Integrator Server and WebSphere Portal Server.

To be clear, the WebSphere management system is about *middleware management*, not *enterprise system management*. The distinction is subtle, but important. Middleware management confines itself to managing the concepts introduced by the middleware and the applications that are hosted by that middleware. Enterprise system management is about managing the entirety of the information system—including the application server, the data management or information integration system, any legacy enterprise integration systems, the network infrastructure, the underlying operating system and hardware, and everything else that contributes an end-to-end flow of information and business automation.

Nonetheless, the middleware management system plays a vital role in enabling the application server. First, it allows customers to manage the application server right out of the box—even if they don't have or use an enterprise management system. It also establishes a consistent and stable definition of the information model on which the application server can base its execution model. For example, the application server can assume that applications will be deployed in a particular way, prepared for execution, and located in a place where they can be safely loaded by the application server. The information model establishes the configuration attributes that affect server behavior, and basic topological concepts such as clustering that affect scaling assumptions for the server. The middleware management system establishes the basic lifecycle elements that affect availability, failover, recovery, and maintenance. Without middleware management, the application server is just an execution shell with limited potential to add value to the enterprise. On the other hand, when the application server is coupled with a management system, its potential for adding value to the business is amplified many fold.

Finally, the middleware management system plays an equally vital role to enterprise systems management as well. In particular, it proxies the application server and its information model to the enterprise—enabling the enterprise management system to leverage that definition as a point of consistency within its overall understanding of the information system.

Managing anything, whether it is people, your checkbook, a business, an information system, or anything else, can only ever be accomplished successfully if you have a clear understanding of the thing that you're managing. That means you have to conceive an image of what it is, how it behaves, including both its actions and reactions, what it is capable of doing (and not), what you want it do, and how to get it to do that. Managing WebSphere is no different.

The basic conceptual model of managing WebSphere is very simple: you create servers, you configure the resources available to each server, you deploy applications to those servers and attach them to the resources available on those servers, and then you start your applications. WebSphere gains a lot of value from the simplicity of that conceptual model.

The practical realities of management can also involve a lot more variation. For example, to get horizontal scalability and continuous availability you will likely want to incorporate several computers and cluster your servers. To protect your applications you will have to create a user registry, set authorization policies, and configure the level of protection you need. To interconnect your applications you will have to configure your messaging network. To optimize the performance and utilization of your system you will have to tune the execution environment. To gain efficiency you may collocate two or more applications on the same server. To maintain isolation between applications you may choose to place different applications on different servers. To maintain your applications you will need to manage the lifecycle of your applications.

Keeping track of all of the possible topology options, configuration parameters, control commands and deployment processes isn't easy. This book is the definitive bible and reference for understanding the conceptual model of administering WebSphere—starting from the architectural premise for topology and administration, through to the largest set of common activities and best practices that I've ever seen on WebSphere administration, and on to a complete listing of all of the user, scripting, command line and programming interfaces supported by WebSphere for managing a WebSphere installation. This is a book worth reading, and leaving at your finger tips for whenever you need guidance on how to manage WebSphere.

My greatest regards go to this team, and to all of you that have found ways to leverage the value of the WebSphere Application Server to benefit your enterprise.

—Rob High

IBM Distinguished Engineer and WebSphere foundation, Chief Architect

Member, IBM Academy of Technology

Preface

This book is part of a series intended to extend your understanding of WebSphere Application Server Version 5. It was written by some of the same team that created the administrative functions of the WebSphere Version 5 product. A great deal of effort went into the WebSphere product, and we put the same effort into making this book. You will find many pieces of inside information about how the administrative tools work and how to get the most from the product on a day-to-day basis.

INTENDED AUDIENCE FOR THIS BOOK

Administration of a product as sophisticated as WebSphere Application Server Version 5 can mean many things to different people. Some people just want to install their applications and run them. Others need to understand the details of the product architecture to plan deployment of their environment. Still others want to write custom Java code that controls one or more instances of WebSphere.

The primary target audience for this book is the administrator who wants to learn about all of the tools shipped with WebSphere Version 5 and how to make the most of those tools. As the title implies, this is a handbook for product administrators. We have tried to create a book that administrators will keep by their side, ready to consult at a moment's notice to recall the details of any specific task.

Substantial information is included about the Java programming interfaces for administration, and those who are interested in writing their own custom administration programs in Java should be able to use the material in Chapter 6 to accomplish this. However, the primary focus of the book is to help the administrator use the tools available with the product out of the box.

The focus of this handbook is on the how, more than the why. We attempt to compile information about how to perform any of the administrative tasks available for the product, using any of the several tools that come with WebSphere. Another book in this series, *IBM® WebSphere®: Deployment and Advanced Configuration* (forthcoming Prentice Hall, 2005), discusses many of the best practices for product deployment strategies, particularly in large enterprise-scale environments. In this administrator's handbook, we attempt to cover the details of how to accomplish each task involved in the various strategies described in that and other books.

WHAT YOU NEED TO KNOW BEFORE READING THIS BOOK

To get the most out of this book, you should have an understanding of basic J2EE concepts. This book does not go into the details of J2EE application components or their development. Another book in this series, *Enterprise Java™ Programming with IBM® WebSphere™*, Second Edition (Addison-Wesley, 2004), is an ideal book to read to learn about the J2EE architecture and development techniques.

To get the most from Chapter 6 of this book, you should know the Java language and how to create and run general-purpose programs (not necessarily J2EE applications) in Java. Because this chapter describes how to create a program that performs administrative functions for WebSphere Version 5, and because all Version 5 administrative tasks are based on Java Management Extensions (JMX), you will be able to get more from the chapter if you have some familiarity with JMX and the JMX programming style. Several books in print currently provide a good foundation in this subject, including *Java™ and JMX: Building Manageable Systems* (Addison-Wesley, 2003).

SOFTWARE NEEDED FOR THE EXAMPLES

The only software needed to test the sample code in the book is the WebSphere Application Server Version 5 product itself. Most examples work in the Base Application Server edition, although some examples require the Network Deployment edition and these are indicated in the text. The required software (WebSphere Application Server Version 5) is available on the CD-ROM that accompanies this book.

Since Version 5.0 was released in late 2002, many subsequent fix packs and point releases have been delivered. Any of the Version 5 releases can be used to try the tasks described in this book. We have made an attempt to specifically indicate when a task is only applicable to a single Version 5 fix-pack release level.

About the Authors

he authors of this book all played significant parts in the development and delivery of WebSphere Application Server administrative features.

LEIGH WILLIAMSON

Leigh Williamson has been working for IBM in Austin, Texas, for 15 years on projects related to distributed computing systems and system management. He holds a Bachelor of Science in Computer Science from Nova Southeastern University, and a Masters in Computer Engineering from University of Texas at Austin. Leigh contributed to the Version 3 and 4 releases of WebSphere and led the team that designed and implemented the new administrative architecture for WebSphere Version 5. He holds several patents in various areas of software design, and is coauthor of the book *Java™ and JMX: Building Manageable Systems*. Prior to working for IBM, Leigh spend many years doing engineering development for TRW and the U.S. Navy.

CHRISTOPHER C. MITCHELL

Chris Mitchell is a Senior Software Engineer at IBM WebSphere development lab in Research Triangle Park, North Carolina. He is the lead architect for WebSphere console and configuration and has been a development team leader through a number of WebSphere releases. Prior to joining IBM, Chris worked for 10 years with companies on object-oriented design and development tools as well as solutions for the health-care industry. Chris currently holds a Bachelor of Science in Computer Science from Ohio University.

SHAWN LAUZON

Shawn Lauzon is a software engineer who has been working at IBM for the past eight years, originally in Rochester, Minnesota, and the past three years in Austin, Texas. A graduate of the University of Wisconsin, he was exposed to computing at an early age when his dad brought home a Radio Shack TRS-80 with a full 4K of memory. He learned to program BASIC on that computer and has continued to write software ever since. He is currently working on the next release of WebSphere with aspect-oriented software design.

LAVENA CHAN

Lavena Chan is a software engineer at IBM in Austin, Texas. She has six years of experience in the middleware field. She holds a Masters of Business Administration from the University of Texas at Austin. Her areas of expertise include install, graphical user interface, application management, and scripting programming.

ROGER CUNDIFF

Roger Cundiff has been developing systems management and component-based software for most of the last 18 years, despite the fact that he doesn't believe it could really have been that long. In 1997 he was the initial member of the development team for management of application servers at the IBM lab in Austin, Texas, and he continues to work on the development of WebSphere Systems Management there today.

Acknowledgments _____

The authors would like to express their gratitude to the technical reviewers whose input has greatly enhanced the content of this book. Particular thanks go to Christopher Vignola who kept the details of the z/OS environment straight and supplied numerous other helpful suggestions for improvement. Rob High, as chief architect for the WebSphere family of products, provided important conceptual feedback as well as great encouragement. Ajay Apte was an essential reviewer for the application management details as well as many great ideas for general book content. Qinhua Wang provided vital input related to configuration programming. James Kochuba went over the scripting chapter with a careful eye, helping to ensure the accuracy of that section. In addition to the technical reviewers, the authors would like to thank John Neidhart and the editors and staff at Prentice Hall for their help, support, and encouragement in the production of this book.

INDIVIDUAL ACKNOWLEDGMENTS

I would like to acknowledge the support of my family, Cheryl and Claire, without whom all of the work would be without purpose. I would also like to thank my coauthors who stuck with the project all the way through and sacrificed their nights and weekends to make this book a reality. I'd like to dedicate my work on this book to my father, who would have loved to have seen it reach completion.

—Leigh Williamson

I would especially like to thank my wife Sherry for her patience and support and my daughter Madison for making this effort worthwhile through her smile.

—Chris Mitchell

I would like to thank my husband, children, parents, and my friend Juniarti Suryakusuma for their support while I was working on this book. My special thanks to Leigh Williamson for giving me the chance to coauthor this book.

—Lavena Chan

To my dad, who brought home our first computer 20-some years ago, and my wife, who encouraged me to complete this book.

—Shawn Lauzon

I would like to thank my wife, Sharon, for her patience, support, and inspiration, and my children, Caitlin and Addison, for bringing me the joy of being a father each day. I also want to thank my parents, Roger and Connie, for making everything possible. We miss you, Mom.

I would like to thank my coauthors for their perseverance in completing this project! I also want to thank Michelle Swenson and the many talented people who make up the WebSphere Systems Management team. I can't imagine working with a better group of people. I especially want to thank Leigh Williamson, to whom I am gratefully indebted for many years of friendship, both personal and professional.

—Roger Cundiff

Introduction to WebSphere Administration

This book continues the series on WebSphere® Application Server Version 5 by focusing on the details of system administration for the product. Once you have developed your J2EE application, and ensured the quality of your application through testing, you are ready to put it into production and use the information from this book to deploy, monitor, tune, and manage your application and the WebSphere Application Server Version 5 environment in which it runs.

IBM® WebSphere® Application Server (hereafter called Application Server) Version 5 provides enhancements to scalability, reliability, Web services, J2EE™ 1.3 certification, and many other areas. Version 5 also provides a completely rewritten infrastructure for you to manage and administer your servers and applications. An open-standards-based management framework, Java™ Management Extensions (JMX), is at the core of the Version 5 management capabilities. New administration tool sets built for Version 5 take advantage of this framework. You can also use the Version 5 administration tool capabilities for your own custom administration programs.

This system administration book discusses a variety of ways to use the Application Server Version 5 management features. Chapter 1 introduces the basic system administration concepts needed to understand Version 5 features. The first important concept to grasp is the new packaging structure for Application Server 5. To understand Application Server administration, you also need to familiarize yourself with the following concepts: servers, nodes and node agents, cells, and the Deployment Manager. It is important that you understand the various processes in the administrative topology and the operating environment in which they apply. Chapter 1 also introduces the four administrative tool sets that are shipped as part of the WebSphere Application Server product.

Chapter 2 completes the foundation concepts needed throughout the rest of the book by delving into the details of the Application Server process internals, distributed administration service product features, administrative security, and the structure of the product configuration files.

Chapter 3 provides a complete reference to the Application Server command-line tools. Each tool is discussed, along with the details of its command-line options.

Chapter 4 is a reference for the Administrative Console program, a sophisticated J2EE Web application that provides the graphical management console for the product. All of the various tasks exposed in the console are covered. This chapter also introduces a set of scenarios for typical administration functions that are carried over to the subsequent chapters for scripting and programmatic administration. These scenarios provide a comparison between how a function can be accomplished through the console, through scripting , and using Java programming interfaces.

Chapter 5 covers the powerful administrative scripting capabilities built into WebSphere Version 5. The wsadmin scripting program supports three operating modes, multiple languages, full extensibility, and complete access to all of the WebSphere Version 5 administration functions.

Chapter 6 delves into the details surrounding programmatic administration, such as writing your own custom management program, extending the Application Server administration system, and using the same Java administrative programming interfaces (APIs) as are used to build all of the other tools shipped with the product.

WEBSPHERE APPLICATION SERVER STRUCTURE

Application Server Version 5 provides an entirely new packaging structure. Several installation images build on one another to incrementally expand the features available to you. Start with the base product installation, and then add features (e.g., extended programming model enhancements or multi-node network deployment capabilities) as you need them. The two basic packages are Base Application Server and Network Deployment.

The WebSphere Version 5 product for z/OS and OS/390 includes both packages, along with an interactive configuration wizard, called the Customization Dialog, with which the WebSphere for z/OS user can configure base application servers and add network deployment functions.

The Base Application Server Package

A Base WebSphere Application Server installation includes everything needed for a single Application Server instance. Additional server definitions can be logically grouped into

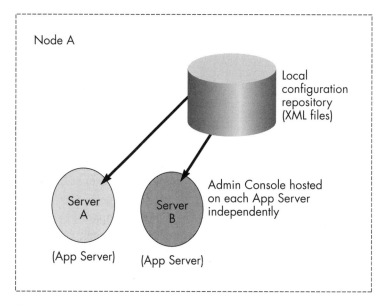

Figure 1.1
Basic Application Server environment.

nodes. A node can contain many servers, but cannot span multiple computer systems. A single computer system can have multiple nodes installed on it, each with multiple managed servers. For example, multiple nodes defined on a large multiuser enterprise server computer makes better use of the system resources, and can isolate projects from one another. Figure 1.1 depicts the base environment.

A limitation of this package on its own is that it does not support the coordination between Application Server instances. Administration is limited to a single server at a time. Although you can create new server definitions from the Base console, you cannot use the console that is running in one server to start, stop, or otherwise manage a different server. The Network Deployment package extends the Base Application Server with capabilities for multiprocess, multinode configuration and control.

The Network Deployment Package

A Network Deployment installation can support a network of computer systems that are configured to run collaborating instances of the Base Application Server installation. The Network Deployment package provides centralized administration and workload management for a set of nodes, referred to as a *cell*. A cell has a master administrative repository that stores the configuration data for all of the nodes in the cell. Figure 1.2 depicts multiple systems in a Network Deployment cell, and shows that a base server can be added to a Network Deployment cell.

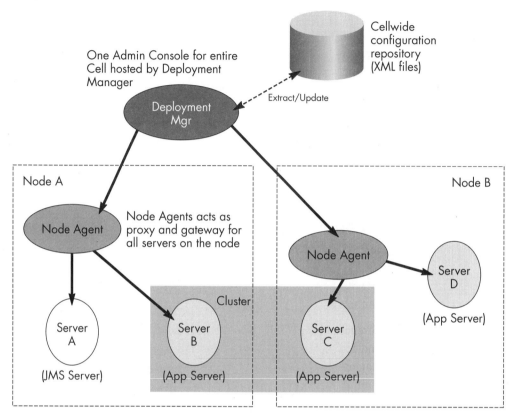

Figure 1.2
Network Deployment environment.

One computer system is designated as the central Deployment Manager machine onto which the Network Deployment package is installed. The central Deployment Manager program that is included in this package manages all of the nodes in the cell. Note that the same computer system that supports the Deployment Manager program can also support one or more federated Base Application Server nodes. The issue of whether or not to configure the Deployment Manager onto a separate computer system is more of a best practice concept pertinent to the subject of availability. For instance, large-scale customers such as those on z/OS enterprise servers might be unwilling to dedicate an entire logical partition (LPAR) to running the Deployment Manager alone. They might want to share system resources of that LPAR with other application server nodes. As with many aspects of Application Server Version 5, the choice of location for the Deployment Manager node and other application server nodes is one for each customer to make based on particular environment and operational policies.

To add a Base Application Server installation to the cell, run the `addNode` program on the base installation (the `addNode` program is fully described in Chapter 3 of this book). After this is completed, a separate node agent administrative server is created that serves as an intermediary between the application servers on the node and the Deployment Manager. Administrative logic that runs in the node agent keeps the configuration data for a node synchronized with the master configuration data for the cell.

Besides grouping servers into nodes, another logical grouping of servers is the *cluster*. A cluster can contain servers on different nodes. All of the servers in a cluster must have the identical application deployment configuration, because the purpose of a cluster is to define servers that collaborate for workload balancing and failover capabilities.

COMPARISON OF THE ADMINISTRATION IN VERSIONS 4 AND 5

Before getting into the details of Application Server 5, it is useful to compare the implementation of system administration in Version 5 with Version 4. Those familiar with Version 4 administration, especially with Version 4 Advanced Edition, will be pleasantly surprised by all of the new management features in Version 5.

There are significant differences between how you would handle administration in Application Server Versions 4 and 5. One of the main differences is that the Version 4 Advanced Edition (AE) requires a database to hold configuration data, whereas no edition of Version 5 requires a database. Version 4 AE administration is based on J2EE Enterprise Java Beans (EJBs) and all of the Version 4 administrative programs are EJB client programs. Version 5 does not use EJBs to store configuration data; therefore, none of the Version 4 administration programs, such as the Swing console, wscp scripting (smapi for v4 on z/OS), and XMLConfig, are compatible with Version 5. Instead, Version 5 relies on Extensible Markup Language (XML) configuration files and industry-standard JMX components to handle management functions.

The Version 4 administration program is a single AdminServer program that serves several functions simultaneously. In Version 4, the AdminServer runs on every node, and every instance of the AdminServer is equivalent to any other. In Version 5, the same functions that were combined in the Version 4 AdminServer have been separated into different specialized administrative programs. The node agent program discussed earlier runs on every node and is specialized to perform node-specific administration functions, such as server monitoring, configuration synchronization, file transfer, and request routing. The single Deployment Manager program manages the entire cell, coordinating with the node agents for the various nodes in the cell.

Unlike Version 4, all administrative functions and programs are applicable to all editions of the product in Version 5. The same scripting program, `wsadmin`, that works for the Version 5 WebSphere Express edition also works for the full Enterprise package, even on the enterprise-class zSeries server machines. The same Administrative Console program, a J2EE Web application based on Java Server Pages (JSPs) and the Jakarta struts framework, works for all editions of Application Server Version 5.

Table 1.1 provides summary comparisons of some of the administrative features between Version 4 AE and Version 5.

Table 1.1   Comparison of Version 4 and Version 5 Administration

Administrative Function	Application Server Version 4 AE	Application Server Version 5
Administrative processes	AdminServer	Node Agent and Deployment Manager
Location of repository data	Relational database	XML configuration files
Graphical interface	"Fat" Swing client	"Thin" Web application
Scripting program	wscp (Tcl syntax) (REXX on z/OS)	wsadmin (Tcl syntax)
Backup of repository data to XML	XMLConfig (different format on z/OS)	None (already in XML)
Debugging utility	DrAdmin (IPCS on z/OS)	wsadmin
Java API	WscpCommand (Part of SMAPI on z/OS)	AdminClient
Program to start the server process	startServer (MVS START command on z/OS)	startServer
Install images	One	Two: Base install and ND install (except for z/OS which is a single image on tape)
Application binary distribution	None	On by default

OVERVIEW OF ADMINISTRATION TOOLS FOR VERSION 5

System administration provides a variety of tools for managing WebSphere Application Server. These tools can be categorized into four general tool sets that are available with most editions of the product:

- Command-line tools
- Administrative Console
- Scripting tool
- Java programming APIs

Individual chapters of this book focus on in-depth details of each of these tool sets, but the following overview provides an introduction to the intended usage for the different tools.

Command-Line Tools

Command-line tools are simple programs that you run from a command prompt to perform specific tasks. Using the command-line tools, you can start and stop application servers, check server status, add or remove nodes, and complete similar tasks. The command-line tools provided with Application Server Version 5 are restricted for use on a single local node.

All of the command-line tools are Java programs that use the same Application Server Version 5 administration APIs as the console and the `wsadmin` tool, which are discussed in the next section. Chapter 3 provides a full list of the command-line tools available with Application Server v5.

Most of the command-line tools print a usage syntax statement if you invoke them with the help option (by entering either `-?` or `-help` as part of the command). Most command-line tools also log their activity under the logs directory for the product. All command-line tools require authentication data when product security is enabled.

Administrative Console

The Administrative Console is a graphical interface that provides many features to guide you through deployment and systems administration tasks. It is extremely useful for helping you start exploring the available management options. Various wizards guide you through the more complicated processes. The Administrative Console program is documented in the Application Server Version 5 InfoCenter. Figure 1.3 shows the WebSphere Administrative Console home page.

The separation of run-time operations from configuration changes is an important concept in Version 5. Run-time requests are delivered to the running server components through JMX operations and take effect immediately. These run-time attribute changes are transient in nature and do not survive a server restart. Configuration changes, which are made in the XML configuration files for the server, are persistent across server restarts. Configuration changes do not take effect immediately; you must restart the server for the new values in the XML configuration files to be picked up.

Most run-time attributes have corresponding persistent configuration settings. However, there are considerably more configuration settings stored in the XML files than there are run-time attributes available for dynamic modification on managed objects while they are running in a server. Separating the two functions makes the distinction clear when you are changing something that will take effect immediately, but is transient as opposed to when

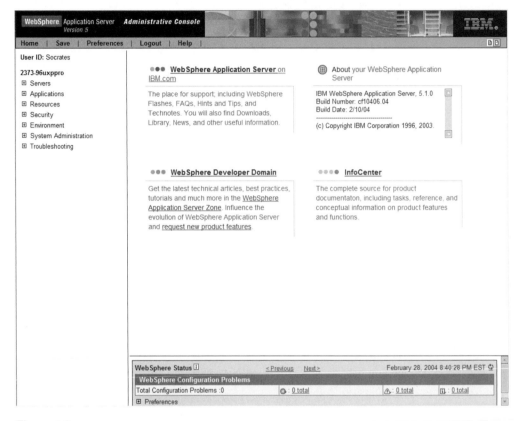

Figure 1.3
WebSphere Administrative Console.

you are making a persistent change. If you want both an immediate run-time change and a persistent configuration change, you need to perform both operations. Figure 1.4 shows a server page in the Administrative Console displaying both the server Runtime and Configuration tab views.

The Base Application Server version of the Administrative Console provides single-server administration capabilities. This Web application runs in the same server that it manages in the base environment. In a Network Deployment environment, the Administrative Console executes in the Deployment Manager server. This lets the console create server clusters that span multiple nodes and manage any process configured on any node within the cell. The Network Deployment environment allows you to manage multiple servers across multiple nodes whether they are clustered or not.

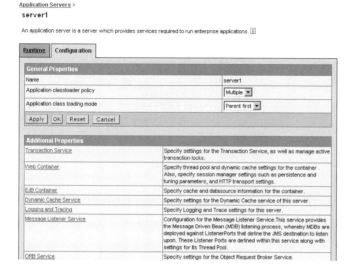

Figure 1.4
Server page in WebSphere Administrative Console.

Use the Administrative Console client program to become familiar with the product and all of its capabilities. You can explore all of the various aspects of the environment in a graphical presentation. Once you have learned many of the details of Application Server Version 5 using the graphical console application, you might find that some of the other administrative tools provide faster access for day-to-day activities.

Scripting Tool

The Application Server administrative scripting program, `wsadmin`, is a powerful, non-graphical command interpreter environment that lets you execute administrative operations interactively or from a script file. The `wsadmin` tool is intended for production environments and unattended operations. The `wsadmin` tool is documented in the Application Server Version 5 InfoCenter. It is built on top of the Bean Scripting Framework that ships with Version 5. This lets the program support several languages for scripting Application Server administrative functions. The initial Version 5 release only supported the Tcl syntax, but additional scripting language support was added in release 5.1 when the Jython syntax was supported.

The `wsadmin` scripting tool has three modes of operation:

- **Interactive mode.** This lets the user enter commands and view the response on a command-line prompt. This mode is useful for learning the scripting tool and its capabilities. It is also useful for prototyping command syntax to verify the options before building a larger script.

- **Batch mode.** This lets the user supply a set of script commands in a file that the tool executes as a program.
- **Command mode.** This lets the user enter a single command from the regular operating system command window and executes this one command, returning control to the operating system command shell.

The wsadmin tool is most often executed as a client attached to a running server. You can also run it in a "local" execution mode where a running server is not required. In this mode, however, the function is limited to only configuration changes because a server run-time is not available to receive operational requests.

The wsadmin tool is primarily intended for rapidly assembling small control programs using the available Application Server administrative functions. You can develop more sophisticated administration programs using the Java API for Application Server administration (described next). However, the combination of full scripting language constructs, such as loops and variable evaluation, along with Application Server administration functions, provides powerful capabilities.

Java Programming API

Application Server v5 supports a Java programming interface for developing administrative programs. All of the administrative tools supplied with the product are written according to the API, which is based on the industry-standard JMX specification.

Using the administrative programming API, you can do the following:

- Write your own custom administration client to perform specific administration functions. The command-line tools available with Application Server Version 5, including the wsadmin tool and the console, are client programs that use the public administration APIs to carry out their tasks. Custom administration client programs can be simple or extremely complex. For example, you could write a client that only lets you start and stop clusters. You could also write a specialized administration client program to monitor certain metrics in the server and adjust configuration settings if the metrics exceed some threshold.
- Extend the basic Application Server administration system with your own custom MBeans that expose the management interface specifically aligned for your requirements. For example, your application might have its own run-time properties that you can adjust to tune the application while it is executing. Your application can implement a JMX MBean that exposes these attributes and other useful operational requests. Using the Version 5 administration programming interfaces, you can add your MBean to the set provided with Application Server, and control your application, along with the rest of the system, using the wsadmin scripting client.

You can even write a custom server extension and expose its functionality to the Application Server administration system as a JMX MBean.

The Application Server administration programming API is fully documented in the java-doc, which is provided with every installation (it is located in the `web/apidocs` directory under Application Server's root installation directory). The Application Server administration API is based on standard JMX interfaces and classes, and the JMX javadoc is also provided with each installation. The `com.ibm.websphere.management` package contains the public Application Server management interface.

Many helper classes and interface definitions are associated with the Version 5 administrative programming APIs. If you plan to create custom administration code, you should familiarize yourself with the public javadoc for the product. Chapter 6 in this book explores the details of how to use this administration programming API, and provides detailed examples of custom administration programs and system extensions.

2

Administrative Concepts and Architecture

B efore launching into the chapters that discuss details of the WebSphere Application Server Version 5 administration tooling, there are some fundamental concepts for Version 5 that are important to absorb. It's important to know how the management logic is structured into each process in WebSphere to have some context in which to understand the following chapters. We therefore cover the administrative architecture for the product in this chapter.

The concepts from this chapter apply to all of the administrative tooling. They represent the foundation on which both the Base Application Server edition and Network Deployment edition management is built. The logic is the same for both Base and Network Deployment; it's just where the code executes that differs between editions of the product. This chapter explains how the two WebSphere editions are the same and where they are different, administratively.

BASE APPLICATION SERVER ADMINISTRATION

In Version 5, the architecture for WebSphere Application Server system management was redesigned. Every process in Version 5 contains an embedded JMX agent, the JMX MBean-Server component. For each process, additional administrative services are built around this central management component.

These Base management services are extended and leveraged to support multiple servers in the Network Deployment edition. A set of distributed management services are built on each other, and they provide the ability to monitor and control Application Server instances on remote nodes in the system.

Anatomy of a Server

WebSphere Application Server Version 5 administration is centered around the JMX specification. That specification (identified as JSR 003 within the Java Community Process)
defines three layers of function:

- *Instrumentation*. The managed resources in JMX are exposed using a standard
  interface—the Managed Bean (MBean) interface. This interface represents all of
  the attributes, operations, and notifications available for the managed resource.
- *Agent*. The JMX Agent acts as a central registry for all MBeans within a single Java
  Virtual Machine (JVM). The Agent exposes an MBeanServer interface so that
  individual MBean instances can be queried and located. There are additional
  management services defined to be available from the JMX Agent, such as a Timer
  service, Monitor service, and Relationship service.
- *Connectors*. The JMX connectors provide communication links between JVMs that
  host a JMX Agent. A connector is the mechanism through which external code can
  obtain a handle to the managed resources of a JVM and manipulate those managed
  resources remotely.

Each managed component of the WebSphere Version 5 run-time is exposed as a JMX
MBean, which is registered with the MBeanServer running in that server JVM. These managed resources are available externally by using JMX connectors to the MBeanServer supplied with the WebSphere product. Application Server V5 supports two JMX connectors:
the RMI/IIOP connector and the SOAP/HTTP(S) connector. This provides a choice of protocols for administration because each protocol has strengths and weaknesses. Additional
connector protocols are planned for future releases.

Each MBean has a unique identifier called the ObjectName, which is used as the target in
scripting and Java APIs to define the managed resource in the run-time to be controlled.
Several chapters in this book discuss MBean ObjectNames, so it is important to know the
MBeans supplied by the WebSphere product and the management purposes represented by
each one.

Documentation for each MBean that is built into WebSphere is installed with the product in
the `web/mbeanDocs` directory under the root installation directory. The documentation
describes the operations, attributes, and notifications that each MBean provides. This documentation is also available in Appendix A.

Figure 2.1 shows the architectural details of how all the pieces fit together.

External tools and programs

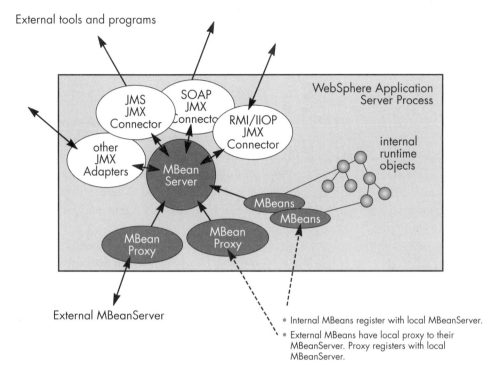

Figure 2.1
Application Server internals.

Considerations for the z/OS Environment

WebSphere Application Server Version 5 uses the exact same code for administration of the product regardless of the computer system on which it is installed. This is pretty amazing when you consider that Application Server Version 5 is available for a wide range of platforms, spanning from small pervasive devices all the way up to the largest mainframe systems. These IBM zSeries Enterprise Servers have special features that ensure high availability and reliability.

WebSphere leverages the enhanced deployment capabilities available on mainframes in many ways. One way in which WebSphere is leveraged is in the architecture for the Application Server itself. Rather than each Application Server representing a single JVM, on z/OS each Application Server is a logical representation of multiple JVMs. The internals of each of these server instances are identical, and match the architecture described previously in the section, Anatomy of a Server. The managed resources are exposed as JMX MBeans. There is an embedded JMX Agent (MBeanServer) in each instance, and JMX connectors provide communication channels into and out of the logical Application Server.

Configuration versus Run-Time Control

An important concept to understand for Version 5 is the difference between configuration and run-time management. All of the configuration data for Application Server Version 5 is stored in XML files. In WebSphere administration terms, configuration means editing these XML files to modify the data used by the run-time when the Application Server process is started. If an Application Server is already running, then modifying its XML configuration files will not result in any immediate change to run-time behavior. Most configuration file changes are only picked up when the server process is restarted.

In contrast, run-time control is a mechanism for sending messages to live running code in the Application Server process. You can send a message to the server run-time to ask it to change the value of a property it is currently using for that process in memory. The run-time will usually comply with these requests, but no persistent record is made of the dynamic change in run-time data. Run-time control represents transient modifications. Configuration changes are persistent, although not immediate.

It is certainly possible to produce an immediate run-time change and also the equivalent persistent configuration change; it requires the invocation of two method calls instead of just one. The reason for this distinction between persistent configuration and transient run-time data is important. It makes clear exactly what behavior to expect when you perform a function. By keeping the mechanisms separate, the system is flexible enough to support situations where one or the other behavior is desired, but not both.

Configuration

Configuration data for WebSphere Application Server Version 5 is stored in several XML files. The server run-time reads these files when started and responds to the component settings stored there. The configuration data includes settings for the run-time itself, such as JVM options, thread pool sizes, container settings, and port numbers the server will use. Other configuration files define J2EE resources to which the server will connect to obtain data needed by the application logic. Examples of these resource definitions include Java DataBase Connectivity (JDBC) datasources, Java Message Service (JMS) queues and topics, JavaMail providers, and J2EE Connector Architecture (JCA) resource adapters. Security settings are stored in a separate document from the server and resource configuration. Application-specific configuration, such as session configuration, cache settings, and deployment target lists, are stored in files under the root directory for each application.

In most cases, changing the data stored in these configuration files will not result in any immediate change in the server run-time behavior. Except for certain application metadata, information in the configuration documents is only read once when the server is started and is not reread later while the server is running. There is a different mechanism that can be used to request that the run-time change a property that it is using while it is running. That mechanism is Run-time Control, which involves sending a message to the run-time that is targeted for a specific managed resource within the server.

Run-time Control

Control of the components that execute as part of the server run-time is achieved by sending those components messages requesting some operation to be performed or to change some attribute value stored in their memory. The messages are delivered across JMX connectors that form the administrative messaging communication system. The server run-time components expose their manageability interfaces as individual JMX MBeans that are remotely accessible to administrative client code.

Application Deployment

The process of deploying applications into a WebSphere Version 5 environment involves several subtasks. The process includes more steps when the target environment is a Network Deployment one, but the basic flow is the same. The main tasks (as illustrated in Figure 2.2) are as follows:

- *Application preparation.* The list of target server run-times for the application are identified; all deployment options are collected; all references declared by the application are resolved; default application bindings are generated if appropriate.

- *Application deployment.* The prepared Enterprise Archive (EAR) file is added to the WebSphere configuration repository; any code that needs to be generated such as EJB stubs or JSP precompilation is processed; a *deployment.xml* file containing the metadata related to the application is created and stored in the repository.

- *Application distribution.* The EAR file stored in the WebSphere configuration repository is transferred to every node on which a target server run-time resides (this task only applies to the multinode Network Deployment environment).

- *Postdistribution processing.* The EAR file is expanded into the file system location where the server run-time will load it, based on the deployment instructions gathered in the preparation step. If the application is already being served by the server, it is stopped and restarted so that the application code is refreshed.

Each of the administration tools delivered with the Version 5 product supports the process of application deployment, but the basic functions are implemented by Java programming interfaces described in Chapter 6. The tools shipped with WebSphere surround and enhance these basic deployment programming interfaces with helper logic to make the process interactive and it is guided by wizard features in the case of the Administrative Console.

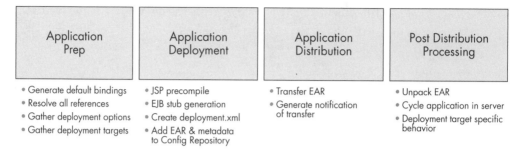

Figure 2.2
Application installation and deployment tasks.

Administrative Security

When system security is enabled, all administrative connections are secure. You must map all administrator user IDs to one of the administrative roles defined by the product. When an administrative client program, such as the console, scripting, command line, or custom program, attempts to perform an administrative function, the user ID of the calling code is obtained and compared to the privileges granted to the role for that particular user. If the user does not have appropriate privileges, the request will be rejected.

The following four roles separate the administrative functions into layers of privilege:

- *Monitor.* This role can view configuration and run-time settings, but cannot modify anything.
- *Operator.* This role can perform run-time operations, but cannot modify the persistent configuration. For example, an operator can start or stop a server, but cannot change the configuration for that server.
- *Configurator.* This role can modify the persistent configuration for the system, but cannot perform run-time operations on live objects. For example, a configurator can install applications into the system, but cannot start or stop a server.
- *Full Administrator.* This role can perform all administrative functions.

NETWORK DEPLOYMENT ADMINISTRATION

In the Base Application Server package, the administrative client programs attach directly to the server process and send administrative requests to that single process. In a Network Deployment environment, there are several special administrative processes, and the administrative client programs can attach to any point in the topology (Deployment Manager, node agent, or managed process). Generally, administrative clients attach to the Deployment Manager because all servers throughout the cell can be controlled from that process.

When a request for an MBean operation is submitted to the Deployment Manager, it is automatically routed to the server on which the target run-time component is executing.

Cell Structure

As described previously, configuration data is stored as a set of files that make up the master configuration repository. In a Base Application Server environment, all documents are stored on the same system as the server. In a Network Deployment environment, the Deployment Manager maintains the full set of configuration documents for the entire cell, and each node in the cell only gets a subset of the documents that apply specifically to that node.

Because each node has the subset of configuration information required for servers defined on that node, you can start and control the servers even if the central Deployment Manager process is temporarily unavailable. Figure 2.3 depicts how administrative commands are routed between the processes in the cell and how different servers read the various parts of the configuration data.

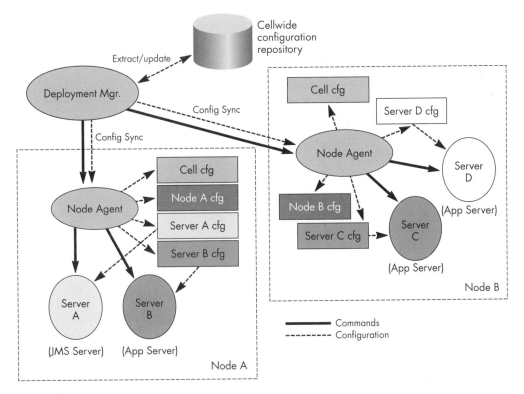

Figure 2.3
Distributed command and configuration routing.

In addition to operational requests (e.g., stopping a server) and configuration requests (e.g., changing an attribute), administrative programs in Version 5 can register as listeners for distributed event notification from any of the MBeans running in the network. Several MBeans generate an event notification when something significant occurs in their logic (e.g., the Server MBean generates notifications when it starts and stops). Administrative clients can register to receive callbacks when these notifications are broadcast.

Building a Cell

A Network Deployment cell is built by first installing the Network Deployment product to create a Deployment Manager administrative process that initially manages an empty cell. Once the Deployment Manager is in place, individual nodes (collections of application servers) can be added to the cell definition.

To add a new node to a cell, the Base Application Server product must be installed on the system to be added. There is an `addNode` utility that ships with the Version 5 Base product that is used to federate a standalone Base node into a cell. You can execute this utility from the Base installation for the node, or from the central Deployment Manager administrative console.

Administrative Agents

Administrative logic for the Network Deployment product executes mostly within special servers designed for this purpose (referred to as administrative agents). The Deployment Manager is designed to provide overall visibility and control over the entire distributed WebSphere cell. It accomplishes this function, in part, by collaboration with the node agents that are the administrative gateway to the group of servers that make up the nodes of the cell.

Specific services hosted by the Deployment Manager include the following:

- Hosts the central admin console web app for the cell
- FileTransferService
- One half of the Configuration synchronization logic
- Node agent status caching
- Configuration Service
- Configuration repository implementation

The node agent has an important set of administrative services also:

- Other half of configuration synchronization
- FileTransferClient
- Application Server process monitoring and restart

- Remote server launching
- Postdistribution application deployment processing

Distributed Administration Services

Within the Version 5 Network Deployment cell, a set of distributed administration services are layered on top of each other to provide a sophisticated distributed management system.

Process Discovery

As servers within a cell start up, they broadcast a special discovery packet so that other parts of the network can learn about the existence of these new processes and link them into the topology of the cell at the appropriate spot. The process discovery logic ensures that any process can terminate at any time and be restarted and rejoin the cell in the same position in the network tree.

Application servers and other leaf processes are discovered by the node agent that aggregates all of the servers for a node. The node agent responds to the Application Server discovery request by establishing a JMX connector link to the Application Server and by reflecting the existence of this server to the rest of the cell (especially the Deployment Manager).

Node agents broadcast a discovery packet also. Node agents are discovered by both Application Servers "beneath" them and by the Deployment Manager for the cell "above" them in the network topology. Figure 2.4 shows the general WebSphere process discovery flow.

JMX Connectors

JMX connectors provide the communication channel into the WebSphere Application Server JVM for administrative requests. JMX connectors expose a remote subset of the standard JMX MBeanServer interface. Because the MBeanServer interface defined by JSR 003 is a

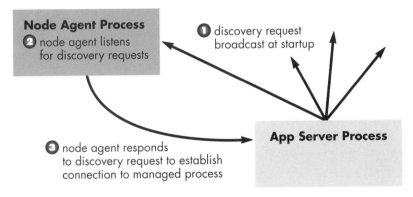

Figure 2.4
WebSphere process discovery.

single JVM interface, certain methods are not appropriate for remote execution. The Web-Sphere JMX connectors only expose MBeanServer methods that can be remotely executed.

There are two JMX connectors shipped with Version 5—a SOAP message over HTTP, and an RMI message over IIOP.

Request Routing

For administrative requests to be entered into the Network Deployment system by client programs attached to JVMs other than where the target MBean is executing, WebSphere Version 5 provides automatic routing of requests through the system to the intended desti-nation. This administrative request routing is based on certain key properties that are set in the ObjectName handle for the target MBean.

MBeans registered through the WebSphere APIs have key properties set that identify the cell, node, and server process in which the MBean is executing. When a request to invoke an operation or access an attribute of that MBean is received by the system, the address key properties of the target MBean are consulted and the request is forwarded from JVM to JVM within the network until all of the address key properties match the target ObjectName (see Figure 2.5).

Distributed JMX Events

The JMX specification includes provisions for managed resources to emit notifications when significant events occur during the resource lifetime. The standard JMX specification defines how registration and broadcast of event notification works within a single JVM. The WebSphere Version 5 system management infrastructure extends the standard JMX notifi-cation behavior to include multiple JVMs in a distributed network.

File Transfer Service

Several administrative tasks involve transferring information in files between systems. The WebSphere Version 5 administrative infrastructure includes a general-purpose file transfer mechanism that uses HTTP to transfer files between the central Deployment Manager and the node agents for each node.

The Deployment Manager has a special system application installed named filetransfer.ear. This program uses the Deployment Manager as the server for HTTP get/put requests that move file contents from one system to another. The node agents all include HTTP client logic that can connect to the Deployment Manager and request uploads or downloads of specific files (see Figure 2.6). Other administrative functions that make use of the file trans-fer service include application installation, distribution, configuration synchronization, and remote log file presentation.

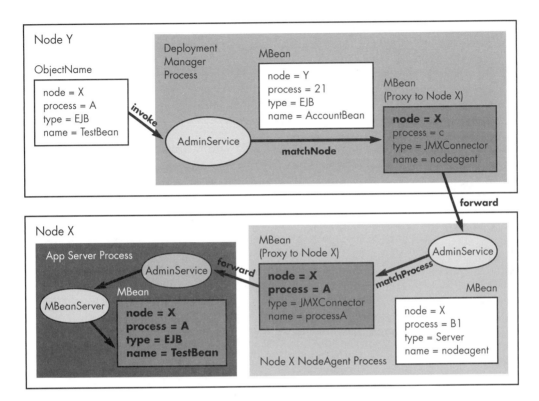

Figure 2.5
Distributed request routing.

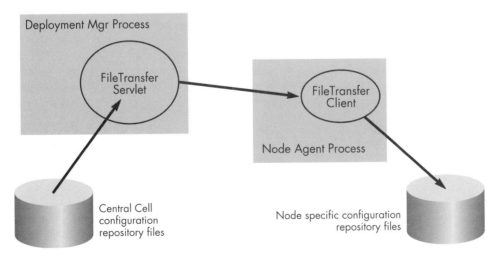

Figure 2.6
File transfer service.

Configuration Synchronization

An important higher level service available in the Network Deployment edition of Web-Sphere Version 5 is configuration synchronization between the master configuration repository and remote nodes. Configuration synchronization builds on basic file transfer services to keep the versions of configuration files stored on the local file system for a node matched to the version stored in the master repository and controlled by the Deployment Manager.

In a Base Application Server environment, the entire configuration applies to a single node, and typically to a single Application Server instance. The configuration is confined to a single file system and is not distributed or replicated in any way.

In a Network Deployment environment, the assumption is that there is no shared file system between the nodes that make up the cell, so the master cell configuration maintained by the Deployment Manager process must be partially replicated to the other nodes in the cell. The node agent for each node collaborates with the Deployment Manager to accomplish this configuration synchronization (see Figure 2.7), and transfer the configuration documents relevant to the node from wherever the master repository exists to the local file system for the node.

A configuration synchronization operation is always initiated by the NodeSync logic that runs in the node agent. In other words, the node always pulls down the configuration docu-

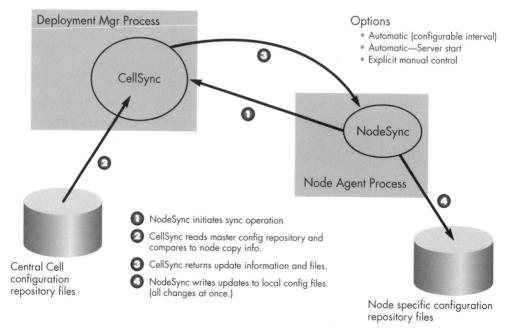

Figure 2.7
Configuration synchronization.

ments from the master cell repository; the Deployment Manager does not push the configuration to the nodes.

There are many things that will cause a node agent to perform a sync operation. The default setup for the product includes an automatic, periodic sync operation that is performed every minute. The time interval is configurable and the autosync function can also be completely disabled. There is an option to have the node agent initiate a sync every time it starts up. The NodeSync MBean exposes operations that allow remote code to request a sync operation be performed. There are thus a number of ways in which a sync operation can be triggered.

The NodeSync MBean exposes two forms of sync operation, blocking and nonblocking. The requestSync operation is nonblocking. It returns immediately and the actual synchronization of the node's configuration occurs over some amount of time after the operation returns. Code that employs the nonblocking requestSync operation can be notified when the sync operation actually completes by registering to receive the websphere.nodesync.complete event notification generated by the NodeSync MBean after each synchorization operation completes. The sync operation of the NodeSync MBean blocks and does not return to the caller until the sync operation completes.

There is the notion of full synchronization exposed in the admin console, which is a means by which the cached data about the state of the repository is flushed and recalculated for all documents in the repository. One of the uses for this full sync function is to pick up any manual changes made to the configuration files in the master repository that did not go through one of the admin tools. Full sync requires examination of every file in the repository and is therefore a very extensive operation that should only be used when it is suspected (or even verified) that the repository on the node does not match the master repository and normal sync does not clear up the problem.

Application Installation and Distribution

Because the main purpose for WebSphere is to provide a platform for hosting applications, the area of application management, installation, and distribution holds significant importance within the administrative function set. WebSphere provides administrative tools to assist with application installation, validate application deployment settings, generate application-specific code, and distribute the application binaries to remote nodes on which the application will run.

The configuration synchronization operation ensures that the files on the node's local disk match those in the master cell repository. Because the EAR file for installed applications is stored in the master configuration repository, this means that it also is transferred to all nodes that contain a deployment target server for that application.

When an application is installed, its EAR file is stored in the configuration repository and replicated by the configuration synchronization mechanism to the appropriate nodes in the cell. On the node, a piece of logic is registered to receive notifications when the sync operation completes. This logic determines if a new or updated version of an application EAR file has been stored in the local repository for the node. If so, the code expands the new or updated EAR file to the configured location where the run time expects to load and execute it.

The EAR expansion logic on the node also includes logic to stop the application prior to expanding the EAR file and restart the application after expansion successfully completes. There is no need to include explicit application stop/restart logic in a script surrounding the application update operation. All that you need to do is use the `-update` option for the `wsadmin AdminApp` command (see Chapter 5 for full details of the `wsadmin` syntax).

WEBSPHERE VERSION 5 CONFIGURATION REPOSITORY

As mentioned previously, Application Server's configuration data is stored in a set of XML documents. Although you typically will not need to manually update or view these files, it is still useful to know the structure and content of these documents. Knowing the configuration repository structure will give you a better understanding of overall system operation. You can modify the configuration files manually; however, unless you know the exact change to make, you should use the administrative tools to modify the configuration files because they can validate changes made to the configuration.

Recall that in a Network Deployment environment, master copies of all documents are stored in the cell repository on the Deployment Manager node. When a change is made to one of these master documents, it is automatically replicated to any of the applicable nodes in the cell. The document on the node is automatically overwritten by the copy from the master repository. For this reason, when updating repository documents in a Network Deployment environment, you should only update documents in the master repository on the Deployment Manager node. The administration tools always update the master configuration files in a Network Deployment environment.

Directory Structure

The repository documents are stored in a directory tree starting at the config directory under the product installation root. At the top of the hierarchy is the cells directory, which contains a subdirectory for each cell. The names of the cell subdirectories match the names of the cells. For example, a cell named mycell has its configuration documents in the directory cells/mycell. In Application Server Version 5, there is always a single cell.

Each cell subdirectory has the following files and subdirectories:

- The *cell.xml* file, which provides configuration data for the cell.
- Files such as *security.xml*, *virtualhosts.xml*, *resources.xml*, and *variables.xml*, which provide configuration data that applies across every node in the cell.
- The clusters subdirectory, which holds a subdirectory for each cluster defined in the cell. The names of the subdirectories under clusters match the names of the clusters. Each cluster subdirectory holds a *cluster.xml* file, which provides configuration data specifically for that cluster.
- The applications subdirectory, which holds a subdirectory for each application deployed in the cell.
- The nodes subdirectory, which holds a subdirectory for each node in the cell. The names of the subdirectories under nodes match the names of the nodes.

Each node subdirectory contains files such as *variables.xml* and *resources.xml*, which provide configuration data that applies across the node. Recall that these files have the same name as those in the containing cell's directory. The configurations specified in these node-level documents override the configurations specified in cell-level documents that have the same name. For example, if a particular variable is in both cell- and node-level variables.xml files, all servers on the node use the variable definition in the node-level document and ignore the definition in the cell-level document.

Each node subdirectory also contains a *serverindex.xml* file that stores the definitions of all ports used by servers on that node. Keeping this information in one document makes it easier to find port conflicts between servers on a node.

Each node directory contains a servers subdirectory with a subdirectory under that for each server defined on the node. The names of the subdirectories match the names of the servers. The server directory always contains a *server.xml* file, which provides configuration data specific to that server. There might also be *security.xml*, *resources.xml*, and *variables.xml* files, which provide configuration data that applies only to the server and overrides the configurations specified in the containing cell and node documents that have the same name.

The names of the application subdirectories match the names of the deployed applications. The original EAR file for the application is stored in each application subdirectory. Also under the application subdirectory is a deployments directory. You can deploy one application multiple times with different bindings for each deployment.

Each deployment subdirectory contains a *deployment.xml* file that contains configuration data about the application deployment. Each deployment subdirectory also contains a META-INF subdirectory that contains a J2EE application deployment descriptor file along with IBM deployment extensions and bindings files. Deployed application directories also have subdirectories for all Web Application Archive (WAR) files and entity bean Java Archive (JAR) files in the application. Only the metadata for the application is stored in the deployment subdirectories. The binary code for the application is stored in the location that the administrator specified when installing the application.

The following is an example WebSphere Version 5 configuration file structure. The names of directories are highlighted in bold and names of files are not highlighted.

```
cells/
  mycell/
     cell.xml
     resources.xml
     virtualhosts.xml
     variables.xml
     security.xml
     nodes/
        nodeX/
           node.xml
           variables.xml
           resources.xml
           serverindex.xml
           servers/
              serverA/
                 server.xml
                 variables.xml
                 resources.xml
              nodeagent/
                 server.xml
        nodeY/
           node.xml, variables.xml, resources.xml, serverindex.xml
           servers/
              nodeagent/
                 server.xml
     applications/
        sampleApp1.ear/
           deployments/
              sampleApp1/
                 deployment.xml
                 META-INF/
                    application.xml ibm-application-ext.xml
        myapp2.ear/
           deployments/
              myapp2/
```

```
deployment.xml
META-INF/
    application.xml, ibm-application-ext.xml,
    ibm-application-bnd.xml
```

Configuration Files, Content, and Structure

Most configuration documents have XML content. Table 2.1 describes the documents and states whether you can edit them using an administrative tool or must edit them directly.

If possible, edit a configuration document using the Administrative Console because it validates any changes that you make to configurations. You can also use one of the other administrative tools (wsadmin or Java APIs) to modify configuration documents. Using the Administrative Console or wsadmin scripting to update configurations is less error prone and likely quicker and easier than other methods.

However, you cannot edit some files using the administrative tools. Configuration files that you must edit manually are explicitly described in the content column in Table 2.1.

Table 2.1 Version 5 Configuration Files

File Name	Location(s) in the Configuration Tree	Content
server.xml	config/cells/*<cell_name>*/nodes/*<node_name>*/servers/ *<server_name>*/	A server definition and its components. This includes the EJBContainer, WebContainer, Naming, Admin, ORB, and other internal components. The launch properties for the server are also stored in this file in the processDefinition element.
resources.xml	config/cells/*<cell_name>*/ config/cells/*<cell_name>*/nodes/*<node_name>*/ config/cells/*<cell_name>*/nodes/*<node_name>*/servers/ *<server_name>*/	Definitions of operating environment resources, including JDBC, JMS, JavaMail, URL, JCA resource providers and factories.
variables.xml	config/cells/*<cell_name>*/ config/cells/*<cell_name>*/nodes/*<node_name>*/ config/cells/*<cell_name>*/nodes/*<node_name>*/servers/ *<server_name>*/	Configuration of variables used to parameterize any part of the configuration settings.

Table 2.1   Version 5 Configuration Files (Continued)

File Name	Location(s) in the Configuration Tree	Content
serverindex.xml	config/cells/*<cell_name>*/nodes/*<node_name>*/	Specify communication ports used on a specific node. This file also contains the list of all deployed applications for each server on the node.
node.xml	config/cells/*<cell_name>*/nodes/*<node_name>*/	Node identity.
security.xml	config/cells/*<cell_name>*/ config/cells/*<cell_name>*/nodes/*<node_name>*/servers/*<server_name>*/	Configure security, including all user ID and password data.
virtualhosts.xml	config/cells/*<cell_name>*/	Configure a virtual host and its MIME types.
cell.xml	config/cells/*<cell_name>*/	Cell identity.
cluster.xml	config/cells/*<cell_name>*/clusters/*<cluster_name>*/	Identify a cluster and its members and weights.
deployment.xml	config/cells/*<cell_name>*/applications/*<application_name>*/	Configure application deployment settings such as target servers and application-specific server configuration.
multibroker.xml	config/cells/*<cell_name>*/	Configure a data replication message broker.
namestore.xml	config/cells/*<cell_name>*/	Provide persistent name binding data.
pmirm.xml	config/cells/*<cell_name>*/	Configure PMI request metrics.
admin-authz.xml	config/cells/*<cell_name>*/	Define a role for administrative operation authorization.
integral-jms-authorizations.xml	config/cells/*<cell_name>*/	Provide security configuration data for the integrated messaging system.
naming-authz.xml	config/cells/*<cell_name>*/	Define roles for a naming operation authorization.

Table 2.1 Version 5 Configuration Files (Continued)

File Name	Location(s) in the Configuration Tree	Content
filter.policy	config/cells/*<cell_name>*/	Specify security permissions to be filtered out of other policy files. This file cannot be edited using admin tooling.
spi.policy	config/cells/*<cell_name>*/nodes/*<node_name>*/	Define security permissions for service provider libraries such as resource providers. This file cannot be edited using admin tooling.
library.policy	config/cells/*<cell_name>*/nodes/*<node_name>*/	Define security permissions for shared library code. This file cannot be edited using admin tooling.
app.policy	config/cells/*<cell_name>*/nodes/*<node_name>*/	Define security permissions for application code. This file cannot be edited using admin tooling.

Most of the XML configuration files in the repository contain elements of the standard WebSphere Configuration Component Model (see Appendix C). An example of the content in these configuration files can be seen in the typical *cell.xml* file shown here.

TYPICAL CONFIGURATION DOCUMENT

```
<?xml version="1.0" encoding="UTF-8"?>

<xmi:XMI xmi:version="2.0" xmlns:xmi="http://www.omg.org/XMI"
xmlns:topology.cell="http://www.ibm.com/websphere/appserver/schemas/5.0/
topology.cell.xmi" xmlns:ipc="http://www.ibm.com/websphere/appserver/schemas/
5.0/ipc.xmi">

  <xmi:Documentation>

    <contact>WebSphere Application Server v5.0 Default Configuration Files
v1.7 7/31/02</contact>

  </xmi:Documentation>

  <topology.cell:Cell xmi:id="Cell_1" name="bluehill"
cellDiscoveryProtocol="TCP" cellType="STANDALONE">

  </topology.cell:Cell>

</xmi:XMI>
```

Each configuration document includes a header containing the namespace for the elements in the document. Note the release version encoded in the schema namespace Uniform Resource Identifier (URI; 5.0/topology.cell.xmi). Future releases will have different namespaces that include additional configuration elements.

Administrative Commands

A fter installation of WebSphere Application Server, the first thing typically done is to start the server with the `startServer` command. This is just one of several administrative commands provided by WebSphere to help you manage your installation. Administrative commands are used to start and stop servers, federate and unfederate nodes, and back up your configuration. A complete list of administrative commands is contained in Table 3.1. This chapter describes describes each command and many of each command's parameters.

Table 3.1   Adminstrative Commands

Name	Description	Product
startServer	Launches the specified server	Base/Network Deployment
startNode	Launches the node agent	Base
startManager	Launches the Deployment Manager	Network Deployment
stopServer	Stops the specified server	Base/Network Deployment
stopNode	Stops the node agent	Base
stopManager	Stops the Deployment Manager	Network Deployment
addNode	Federates the local node into a Network Deployment cell	Base
removeNode	Unfederates the local node from the current Network Deployment cell	Base
backupConfig	Backs up the cell configuration	Base/Network Deployment
restoreConfig	Restores a previously backed up configuration	Base/Network Deployment
syncNode	Synchronizes the node's configuration with the cell	Base
cleanupNode	Erases a partially removed node from the cell	Network Deployment

There are a number of parameters that are common to all of the commands. You can pass either –help or -? to any of the commands to get help about the command. The -quiet option can be used to suppress most of the output from the tool. The -trace option outputs additional tracing information to the log file, and the -logfile option overrides the normal location of the log file (by default it goes to the WebSphere logs directory or some subdirectory therein). By default, the contents of the logfile are appended with each command executed; however the -replacelog parameter will cause the log file to be overwritten.

The -username and –password options can be used to specify the user name and password to those commands that need them. Whenever you connect to a server and security is enabled, the user name and password are required. If you specified this information in *sas.client.props* or *soap.client.props* it will be read from there. If not, the information must be passed on the command line. Because almost all commands connect to a server, this information is usually required. Starting a server, does not require the user name and password because it is starting, not connecting to, a server. The stopServer command, however, does require a user name and password.

SERVER MANAGEMENT COMMANDS

Starting Servers

The startServer, startNode, and startManager commands are used to launch various types of servers. With the startServer command you can start any server on the local machine. The startNode and startManager commands are provided for convenience to start the node agent or Deployment Manager servers. Because startNode and startManager are aliases for appropriate startServer commands (startServer nodeagent and startServer dmgr), all discussion of startServer applies equally to the other two commands, except that you do not provide a server name on the command.

With the simplest version of startServer you only provide the name of the server (startNode and startManager do not require any parameters):

```
C:\WebSphere\AppServer\bin>startServer server1
ADMU0116I: Tool information is being logged in file
           C:\WebSphere\AppServer\logs\server1\startServer.log
ADMU3100I: Reading configuration for server: server1
ADMU3200I: Server launched. Waiting for initialization status.
ADMU3000I: Server server1 open for e-business; process id is 2512
```

The first line tells you that startServer.log contains some information about this invocation of startServer. The next line shows that the configuration of server1 is being read to determine how it is to be launched; specifically, the server.xml file is read and the <process-Definition> stanza is parsed to determine the correct JVM parameters to use. Next the server itself is launched in a separate process. The `startServer` command waits until either the server is initialized successfully or it fails for some reason. In this example the server is launched successfully, and can be referred to by the process ID (PID) given, 2512. At this point the `startServer` command is finished and returns to the command line. If you don't want the command to wait for the server to start, you can pass the `-nowait` parameter; after parsing the configuration and launching the server the command will return.

It is important to note that there are really two separate processes involved in starting the server in this way. The first is the `startServer` command itself, also known as the launcher; the other process is the server that is launched. When the command completes, there is only one process remaining, the server process. The *startServer.log* file only logs information about the launcher process. To see information about the server itself, you need to go to the *SystemOut.log* file, which is located in the same directory as the *startServer.log* file. When the server fails to start successfully, it is the *SystemOut.log* that almost always contains the most important information, rather than the *startServer.log* file.

Another consequence of there being two separate processes is that if you set anything in the *startServer.bat* or *.sh* file, you should not expect those settings to be passed to the server. In general, JVM options should be specified in the *server.xml* file. However, you can also generate a command that is used to directly launch the server with the `-script` option. The following command creates a new file *startServer1.bat* that can then be used to launch server1 directly.

```
C:\WebSphere\AppServer\bin>startServer server1 -script startServer1.bat
ADMU0116I: Tool information is being logged in file
            C:\WebSphere\AppServer\logs\server1\startServer.log
ADMU3100I: Reading configuration for server: server1
ADMU3300I: Launch script for server created: startServer1.bat
```

The benefit of generating a script is that the server1 configuration only needs to be parsed once. However, be aware that any change you make to the server1 process definition will not be picked up unless you regenerate the script. The other benefit of generating a script is that you can provide settings to debug the server.

Stopping Servers

The commands to stop servers are quite similar to the commands to start servers. There are three commands to stop servers: `stopServer`, `stopNode`, and `stopManager`. Again, the latter two commands are aliases for `stopServer nodeagent` and `stopServer dmgr`. Again, the only required argument to `stopServer` is the server name:

```
C:\WebSphere\AppServer\bin>stopServer server1
ADMU0116I: Tool information is being logged in file
           C:\WebSphere\AppServer\logs\server1\stopServer.log
ADMU3100I: Reading configuration for server: server1
ADMU3201I: Server stop request issued. Waiting for stop status.
ADMU4000I: Server server1 stop completed.
```

The *stopServer.log* contains information about the tool, and *SystemOut.log* contains information from the server on how the stop is progressing.

Server Status

The serverStatus command is used to examine whether servers are accepting calls. You can determine the status of any server on the local system by passing the server name to the command:

```
C:\WebSphere\AppServer\bin>serverStatus server1
ADMU0116I: Tool information is being logged in file
           C:\Program
Files\WebSphere\AppServer\logs\server1\serverStatus.log
ADMU0500I: Retrieving server status for server1
ADMU0508I: The Application Server "server1" is STARTED
```

You can get the status of all the servers in the system by passing -all instead of the server name:

```
C:\WebSphere\AppServer\bin>serverStatus -all
ADMU0116I: Tool information is being logged in file
           C:\WebSphere\AppServer\logs\serverStatus.log
ADMU0503I: Retrieving server status for all servers
ADMU0505I: Servers found in configuration:
ADMU0506I: Server name: server1
ADMU0509I: The Application Server "server1" cannot be reached. It appears
           to be stopped.
```

Note that if a server is running but having communication problems, it might still be reported as stopped.

NETWORK DEPLOYMENT COMMANDS

This class of commands deals with the configuration of the local node in relation to a cell. Commands allow you to federate a node into a cell (addNode), defederate a node from a cell (removeNode), or in certain situations, get the configuration from the Deployment Manager copied to the node.

Federation

The process of federation takes a stand-alone node and adds it as part of a cell. After a node is federated, it can be administered from the Deployment Manager server, along with all the other nodes in the cell. Node federation also creates the node agent process, which allows the Deployment Manager to communicate with all of the servers in the node.

To federate a node, run the addNode command from the node you want to federate, specifying the location of the Deployment Manager for the cell. In the following example, a node called my-node is being federated to a cell named my-cell, which has Deployment Manager located on the my-dmgr-host machine. As you can see, the only required parameter is the name of the machine on which the Deployment Manager is located:

```
C:\WebSphere\AppServer\bin>addnode my-dmgr-host
ADMU0116I: Tool information is being logged in file
           C:\WebSphere\AppServer\logs\addNode.log
ADMU0001I: Begin federation of node my-node with Deployment Manager at
           my-dmgr-host:8879.
ADMU0009I: Successfully connected to Deployment Manager Server: my-dmgr
           host:8879
ADMU0505I: Servers found in configuration:
ADMU0506I: Server name: server1
ADMU2010I: Stopping all server processes for node my-node
ADMU0512I: Server server1 cannot be reached. It appears to be stopped.
ADMU0024I: Deleting the old backup directory.
ADMU0015I: Backing up the original cell repository.
ADMU0012I: Creating Node Agent configuration for node: my-node
ADMU0014I: Adding node my-node configuration to cell: my-cell
ADMU0016I: Synchronizing configuration between node and cell.
ADMU0018I: Launching Node Agent process for node: my-node
ADMU0020I: Reading configuration for Node Agent process: nodeagent
ADMU0022I: Node Agent launched. Waiting for initialization status.
ADMU0030I: Node Agent initialization completed successfully. Process id
           is: 2764
ADMU0523I: Creating Queue Manager for node my-node on server jmsserver
ADMU0525I: Details of Queue Manager creation may be seen in the file:
           createMQ.my-node_jmsserver.log
ADMU9990I:
ADMU0300I: Congratulations! Your node my-node has been successfully
           incorporated into the my-cell cell.
ADMU9990I:
ADMU0306I: Be aware:
```

```
ADMU0302I: Any cell-level documents from the standalone my-node
           configuration have not been migrated to the new cell.
ADMU0307I: You might want to:
ADMU0303I: Update the configuration on the my-cell Deployment Manager
           with values from the old cell-level documents.
ADMU9990I:
ADMU0306I: Be aware:
ADMU0304I: Because -includeapps was not specified, applications installed
           on the standalone node were not installed on the new cell.
ADMU0307I: You might want to:
ADMU0305I: Install applications onto the my-cell cell using wsadmin
           $AdminApp or the Administrative Console.
ADMU9990I:
ADMU0003I: Node my-node has been successfully federated.
```

The process of node federation consists of several small steps:

1. Connect to my-dmgr-host to ensure that it can be reached and to verify other details about the cell:
   ○ The Deployment Manager version must be the same or greater than the node's version.
   ○ There cannot be any other addNodes or removeNodes in progress.
   ○ The Deployment Manager must be able to contact the node by its hostname.
   ○ The clocks of the two machines must be within 5 minutes of each other.
2. Stop all of the servers on the node.
3. Back up the existing config directory to the config/backup directory (any prior backup is overwritten).
4. Create the node agent server configuration.
5. Contact the Deployment Manager to add this node to its cell.
6. Copy the cell's configuration documents to the node.
7. Update setupCmdLine and wsadmin.properties with new cell information.
8. Start the node agent.
9. If embedded messaging is installed, create the JMS server.

By default the Deployment Manager is contacted on port 8879 with the SOAP connector. You can use a different port by specifying it after the Deployment Manager hostname, and can use a different connector with the -conntype argument (e.g., -conntype RMI). You can also choose to not have the node agent automatically launched by passing the -noagent parameter.

In a Network Deployment installation, applications are installed onto the cell, not onto an individual node. Because of this, after federation is complete, applications that were installed on the node are no longer available. Applications that should be available to the new cell should be then installed onto the cell by the normal method. The `addNode` command does not automatically add applications from the node to the cell because applications that already existed with the same name (and whose functionality might not be the same) would be overwritten by the new application. Additionally, because `removeNode` does not remove applications, the sequence `addNode–removeNode–addNode` would cause the second `addNode` to have errors because applications already exist. However, if you understand these issues, using the `-includeApps` option will attempt to add all the applications from the node to the cell.

Defederation

At times, you might want to defederate, or remove a node, from a cell. For example, you might want to remove a node from one cell before adding it to another. To do this, simply run the `removeNode` command:

```
C:\WebSphere\AppServer\bin>removeNode
ADMU0116I: Tool information is being logged in file
           C:\WebSphere\AppServer\logs\removeNode.log
ADMU2001I: Begin removal of node: fatboyslim
ADMU2026E: Node fatboyslim is not incorporated into any cell.
```

The processing of `removeNode` is fairly straightforward. First the Deployment Manager is contacted and prompted to begin `removeNode` processing; this deletes the config documents for the node from the cell. After the documents are deleted, the cell no longer has any knowledge of the node. Processing at this point continues on the node by deleting the files in the config directory, and then copying the files from the config/backup directory into the current config directory. Recall that the files in this directory are created during `addNode`; in effect, this returns the node configuration to the same state that it was in before the `addNode` occurred. At this point `removeNode` processing is complete, and the node is thus returned to a base configuration. Note that because the files copied are those that existed at the time of `addNode`, any changes made since then will be lost.

There are very few options specific to `removeNode`. Important at times is the `-force` option, which causes the `removeNode` command to continue even if it would normally fail. For example, if the Deployment Manager cannot be contacted, usually processing will stop with a failure stating the dmgr is down. However if `-force` is specified, the command will continue to convert the node to its prefederated state without modifying the Deployment Manager. This is useful if the Deployment Manager has been uninstalled, or if a previous `removeNode` was interrupted before completion. Note that at this point if the dmgr is again started, the `cleanupNode` utility should be run (see later). Also listed is a `-nowait` parameter for `removeNode`; however, this option does nothing.

CleanupNode [Troubleshooting, Network Deployment Only]

In some situations you might want to remove a node from a cell and not be able to through `removeNode`. For example if the node is a machine that no longer exists, you won't be able to go to the node and run the `removeNode` command. Also, if you ran the `removeNode` with the `-force` option and the `dmgr` again became available, the `removeNode` could not be run because the node is no longer a part of the cell. In situations such as these, the `cleanupNode` command can be used to remove the node from the cell configuration:

```
C:\WebSphere\DeploymentManager\bin>cleanupNode my-node
ADMU0116I: Tool information is being logged in file
           C:\WebSphere-5.0.2\DeploymentManager\logs\cleanupNode.log
ADMU2001I: Begin removal of node: my-node
ADMU2018I: Node my-node has been removed from the Deployment Manager
           configuration.
ADMU2024I: Removal of node my-node is complete.
```

It should be emphasized that `cleanupNode` is not a replacement for `removeNode`. The `cleanupNode` command should only be used in cases in which the system is in a state where `removeNode` does not work, as in the preceding example. Because `cleanupNode` only runs on the Deployment Manager, any existing federated nodes will be in a "zombie" state, where the node thinks it is part of the cell, but the Deployment Manager thinks that it is not. However, even this state can be resolved by running `removeNode -force` (the `-force` option is needed because otherwise processing will fail when the dmgr sees the node is not part of the cell). In short, this is a useful command to use if `removeNode` does not work.

SyncNode [Troubleshooting]

Another utility that is not generally needed but is useful in some cases is `syncNode`. Recall that by default the Deployment Manager periodically copies configuration documents to the node when changes are made so that the cell and node documents are in sync. The node agent is required to perform the sync because the dmgr contacts the node agent to perform the operation. However if the node agent cannot be started (e.g., because of a corrupted configuration file) sync will not occur. In a case such as this, running the `syncNode` command will bring the node configuration documents up-to-date with those in the cell. Like the `addNode` command, `syncNode` requires the hostname of the Deployment Manager to run:

```
C:\WebSphere\AppServer\bin>syncNode my-dmgr-host
ADMU0116I: Tool information is being logged in file
           C:\WebSphere\AppServer\logs\syncNode.log
ADMU0401I: Begin syncNode operation for node my-node with Deployment
           Manager my-dmgr-host: 8879
ADMU0016I: Synchronizing configuration between node and cell.
ADMU0402I: The configuration for node my-node has been synchronized with
           Deployment Manager my-dmgr-host: 8879
```

Note that the syncNode command can only be executed if the node agent is stopped.

BACKUP/RESTORE COMMANDS

A pair of simple utilities allows you to back up your configuration to a file and to restore it from that file at a later time. They are not meant as migration tools, nor as a replacement for removeNode. Instead, they should be used as part of a fail-safe strategy in case unforeseen incidents occur.

Backing Up Your Configuration

The backupConfig command takes a snapshot of the contents of your config directory and stores it as a zip file. To ensure that config documents are not changed during a backup, all servers are stopped before the backup is made; this can be disabled with the -nostop option.

```
C:\WebSphere\AppServer\bin>backupConfig
ADMU0116I: Tool information is being logged in file
           C:\WebSphere\AppServer\logs\backupConfig.log
ADMU5001I: Backing up config directory C:\WebSphere\AppServer\config to
           file C:\WebSphere\AppServer\bin\WebSphereConfig_2003-10-26.zip
ADMU0505I: Servers found in configuration:
ADMU0506I: Server name: server1
ADMU2010I: Stopping all server processes for node my-node
ADMU0510I: Server server1 is now STOPPED
..........................................................................
............................................
..........................................................................
..............................
ADMU5002I: 227 files successfully backed up
```

By simply calling the command, a file starting with "WebSphereConfig_" and ending with the current date is saved into the current directory. If a file of that name already exists, the name is appended with an _x, where x is a number that makes the name unique on the file system. If a different name or location is desired, it can be passed to the tool (e.g., `backup-Config c:\temp\myConfigFile.zip`).

Restoring Your Configuration

The `restoreConfig` command is the opposite of the `backupConfig` command; it takes a file created by `backupConfig` and uses it to create a new configuration for the local server. You must provide it with the name of a backup file with which to extract the configuration information. The config directory is determined by the CONFIG_ROOT variable in *setupCmd-Line.bat* or *setupCmdLine.sh*, as usual. If this directory already exists, it is renamed by adding *.old* to the directory name, with a number at the name to guarantee uniqueness.

```
C:\WebSphere\AppServer\bin>restoreConfig WebSphereConfig_2003-10-26.zip
ADMU0116I: Tool information is being logged in file
           C:\WebSphere\AppServer\logs\restoreConfig.log
ADMU0506I: Server name: server1ADMU0505I: Servers found in configuration:
ADMU2010I: Stopping all server processes for node fatboyslim
ADMU0512I: Server server1 cannot be reached. It appears to be stopped.
ADMU5502I: The directory C:\WebSphere\AppServer\config already exists;
           renaming to C:\WebSphere\AppServer\config.old
ADMU5504I: Restore location successfully renamed
ADMU5505I: Restoring file WebSphereConfig_2003-10-26.zip to location
           C:\WebSphere\AppServer\config
...............................................................................
.....................................................
...............................................................................
.................................
ADMU5506I: 227 files successfully restored
ADMA6001I: Begin App Preparation -
ADMA6009I: Processing complete.
```

OTHER COMMANDS

There are a number of other commands that aren't specifically administration commands, but are still useful to understand. Because these are not administrative commands, they do not conform to the general command syntax described at the beginning of this chapter.

EAR Expander

EARExpander is a bit of a misnomer; it can be used to expand EAR files to a directory structure, but it can also be used to collapse an already-expanded EAR directory structure into an EAR file. With it you can make simple changes to an EAR file by expanding it, making some changes, and then collapsing it into an EAR file again.

The EARExpander command requires the name of an EAR file (the source for expand or destination for collapse), a directory (the source for collapse or destination for expand), and the type of operation you want to perform (expand or collapse). The following example shows expansion of DefaultApplication.ear into the C:\temp directory.

```
C:\WebSphere\AppServer\bin>EARExpander -ear
..\installableApps\DefaultApplication.ear -operationDir c:\temp\defaultApp
-operation expand
ADMA4006I: Expanding ..\installableApps\DefaultApplication.ear into
c:\temp\defaultApp
```

You could make modifications to the files in the EAR at this point. Then to collapse the modified directory into a new EAR file, simply run the same command with slightly different arguments:

```
C:\WebSphere\AppServer\bin>EARExpander -ear
..\installableApps\new_DefaultApplication.ear -operationDir
c:\temp\defaultApp -operation collapse
ADMA4007I: Collapsing c:\temp\defaultApp into
..\installableApps\new_DefaultApplication.ear
```

Creating Additional WebSphere Instances

It is sometimes useful to be able to have multiple WebSphere installations on the same host computer; for example you might want to have a separate cell for prototyping configuration changes, separate from the production cell. Because WebSphere is sold on a per-CPU basis, this can result in cost savings compared to having WebSphere installed separately on multiple systems. However with multiple installations there are multiple copies of many files that never change, resulting in unnecessary disk utilization. WebSphere Version 5 provides the ability to create multiple WebSphere instances on the same host; each instance has its own copy of configuration files and other per-node files, while sharing the server binary files. The wsinstance command is used to create or delete WebSphere instances. In the following example the wsinstance command is used to create a new instance named myInstance on the host myHost, which is rooted at C:\MyInstanceDir. Note that the wsinstance command is located in the wsinstance subdirectory of the bin directory:

```
C:\WebSphere-5.0.2\AppServer\bin\wsinstance>wsinstance -name myInstance
-path c:\MyInstanceDir -create
Usage:
wsinstance.bat(sh) -name instanceName -path instancePath -host myHost
[-startingPort startingPort] -create|-delete  [
-debug]


C:\WebSphere-5.0.2\AppServer\bin\wsinstance>wsinstance -name myInstance
-path c:\MyInstanceDir -host myHost -create
[wsNLSEcho] Creating new wsinstance with name myInstance
[wsNLSEcho] Instance location   : c:\MyInstanceDir
[wsNLSEcho] Instance node name  : myHost_myInstance


[wsNLSEcho] Start creating instance

[wsNLSEcho] Creating configuration folder for new instance.
[wsNLSEcho] Successfully created configuration folder for new instance.


[wsNLSEcho] Creating required folders for new instance.
[wsNLSEcho] Successfully created required folders for new instance.


[wsNLSEcho] Genrating user script for new instance.
[wsNLSEcho] Genrated user script. c:\MyInstanceDir/bin/setupCmdLine.bat
for  new instance.


[wsNLSEcho] Updated port numbers for new instance.
[wsNLSEcho] See file myHost_myInstance_portdef.props for list of ports
being used by the new instance.


[wsNLSEcho] Creating MQ QueueManager for the new instance.
[wsNLSEcho] Created MQ QueueManager for the new instance. See
createMQ_myHost_myInstance.server1.log file for log messages.


[wsNLSEcho] Installing Admin Application on the new instance.
[wsNLSEcho] Completed installing admin application on the new instance.
See installAdmin_myHost_myInstance.log file for log messages.


BUILD SUCCESSFUL
Total time: 4 minutes 0 seconds
```

The result of this command is a new instance with a base node named myHost_myInstance. A new server1 application server is also created in the new node. The new node is not federated into any cell, even if the node from which `wsinstance` was run is part of a cell. The new node can now be used the same as any Base server, or can be federated into a cell for a Network Deployment installation. Changes made to the myInstance configuration are separate from the Base instance, servers can be started and stopped independently, and applications can be installed to either instance independently.

The `wsinstance` command can also be used from a Network Deployment installation to create a new Deployment Manager instance. The resulting instance includes a new node and a new Deployment Manager server, instead of an application server. Like the Base instance, all configuration changes to the Network Deployment instance are separate from the Base instance.

With multiple servers running on the same system, it is important to keep in mind the port numbers need to be unique. Recall that the Deployment Manager and a base server both use a default SOAP port of 8880, so you cannot run both servers at the same time without modifying the port numbers. New instances created with `wsinstance` attempt to give unique port numbers by incrementing the port number used, so a new instance created from a base installation by default uses port 8881 for SOAP communication. However if a second instance is created, it will also use port 8881, forcing you to either not run servers at the same time, or to change the port numbers after instance creation. However `wsinstance` provides an optional argument `-startingPort`, which can be used to set unique new port numbers for all the ports generated in the instance. For example by specifying `-startingPort 8885`, ports 8885 to 8889 are used by the HTTP transport service, port 8893 for SOAP communication, and so on. To prevent duplicate port numbers, you should ensure there are at least 15 ports available for use, beginning at the starting port that is given.

Instances can also be deleted with the `wsinstance` command. Instead of specifying `-create` to create the instance, specify `-delete` to remove the instance. Although in Version 5 this simply deletes the instance configuration files, you are encouraged to delete the instance in this manner to prepare for future enhancements to the command. Any files remaining in the directory after deleting the instance can safely be removed.

Using Ant to Automate WebSphere Commands

The commands examined in this chapter are executed by opening a command prompt and manually entering the command and waiting for a response. For day-to-day use this is fine, but often it is useful to run commands in an automated fashion. Ant (*http://ant.apache.org*) is a general-purpose, open-source Java-based build tool that is commonly used to perform a large set of tasks. WebSphere provides a set of Ant tasks that perform some of the commands just discussed inside a standard Ant build file. Additionally there are tasks for executing any wsadmin command, application administration, Web Service Definition Language (WSDL) generation, and other J2EE-related activities. A general overview of the Ant tasks is presented here; for more information refer to the API documentation for the com.ibm.websphere.ant.tasks package. WebSphere ships with Ant included, so there is no separate installation necessary.

With Ant, the file build.xml contains all the commands that will be executed when the ant command is executed. The following is a simple build.xml file that starts the node agent and server1 processes:

```
<?xml version="1.0"?>
<project default="startNodeWithServers" basedir=".">
  <taskdef name="wsStartServer"
classname="com.ibm.websphere.ant.tasks.StartServer"/>
  <target name="startNodeWithServers">
    <wsStartServer server="nodeagent"/>
    <wsStartServer server="server1"/>
  </target>
</project>
```

First we define a task by the name of wsStartServer that uses the StartServer class. Then we create a target startNodeWithServers, which first starts the node agent with the wsStartServer task, and then starts server1 with the same task. To execute the build file, run the ws_ant command provided in the WebSphere bin directory. Your current directory should contain the *build.xml* file:

```
C:\startNode>\WebSphere\AppServer\bin\ws_ant
Buildfile: build.xml

startNodeWithServers:
[startServer] ADMU0116I: Tool information is being logged in file
[startServer]
C:\WebSphere\AppServer\logs\nodeagent\startServer.log
[startServer] ADMU3100I: Reading configuration for server: nodeagent
[startServer] ADMU3200I: Server launched. Waiting for initialization
status.
[startServer] ADMU3000I: Server nodeagent open for e-business; process id
is 2668
[startServer] ADMU0116I: Tool information is being logged in file
[startServer]
C:\WebSphere\AppServer\logs\server1\startServer.log
[startServer] ADMU3100I: Reading configuration for server: server1
```

```
[startServer] ADMU3200I: Server launched. Waiting for initialization
status.
[startServer] ADMU3000I: Server server1 open for e-business; process id
is 1932

BUILD SUCCESSFUL
Total time: 1 minute 16 seconds
```

As you can see, the output to the command is nearly identical to running startNode followed by startServer server1. Of course in this case it would probably be easy to write a script that simply performs these two commands. The benefit of using the Ant tasks is when you want to combine WebSphere tasks with other Ant tasks, such as building application source code. For example, you can compile your code, generate a jar file, run the deploy tool (with wsejbdeploy task), and install the application (wsStartApp). You can also use the wsadmin task to execute any command that would normally be run from the wsadmin scripting tool, including executing scripts. For example, the following build script executes the *myScript.jacl* script on the application server my_server:

```
<?xml version="1.0"?>
<project default="runMyScript" basedir=".">
  <taskdef name="wsadmin" classname="com.ibm.websphere.ant.tasks.WsAdmin"/>
  <target name="runMyScript">
    <wsadmin script="myScript.jacl" host="my_server" port="8880"
conntype="SOAP"/>
  </target>
</project>
```

WebSphere Administrative Console

This chapter provides detailed coverage the WebSphere Administrative Console (referred to as "console"), a sophisticated J2EE Web application that provides the graphical management console for administering WebSphere Application Server. The WebSphere Administrative Console supports a full range of administrative activities for WebSphere Application Server.

ADMINISTRATIVE CONSOLE ENVIRONMENT

The console provides a graphical management console for configuring, managing, and controlling WebSphere Application Server.

Administrative Console Overview

The console (see Figure 4.1) was designed so that systems management tasks for all aspects of managing the server environment could be made available to systems administrators using standard Web browser technology. The console was also built to be flexible because the tasks provided to administrators vary by WebSphere server product (Base, Network Deployment, or Express edition) as well as by platform (non-z/OS platforms and z/OS). In WebSphere Version 5, the tasks for add-on product features such as Network Deployment get added to the basic console provided in the Base product in a seamless manner to form a single administrative solution.

In addition, the console was built to be secure. When security is enabled for the server environment, all access to the console is tightly guarded using J2EE security mechanisms, and authorization to perform tasks within the console will be restricted to allow only administrators assigned to the roles of the tasks being performed. However, the WebSphere Version 5 console does not further restrict access to individual managed objects; for example, all administrators

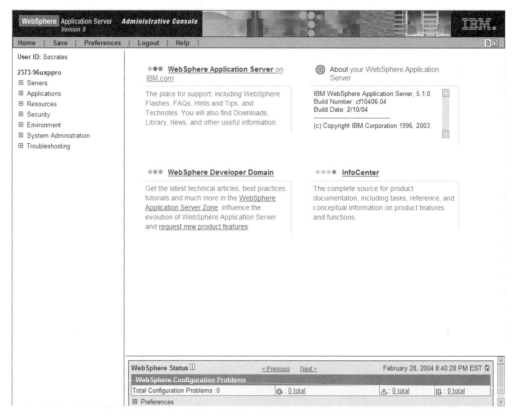

Figure 4.1
WebSphere Application Server Administrative Console.

with the Configurator role will be able to configure all nodes and servers within the cell. To have finer grained control of administrative security through the console, you will need to use WebSphere configuration instances (cells), setting security in each cell appropriately.

The console was designed to scale up with the server environment being managed. The console can manage a single server environment as well as multiple nodes with multiple servers (in the Network Deployment product). Management tasks were built to be able to meet the scalability requirements of the WebSphere products.

The console is a Web application provided as an optional feature that can be selected for installation through the WebSphere product installer. The default installation option is to install the console during both the Base and Network Deployment product installations. However, if you do not want or need the console to be installed, use the Custom install options of the installer to disable the automatic installation and deployment of the console, as shown in Figure 4.2. When installed in the Base environment, the console application is

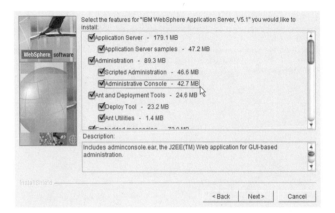

Figure 4.2
Custom install option for WebSphere Administrative Console.

deployed by the product install into the default Application Server (alongside sample appli-cations and other user applications). In a Base product installation, the default Application Server must be started before attempting to access it through a Web browser. You can use the command startServer server1 to start the default server after installing the Base product (see Chapter 3 for details of the startServer command).

In the WebSphere Network Deployment environment, the console is deployed by the prod-uct install into the Deployment Manager agent. The Deployment Manager agent must be running to access the console via a Web browser. When Base nodes are federated into a WebSphere Network Deployment multinode cell using the addNode command, the addNode command removes any Base console instances from servers of the node being added, so that the console is only run in the Deployment Manager in the WebSphere Network Deploy-ment environment. The WebSphere Network Deployment version of the console adds in additional multinode, multiserver, and cluster management tasks related to the distributed management features of the WebSphere Network Deployment product. Table 4.1 summa-rizes the tasks that are available in the navigation tree and shows the additional tasks added by each WebSphere add-on product (or platform).

Table 4.1   Available Tasks in the Navigation Tree

Category or Task	Product	Description
Servers	All	Category containing tasks related to the management of servers within the WebSphere environment.
Application Servers	Base	Task for working with Application Server configurations and operations management of servers. There are many additional server management subtasks available when working with individual servers within this task.
Messaging Servers	Network Deployment	Task for working with stand-alone messaging servers. There are many additional server management subtasks available when working with individual servers within this task.
Clusters	Network Deployment	Task for working with server clusters in the cell.
Cluster Topology	Network Deployment	Task for viewing the cluster topology in the cell.
Applications	All	Category containing tasks related to the management of enterprise applications deployed in the environment.
Enterprise Applications	Base	Task for working with enterprise applications. There are many additional application management subtasks available when working with individual applications within this task.
Install New Application	Base	Task for installing and deploying a new enterprise application into the WebSphere environment.
Resources	All	Category containing tasks related to the management of resource connections within the server environment.
JDBC Providers	Base	Task for working with database connections used by applications.
Generic JMS Providers	Base	Task for working with messaging-related resource connections for non-IBM messaging products used by applications.
WebSphere JMS Provider	Base	Task for working with messaging-related resource connections for the embedded WebSphere messaging provider used by applications.

Table 4.1   Available Tasks in the Navigation Tree (Continued)

Category or Task	Product	Description
WebSphere MQ JMS Provider	Base	Task for working with messaging-related resource connections for external IBM MQ Series used by applications.
Mail Providers	Base	Task for working with external mail server connections used by applications.
Resource Environment Providers	Base	Task for working with settings for resource environment entries.
URL Providers	Base	Task for working with Uniform Resource Locations (URL) protocol handlers used by applications.
Resource Adaptors	Base	Task for working with Enterprise Information System connections that can be used by applications.
Security	All	Category containing tasks related to security management features.
Global Security	Base	Task for enabling and configuring global security settings for the entire cell.
SSL	Base	Task for configuring Secure Sockets Layer (SSL) protocol.
Authentication Mechanisms	All	Category containing tasks related to the administration of authentication mechanisms.
LTPA	Base	Task for configuring Lightweight Third Party Authentication (LTPA) protocol settings.
User Registries	All	Category containing tasks related to the administration of user registries.
Local OS	Base	Task for configuring use of the local operating system's user registry as the user registry for the cell.
LDAP	Base	Task for configuring the use of Lightweight Directory Access Protocol (LDAP) to use an external LDAP server as the user registry for the cell.
Custom	Base	Task for configuring the use of a custom user registry implementation as the user registry for the cell.
JAAS Configuration	Base	Category containing tasks for configuring standard authentication and authorization for the cell.

Table 4.1   Available Tasks in the Navigation Tree (Continued)

Category or Task	Product	Description
Application Logins	Base	Task for configuring the application logins.
J2C Authentication Data	Base	Task for configuring credentials (user IDs and passwords) that can be used for connecting to external resources such as databases.
Authentication Protocol	All	Category containing tasks related to authentication protocol configuration.
CSIv2 Inbound Authentication	Base	
CSIv2 Outbound Authentication	Base	
CSIv2 Inbound Transport	Base	
CSIv2 Outbound Transport	Base	
SAS Inbound Transport	Base	
SAS Outbound Transport	Base	
Web Services	All	Category for tasks related to security for Web Services.
Properties (Web Services)	Base	(since 5.0.2) Web Services security settings.
Trust Anchors	Base	(since 5.0.2) Web Services security.
Collection Cert. Store	Base	(since 5.0.2) Web Services security.
Key Locators	Base	(since 5.0.2) Web Services security.
Trusted ID Evaluators	Base	(since 5.0.2) Web Services security.
Login Mappings	Base	Tasks for configuring login mappings (credential mappings).
Environment	All	Category containing tasks for configuring miscellaneous aspects of the cell environment.
Update Web Server Plugin	Base	Task for regenerating the plug-in configuration file that must be used with the external Web servers that route requests into application servers.
Virtual Hosts	Base	Task for configuring virtual hosts, MIME types and host aliases used for Web applications.
Manage WebSphere Variables	Base	Task for configuring variables and path mappings used to virtualize file system paths in WebSphere configurations.

Table 4.1   Available Tasks in the Navigation Tree (Continued)

Category or Task	Product	Description
Shared Libraries	Base	Task for configuring code and resource libraries (e.g., jars) that can be shared by multiple applications.
Internal Replication Domains	Network Deployment	Task for configuring memory-to-memory replication domains for use by data replication services.
Naming	All	Category containing tasks for configuring naming and directory support.
Namespace Bindings	Base	Task for configuring how names are bound into JNDI namespaces for use by applications. This task can be used for federating namespaces together.
CORBA Naming Service Users	Base	Task for configuring users that can access CORBA naming and directory entries.
CORBA Naming Service Groups	Base	Task for configuring groups of users that can access CORBA naming and directory entries.
System Administration	All	Category containing tasks related to configuring the WebSphere console and the management agents within the cell.
Cell	Network Deployment	Task for configuring high-level settings of a cell.
Deployment Manager	Network Deployment	Task for configuring Deployment Manager server settings.
Nodes	Network Deployment	Task for configuring node information for the nodes in the cell.
Node Agents	Network Deployment	Task for configuring node agent server settings for each node in the cell.
Console Users	Base	Task for configuring users who are administrators with rights to use the console and subtasks for setting role-based permissions for console administrators.
Console Groups	Base	Task for configuring groups of users who are administrators with rights to use the console and subtasks for setting role-based permissions for console administrators.
Troubleshooting	All	Category containing tasks related to viewing logs, working with configuration problems, and tracing performance.

Table 4.1   Available Tasks in the Navigation Tree (Continued)

Category or Task	Product	Description
Logs and Trace	Base	Task for configuring logging and tracing settings for servers.
Configuration Problems	Base	Task for viewing configuration problems that systems management has detected in the cell. This task contains subtasks for configuring frequency and depth of configuration validation.
PMI Request Metrics	Base	Task for configuring PMI request metrics for tracing request performance through the servers.

Accessing the Administrative Console

By default, the console is accessible by pointing your Web browser to `http://<your_server_name>:9090/admin` where `<your_server_name>` is the fully qualified hostname for the machine with the WebSphere Application Server installation. On Network Deployment installations, remember that the console is running only on the Deployment Manager agent and to use that machine's hostname in place of `<your_server_name>` when connecting your Web browser to the console. Also by default, when security is enabled in the server environment, incoming connections to the 9090 default port will be automatically redirected to use HTTPS on port 9043 without additional configuration.

On WebSphere z/OS Version 5.0, by default the console is accessible on `http://<your_server_name>:9080/admin` because there is only one default virtual host defined on the z/OS cell, which is shared with sample applications and user applications running on the default server.

If you have specified custom ports to use for the console during the installation, such as when using multiple wsinstance configuration instances per product installation, you will need to use the console ports that you have configured for each individual configuration instance.

The console is made up of several frame areas—the Banner area, the Menu Bar area, the Navigation area, the Content area, and the Status area (see Figure 4.3).

The Banner area is just an image with the IBM logos, and can be hidden through a user preference to increase the screen area usable for performing tasks through the console.

The Menu Bar includes a list of actions that are always accessible to the administrator. These include access to the product home page, the console's user preferences, logout, and help contents.

The Navigation area includes a list of all the tasks that the administrator is authorized to perform. Tasks the administrator is not authorized to perform will not appear in this view.

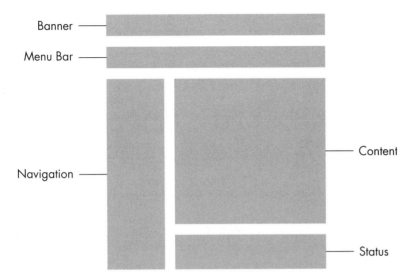

Figure 4.3
WebSphere Administrative Console frame areas.

Management tasks that are displayed in this view are categorized into high-level functional categories based on the primary purpose that the tasks provide the administrator. When tasks are selected from the Navigation area, the task page is displayed in the Content area where you begin working on the task.

The Status area is where important messages, events, or status information is displayed. Examples of the type of information found in this area include summaries of the number of events of various severities that have been logged by servers in the environment, or outstanding configuration problems that need to be resolved in the cell. Additional add-on features can provide additional status or feedback to the administrator in this view.

The Content area is where the details of each task are displayed. Content displayed in this area varies depending on the task being performed by the administrator.

Administrative Console Settings

The WebSphere console provides features for storing per-user preferences. Some of the customizable preference are global and apply to the entire console and all tasks within an administrator's session, whereas others are specific settings for individual management tasks.

Global Preferences

There are a few global console preferences provided directly from the Preferences link on the main Menu Bar (see Figure 4.4).

Preferences

User Preferences

Preferences		
Enable WorkSpace Auto-Refresh	☑	Turn on WorkSpace Auto-Refresh
Do not confirm WorkSpace Discards	☐	No Confirmation on WorkSpace Discard
Use Default Scope	☐	Use Default Scope (Admin Console Node)
Hide/Show Banner	☑	Show Banner
Hide/Show Descriptions	☑	Show Descriptions
Apply Reset		

Figure 4.4
WebSphere Administrative Console global preferences settings.

- *Do not confirm workspace discards.* When this option is enabled, the administrator will not be prompted when the Discard Changes action is selected during the synchronize local configuration changes with master repository task.

- *Use default scope.* When enabled, this option specifies to always automatically use the node that the console is running on when displaying the scope panel for configuration settings that can be applied to multiple contexts. This setting should never be used in WebSphere Network Deployment environments.

- *Hide/Show console banner.* When enabled, this option specifies to show the console banner image. To free up additional screen space for working on tasks, this setting can be disabled, causing the IBM logo banner to not appear for the current administrator.

- *Hide/Show descriptions.* When this option is enabled, the console will display field-level help descriptions next to every field within management tasks (wherever field help is available). Expert administrators who are already familiar with most WebSphere configuration settings might find disabling this option useful, as it increases the amount of data that can be displayed in the Content area of the console for management tasks.

Preferences

Each management task provided through the console can have its own special set of user preferences. For example, on the Servers view the settings shown in Figure 4.5 are available as user preferences specific to the Servers management task. User preferences persist across sessions per administrator, so that the next time an administrator performs the same task the previous settings are recalled. Examples of task-level user preferences are to set the number of rows to display in collections of objects, or to remember the filter/search criteria entered for a collection.

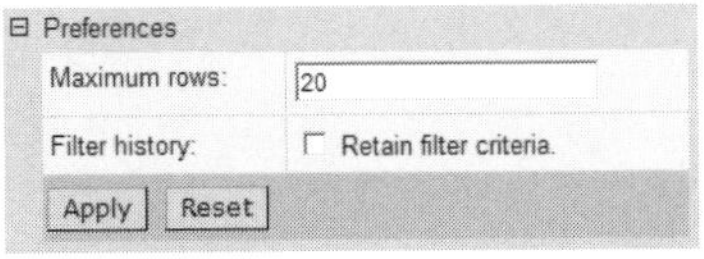

Figure 4.5
WebSphere Administrative Console example preferences settings for a management task.

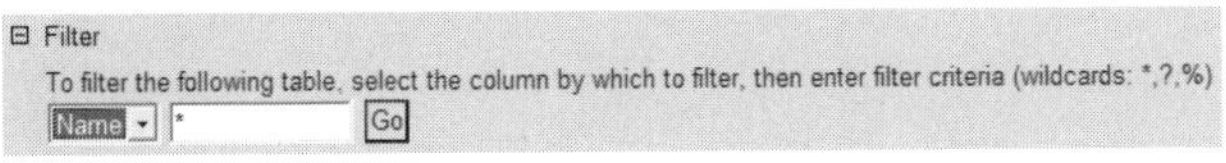

Figure 4.6
WebSphere Administrative Console example filter settings for a management task.

Filter

Another panel that appears on many configuration tasks that display large collections of managed resources is the filter criteria entry panel (see Figure 4.6). Each type of managed resource has a different set of attributes that can be used to search or filter the set of items shown to the set of items that match the filter, rather than the entire collection of items defined within the cell. Administrators can use the filter scope entry panel to quickly narrow the set of items in a collection to the ones they are interested in managing. For most text fields, the filter entry panel accepts simple wildcard patterns for matching entries. In most panels, filter criteria entered by an administrator can be saved with the administrator's user preferences (see the Preferences panel for the task that the filter settings are applied on for a list of available task preferences) so that the next time the task is viewed, the previous filter criteria are automatically applied.

Scope

Configuring settings that can exist within variable configuration scopes in WebSphere is one of the more difficult things that first-time users encounter. Certain types of configuration settings can be set within the cell, node, and server configuration contexts and typically an override policy applies when resources with the same name or JNDI name are defined in two or more of these contexts and are visible to a server (see Figure 4.7).

Each node in WebSphere has its own stand-alone slice of the master configuration repository that it synchronizes with the master copy according to a synchronization policy. When an Application Server starts up, it must derive its configuration by looking at the configuration tree for the node. For configuration settings that can be defined within multiple scopes for that node, such as variables (stored in *variables.xml*) or resource definitions (stored in *resources.xml*), the server loads up the configuration settings from cell, node, and server scopes and then combines the settings together to form a single list of configuration settings

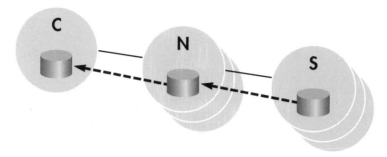

Figure 4.7
Multiple configuration scopes with overriding.

that apply to the server. When it combines the settings from the multiple scopes it uses a predefined lookup order starting with those settings at the cell scope, going to the node scope, and finally moving to the server scope. If the server encounters settings with the same name (or JNDI name in the case of resource definitions), it replaces definitions defined at higher scopes with the definitions defined at lower scopes (i.e., settings with the same name at the server scope override those at that node scope, which override the settings at cell scope). The server then uses the final merged list as its settings.

When variable scoping is possible for configuration tasks, a scope selection panel similar to the one shown in Figure 4.8 will be displayed for the task.

Figure 4.8
Example scope selectors panes that appear on tasks that work with configuration data in multiple scopes.

The scope selection tile looks and functions differently in Base and Network Deployment server environments. In Base environments, because there is only one node, only the server name is selectable. The cell and node name are preset. In Network Deployment environments, where there are multiple nodes, a Browse button appears next to the Node and Server name entry fields so that you can specify the node or server as part of the scope identifier used to determine for which scope you will be modifying configuration settings (see Figure 4.9).

Select a Server Scope

Select a Server from the list that with be used to set the current scope. ⓘ

Total: 2	
⊞ Filter	
Server ↕	**Node**
○ MyApplicationServer	2373-96uxppro
○ server1	2373-96uxppro
[OK] [Cancel]	

Figure 4.9
Selecting a server name as part of identifying a scope of configuration.

Something that might not be immediately apparent on the scope pane is that you can select either cell scope, node scope, or server scope. If you only select the cell scope any names you place in the node or server name fields are ignored, and you will be working within the cell scope directly. If you select node scope and specify a node name but not a server name you will be working directly in the specified node's scope. If you select server scope and specify a node name and server name, you will work directly in the specified server scope.

Once you select and specify scope identifying information and click Apply, you will only be looking and able to work with the configurations in that single scope, not any configuration settings that might be in higher level scopes that you might be overriding. For this reason, it is always good practice before configuring variable-scoped configuration settings of a server to switch among all three scopes and look at the resources specified in those scopes (possibly keeping separate browser windows open for quick reference) so that you know exactly what resources are already defined for which you could be overriding the definitions inadvertently.

Unfortunately, at the time of this writing, there is not a good "flattened" view of variable scoped configuration settings from the server perspective that is available for administrators through the WebSphere console.

Accessibility Mode

The console officially supports Microsoft Internet Explorer 5.5 Service Pack 2 and higher Internet Explorer 6.0 and higher, and Netscape 4.79, but can work with Mozilla 1.4 and higher and other browsers. The console can run in a special accessibility mode that is intended to provide accessibility enablement for visually impaired users. This mode is also useful for using unsupported browsers with slightly non-standard JavaScript support (e.g., KDE Konqueror or Mac OS X/Safari), although it is not as visually appealing or easy to use. Disable JavaScript in your browser to have tasks rendered without full JavaScript capabilities in accessibility mode.

Separation of Configuration Management from Operational Management

An important convention used within all WebSphere configuration tasks that enforces the split between configuration management and operations management is that the configuration tasks are the primary focus of management and navigation (because configuration is always accessible). Configuration data and subtasks for configuration management are always displayed on a Config tab on the managed object's primary configuration task page, and operations management subtasks, views, and active data are always displayed on the Runtime tab available from the managed object's primary configuration task page. The operations management views are only made available from the configuration tasks of objects that correspond to the managed object when connections to the managed object are established. It will not be possible for an administrator to see the active state of a managed object or to perform operations management tasks on an object in the environment until the object is running and is connected to systems management agents. Most managed objects that have an operational state or tasks that can be performed must first be started using a Start command or a Connect command to make the object run in the environment or create a connection to an object that is already running in the environment.

Role-Based Filtering of Tasks

As discussed earlier, WebSphere administrators can be assigned to perform one of four key roles:

- Administrator
- Configurator
- Operator
- Monitor

The console automatically filters tasks (pages and links), actions (buttons), and views (data displayed) on these tasks based on the security role(s) assigned to the administrator who is using the console. Filtered items cannot be seen by the administrator, and superuser administrators need to be aware of this if working with other administrators who have not been given full permissions of Administrator role in the cell. If any of the features described in this chapter do not appear in your console when running with security enabled, check your role assignments using the Console Users tasks described in later sections.

Common Tasks

There are a number of common tasks related to working with the console itself and the WebSphere environment in general, such as how to log in and out of the console, as well as peculiarities of saving and synchronizing configuration changes.

Login

After you open the URL to access the console, a logon page appears. Because security is disabled out of the box, the first time you log in as administrator, the unsecured logon page is shown (see Figure 4.10). The unsecured logon page prompts you to enter only a user ID, and not a password. On this page, any user ID you enter will not be checked against any user registry, and the user ID is only used to establish a session and workspace for administrative changes.

Figure 4.10
WebSphere Administrative Console logon page with security disabled.

Once security has been enabled in the server environment, subsequent access to the console will display the secure login page. Your browser should also prompt you that the CA Root certificate is not trusted for the login page. Initially, an administrator can enable trust and begin using the console by installing the default self-issued certificate provided by IBM into the browser's trusted root certificate store; however, in a production environment the administrator will want to change the certificate of the console to one issued by the company running the console or trusted authority.

The secure login page prompts for both a user ID and a password (see Figure 4.11). Information entered on the secure login page will be checked against the current user registry in use and password credentials will be verified before access is permitted to other areas of the console.

Figure 4.11
WebSphere Administrative Console logon page with security enabled.

After authenticating with the console, if the administrator already has an open session to the console (possible through another browser window), the console informs the administrator of this situation and gives three options for resolving it:

- *Logout the other user with the same user ID.* The administrator can recover any configuration changes that were being made within the other administrator's session.

- *Return to the login page*. The administrator can return to the login page and authenticate as a different console user.
- *Return to the login page and wait*. The administrator can return to the login page and wait for the other user to log out or for the other user's console session to timeout (typically 20 minutes).

If the console detects local workspace changes that were made in a previous session by this administrator, the console prompts the administrator to either continue using the changes as they were left in the prior session or to completely discard all pending changes from the previous session and continue with a fresh workspace.

The console then displays the main console frame and home page. If pending changes were detected and the administrator decided to continue using the pending changes, it might be a good idea to synchronize the changes with the master configuration repository at this time before making further changes, depending on the completeness and validity of the previous configuration changes (see the section titled Save for further information regarding local workspace synchronization).

Home

The home page of the console (see Figure 4.12) displays the product information for the WebSphere environment being managed through the console. From this page the administrator will find links to important IBM Web sites and other product information. Add-on features for WebSphere may append additional information to the home page relevant to them. Always make sure to check the console home page for new links and information after installing additional WebSphere add-on products such as Network Deployment and Express edition. If this is the first time you are using the product, make sure you visit each of the various links on the home page and familiarize yourself with the available information.

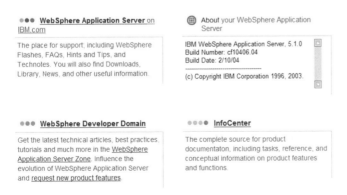

Figure 4.12
WebSphere Administrative Console home page.

Save

Unlike operational management tasks such as starting and stopping servers, as an administrator makes configuration changes through configuration tasks in the console, each configuration change is saved to a local workspace assigned to that administrator. The workspace keeps the changes separate from changes being made by other users, and these changes are also not automatically synchronized with the master repository. Therefore, servers will not automatically pick up configuration changes if the administrator has not yet synchronized local workspace changes with the master configuration repository.

When the console detects that there are local configuration changes that have not yet been synchronized with the master repository, it displays the important working message shown in Figure 4.13 at the top of the Content area page.

Figure 4.13
Important local change notification message.

The administrator must make a conscious decision to synchronize local workspace changes with the master repository, as configuration changes can have a dramatic effect on a production server environment. To perform the synchronization task, the administrator must either select the Save menu item from the Menu Bar, or click the Save hyperlink in the important local changes warning message area (see Figure 4.13).

The Save menu item allows an administrator to synchronize all local configuration changes to the master configuration repository (see Figure 4.14; it might be useful to think of the Save action as Synchronize Local Workspace with Master Configuration). During the local-to-master configuration synchronization task, an administrator might need to resolve configuration conflicts. The administrator is also given the opportunity to completely discard all configuration changes made since his or her last local-to-master configuration synchronization. Merely synchronizing the local configuration changes to the master configuration repository will not be enough to cause the components running in the server environment to pick up the changes—especially in a production-mode Network Deployment environment. Remember that servers that are already running are using the configuration that was in place on the server's node at the time the server was started. The servers will (typically) need to be restarted to pick up the latest changes from the master configuration repository.

In a Network Deployment distributed environment with multiple nodes in a cell, the nodes have to resynchronize their local "node" copies of the configuration from the master reposi-

Save

Save your workspace changes to the master configuration

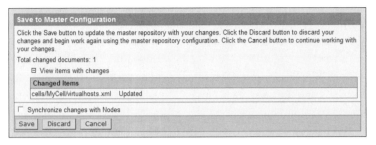

Figure 4.14
WebSphere Administrative Console Save Local Changes to Master Repository page showing files that have been changed in the administrator's local workspace.

tory before the changes that are stored in the master configuration repository become usable by the server components on that node. The master repository to node synchronization is different from local workspace synchronization where administrators are pushing changes into the configuration repository. In the master repository to node synchronization, nodes pull the "latest" configuration from the master repository. In Network Deployment environments, it is possible that the automatic node synchronization service that is configured by default has been disabled by an administrator, requiring each node to be manually synchronized with the master repository. Turning off automatic node synchronization can give you an extra level of control and predictability in large-scale production server environments.

When more than one administrator is making changes to the console environment, configuration conflicts might occur in the environment. One example scenario where this occurs is when the first administrator begins making changes to settings on the same server that a second administrator was also changing, but the second administrator synchronized with the master configuration repository after the first administrator began making changes.

At the time of this writing, WebSphere only allows very coarse-grained (document-level) conflict resolution in these situations. When a conflict is detected during the synchronization of local changes to the master repository, a summary of changes is displayed to the administrator, and the administrator must choose to either overwrite the configuration in the master repository with all changes in the local workspace, or to discard all changes in the local workspace. In WebSphere Version 5, there is not finer grained control for configuration conflict resolution than all-or-nothing replacement.

Logout

An administrator can log out of the console by using the Logout link on the main menu. If there are configuration changes that have been made during the administrator's session, the configuration synchronization view is displayed as a reminder that changes were made that need to be synchronized with the master configuration repository before they will become active for the cell (see Figure 4.11). There is also an option to discard all of the changes made during the administrator's session. If there are no pending changes, or the administrator has resolved what to do with pending changes, the administrator's session is terminated and the administrator will not be allowed to perform administrative tasks through the console again until re-authenticated (via the logon page).

Session Timeouts

By default, the console is configured to automatically log out users that have not actively used the console for a period of 20 minutes. This feature is called automatic session timeout. When an administrator's session has timed out, all pending work is saved automatically in the administrator's local workspace that was associated with his or her session. The administrator is not allowed to perform further tasks within the console until reauthenticated (via the logon page).

The next time the administrator logs into the console, a pending changes page will be displayed prompting the user to recover pending changes from a previous session (these are actually all changes since the last time that administrator synchronized the local workspace with the master configuration repository). The administrator can then choose to continue with the previous changes or discard them and continue with a new session.

Security Cookie Timeouts

When using authentication mechanisms such as LTPA, cookies might be used by the authentication mechanism to track single sign-on. If timeout periods have been configured for cookies used in the underlying authentication mechanism of the console, they will typically be configured with a timeout period, after which they will expire. Once the cookie has expired, all pending work is saved automatically in the administrator's local workspace that was associated with his or her session. The administrator is not allowed to perform further tasks within the console until reauthenticated (via the logon page).

The next time the administrator logs into the console, a pending changes page will be displayed prompting the administrator to recover pending changes from a previous session (these are actually all changes since the last time that administrator synchronized the local workspace with the master configuration repository). The administrator can then choose to continue with the previous changes or discard them and continue with a new session.

ADMINISTRATIVE CONSOLE TASK REFERENCE

The remainder of this chapter describes each of the WebSphere Application Server management tasks available through the console.

Manage Servers

Tasks are provided for configuring and managing each of the four types of servers that can be managed within the WebSphere environment, namely:

- Application Servers
- JMS servers (Network Deployment)
- Node agents (Network Deployment)
- Deployment Manager (Network Deployment)

Application Servers

Application Server configurations can be created, deleted, and edited through the Administrative Console. In the Base environment, operations management actions are not provided through the console because the services of a node agent are required for launching and terminating processes on nodes, even though it is possible to create more than one server configuration through the console. Instead, use the `startServer` and `stopServer` commands in a shell prompt to start and stop servers in the Base environment. In the Network Deployment multiple-node management environment, more than one server can be started and stopped using the console and these additional actions are added automatically to the list of available server actions in the console.

The primary task for working with application servers may be found under the "Servers" category on the Navigation pane of the console (see Figure 4.15). Selecting this task displays a view containing a searchable table of application servers that an administrator can use to browse through the application servers defined for a node or cell.

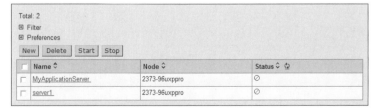

Figure 4.15
Application Servers management task.

If you access the Network Deployment console immediately after installing the product, you might be surprised to find that no application servers are available in the Application Servers task, and no nodes are configured in the Nodes task. This is because nodes have not been federated into the cell that the console is managing (via the addNode command).

In the WebSphere Network Deployment console, in addition to being able to find servers by name or name of the node on which they are configured, you can use the Application Servers view as a simple way to quickly determine the operational status (started, stopped, synchronizing, etc.) of a set of the servers in the cell. Operational status is not provided in the Base console Application Servers table; however, you can find the operational status of a server by visiting the Runtime tab on the server's detailed configuration page. Each time you refresh the servers table, the current operational status indicator will be updated with the latest status from the server agents. Some administrators like to keep this view of servers open in a separate browser window (perhaps in full screen) once an environment is in production, and then refresh it periodically. In large environments, keep in mind that it could take a while to display the active operational status of a large number of servers in the view because each server is being queried individually for its status asynchronously. It could take longer to retrieve the status of some servers than others, but as long as the table is displayed in your browser, the pending status queries will continue to update as results are available, updating the status displayed in the view as each status query completes.

If you find that this view takes too long to appear, try setting the number of servers displayed in your view lower and page through the servers, or enter more specific search criteria so that a smaller set of servers is viewed at one time. By default, the console shows only the names and operational status of the first 10 application servers configured that match the specified search criteria, but administrators typically change the user preference for number of servers to be displayed to a larger number (typically 100 or 200 in large environments).

You can create additional application servers on each node through the console if needed. To create a new application server for a node, use the New subtask on the Application Server collection view. The console will display the Create New Server subtask panel (see Figure 4.16). Select the name of the node that the server will be created on and then enter a name for the new Application Server that is unique for servers on the same node.

Usually, the new Application Server will need to be able to be running at the same time as other Application Servers on the node, and will require using a different set of endpoints (ports) to be configured for the server on which to listen for inbound connections. The ports that the new server will listen on for various connections must not conflict with other ports already in use on the machine, so by default the Generate Unique HTTP Ports check box is enabled. If for some reason in your environment the new server will never be running at the same time as other servers on the same node, you can disable this check box. For a variety

Create New Application Server

Create New Application Server

→ Step 1 : Select an application server template

You may either select an existing application server as a template for the new one, or use the default application server template.

Select node	MyCell/2373-96uxppro ▾	The node that is selected on this step will determine the server processes available from which to choose on the next step.
Server name	* [ ]	Logical name for server. Name must be unique within cell.
Http Ports	☑ Generate Unique Http Ports	Generates unique port numbers for every http transport that is defined in the source server, so that the resulting server that is created will not have HTTP Transports which conflict with the original server or any other servers defined on the same node.

Select template	⦿ Default application server template
	  default/server1 ▾
	○ Existing application server
	  MyCell/2373-96uxppro/server1 ▾
		Using an existing application server as a template will basically copy the configuration for the selected server.

[Next] [Cancel]

Step 2 Confirm new application server

Figure 4.16
The Create New Server subtask.

of reasons, it is not possible for WebSphere to know what non-WebSphere applications might be using the unique ports that it generates for the new Application Server, and its port generation algorithm only takes into account the ports that it knows are configured for other WebSphere-managed servers on the same node. The administrator must verify that the ports used by the new server do not conflict with ports used by other applications or services running on the same machine as the new server, find an available open port to use if conflicts are found, and configure the ports used by the new server with the nonconflicting ports. If you find that your server will not start up after creating it, check for port conflicts. This is one of the most frequent problems that administrators must be able to resolve in the environment using their operating system's tools for showing ports in use. On Microsoft Windows platforms, using the netstat –a –o shell command in conjunction with the PID of the running processes that is available in the Windows Task Manager is one of the easiest ways to find which ports are in use by a process. You should also examine your server startup logs to find the PID and ports that they are running under and keep track of these in a table for future reference. If you find that you cannot connect to Web applications on the new server, make sure you are using the proper endpoint for the new server.

The last choice on the Create New Server subtask panel is to choose where the new server will get its default configuration settings from. There are two ways for a server to get its settings, either by copying the configuration settings of another server (that can be defined on a different node), or by copying the default out-of-the-box server template that is provided by

WebSphere. If you already have a server configured, and want this new Application Server to have exactly the same settings, select the Existing Application Server radio button and choose the existing server's name from the dropdown list. Otherwise, click Next and the console will display a summary of how the new server will be created, along with any potential issues that might arise because of the new server getting created. Make sure to review these important messages and then click Finish to complete creation of the new server.

Once servers exist, they can be configured and managed by selecting the hyperlink of the server name from the table of servers in the Application Servers task. The console displays the Application Server top-level configuration page with additional configuration subtasks (Figure 4.17). If the server is already running, a Runtime tab will appear next to the Configure tab displayed on this page. Active settings from the running Application Server process(es) and operational management tasks related to Application Server management are available from the Runtime tab.

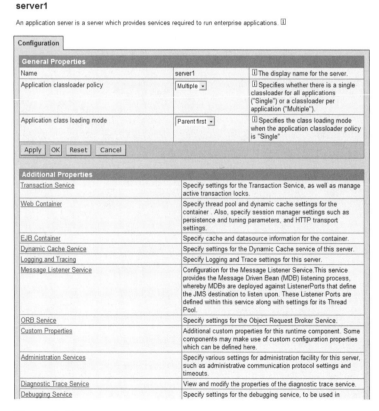

Figure 4.17
The Server Configuration subtask.

Clusters (Network Deployment Only)

In the WebSphere Network Deployment product, server clusters can be configured through the console using the `Clusters` task.

When creating new server clusters, the console first prompts for cluster-wide configuration settings (see Figure 4.18). If memory-to-memory replication is being used as a fast option for session management for applications that will be running within the server, you might need to create a replication domain to be used for the servers within the cluster. When creating the cluster for the first time, you can choose to use the configuration of a server that already exists within the cell to add to the cluster, so that it is the first cluster member.

Create New Cluster

Create New Cluster

→ Step 1 : Enter Basic Cluster Information		
Cluster name:	∗ MyCluster	The name of this cluster.
Prefer local:	☑ Prefer local enabled	Enable or disable Node scoped routing optimization.
Internal replication domain:	☐ Create Replication Domain for this cluster	If this option is selected, a Replication Domain will be created and the name will be set as the Cluster name
Existing server:	⦿ Do not include an existing server in this cluster ○ Select an existing server to add to this cluster Choose a server from this list: MyCell/2373-96uxppro/server1 ▾ Weight: 2 ☐ Create Replication Entry in this Server	Choosing existing Server as a Cluster Member. A list of Servers which are not already a part of existing Clusters is provided. You can specify the weight for this Cluster Member. You can also choose if a Replication Entry needs to be created in this Server for internal replication.

Next Cancel

Step 2 Create New Clustered Servers
Step 3 Summary

Figure 4.18
Creating a new cluster.

Next, cluster members must be established for the cluster (see Figure 4.19). For each server that will be part of the cluster, select the node on which the clustered server will reside, and specify whether unique HTTP ports should be generated automatically for the new cluster member (so that its ports won't conflict with other Application Servers that might already be defined to run on the same node. Finally, select a server configuration to use that will define the server configuration to use for every member in the cluster.

Each cluster member has its own copy of configuration data. When configuration settings are changed for one member, be sure to make the same exact change to other cluster members' server configurations (if necessary). Most server configuration settings will need to be exactly the same for all members of a cluster. Once the cluster has been created, subtasks

Step 1   Enter Basic Cluster Information

→ Step 2 : Create New Clustered Servers

Enter information about the new server below, and then use the Apply button to add it to the list of cluster members that will be created for this cluster. Use the Edit button to edit the properties of a server already included in the list. Use the Delete button to remove a server from the list.

Name:	* [ ]	The name of the new cluster member
Select Node:	[2373-96uxppro ▼]	The new cluster member will be created on the selected node
Weight:	[2]	Controls the amount of work directed to the application server. If the weight value for the server is greater than the weight values assigned to other servers in the cluster, then the server will receive a larger share of the servers' workload.
Http Ports	☑ Generate Unique Http Ports	Generates unique port numbers for every http transport that is defined in the source server, so that the resulting server that is created will not have HTTP Transports which conflict with the original server or any other servers defined on the same node.
Replication entry:	☐ Create Replication Entry in this Server	If selected, a replication entry will be created for the new cluster member
Select template:	⦿ Default application server template [server1 ▼] ○ Existing application server [MyCell/2373-96uxppro/server1 ▼]	Cluster members must be created using either a default template or an existing application server as a model. Each member is required to use the same model.

[Apply]

[Edit] [Delete]

| ☐ Application servers | Nodes | Weight |

[Previous] [Next] [Cancel]

Step 3   Summary

Figure 4.19
Adding member servers to a cluster.

are available on the cluster detail page for modifying the members, which is often necessary to perform manually as nodes are added to and from the cluster.

In addition to creating and deleting clusters and their members, commands are provided through the console for starting and stopping the entire set of servers within the cluster as a whole. Cluster members can also be started and stopped individually.

Manage Applications

Enterprise Applications

Enterprise applications can be installed, configured and managed through the console using the tasks under the Applications category.

To install a new enterprise application (.ear) or a stand-alone module (.jar or .war), use the Install New Application task, or use the Enterprise Applications tasks and click Install (both tasks do the same thing). Next, you will be prompted for the location of the application's binaries. Either they are on the machine that your browser is running on (local machine), or they must be somewhere within the server environment that is accessible from the DMgr (server path). Pick the appropriate check box.

If the files reside on the machine running the Web browser (or are accessible from it using the Web browser's file browsing function), find the file and select Next. The browser will transfer the file to a staging area on the Deployment Manager where it will stay temporarily during the installation process.

On WebSphere Network Deployment, if the files reside on a server machine that is a node within the cell, and you are running with Administrator role privileges, you will be able to use a special remote file browser to browse the file systems of the server nodes and transfer the application's binaries from a node up to a staging area on the DMgr node. On WebSphere Base, the remote file system browser is not available, as it makes use of the node agent file transfer services; however, you can manually enter a path (a server file system path—not a local file system path) to the location of the application binaries.

Once the application binaries are in the DMgr staging area, depending on the types of modules and components detected inside the application's archive, you will be prompted for additional information regarding how you want to deploy the components within the application. There is a wealth of information related to application installation settings that can be found in the WebSphere InfoCenter provided with the product (as well as on the IBM Web site).

Once it is deployed and running, you can use the Enterprise Applications task to stop and start the application (and its modules). Unfortunately, there is currently not a trace or log view other than the server log for viewing trace and log output for applications. You will need you use your application's own logging mechanisms to get application-specific messages.

Manage Resources

Resource definitions configured within a cell allow WebSphere servers running within the cell to connect to the resources that might or might not be managed directly by WebSphere. For example, various database servers might host the databases containing data used by applications deployed on WebSphere servers. For those applications to access or connect to the databases residing in the externally managed database servers, a description of the connection properties must be defined within the WebSphere environment, specifying what client driver to use for the external database vendor's product remotely, as well as how to locate the database residing within the database server, and how to authenticate with that database. The same pattern applies to many other types of resources. WebSphere provides tasks used for configuring these resource definitions so that applications can make use of the external resources at run time (indirectly via JNDI name lookups as defined by the J2EE specification). Every resource defined within a WebSphere cell must have a unique JNDI name configured for it. This JNDI name is often referred to as the "physical" JNDI name. The physical JNDI name is the name used for identifying the resources known to the Web-

Sphere server infrastructure. Every J2EE application uses logical JNDI names to specify the application's requirements for connectivity to resources with specific properties. When applications are deployed into the WebSphere server environment, the logical JNDI names must be mapped to the physical JNDI names of resources that can fulfill the requirements of the application.

Use the resource configuration tasks in this section to define resources and their physical JNDI names either prior to or immediately after deploying applications into the environment. Most resource types can have connections defined for them for a specific vendor's product version (the "providers" of the external resources). To actually make a connection between the WebSphere server and the external product, the client-side libraries (often called drivers) must be installed on every node that will make use of the resources of the external product. In a heterogeneous environment consisting of multiple operating system platforms and versions, you will need to take extra care to ensure that the proper libraries (possibly including native code such as .dll's or .so's) are installed on each node that needs to access the external resource using the connection definitions.

WebSphere requires that resource connection definitions be provided by resource provider type. This means that you will need to know the resource provider that is being used to find your resource connection definitions. Unfortunately, WebSphere does not currently provide a view of all resources for all providers.

WebSphere resource connection definitions are also variably scoped with overrides, such that resources with physical JNDI names defined at the server scope will override resources of same type and name defined at the node or cell scope. It is a good practice to make sure that the scope in which resources are defined most closely matches how the resources will need to be accessed. This means that if a particular resource needs to be accessed only from the applications running on one server, then you should define only the resources in that server's scope. If a particular resource needs to be accessed only by applications running on multiple servers on one or more nodes, then only define the resources in the node scope for the nodes that need them. In larger environments, if all or almost all of the nodes in the cell will need to access the same resource (this is rare), only then use the cell scope to configure resources. Remember, if you use the cell scope you still need to ensure that the client drivers are installed on every node in the cell, and every node in the cell will need to be homogenous. For this reason, we do not recommend using the cell scope for configuration of resource connections.

WebSphere provides tasks for configuring resources for database connectivity, message brokers, mail accounts, enterprise information systems, and administrative objects for managed resources, among other miscellaneous types of resources. The full set of configuration settings possible for various resource providers is beyond the scope of this book. See the WebSphere Info Center for specific information regarding configuring specific types of resources.

Manage Security

Global Security

The Global Security task (see Figure 4.20) is used when an administrator is ready to secure access to an Application Server environment. To enable security, check the Enabled field. By default, the first time the Global Security Enabled field is checked, Enforce Java2 Security is turned on automatically. If you have not configured a user registry or authentication mechanisms prior to enabling security, WebSphere defaults to use the Local OS user registry and LTPA authentication mechanism. If an LDAP directory will be used for the user registry, configure the connection to LDAP prior to enabling security.

Global Security

Specifies global security configuration for a managed domain. The following steps are required to turn on security. 1) Select the desired User Registry from the left navigation panel and set the properties in that panel. 2) Enable security in this panel. ⓘ

Configuration		
General Properties		
Enabled	☐	ⓘ Enables security for this WebSphere domain.
Enforce Java 2 Security	☐	ⓘ If Java 2 Security is enabled and the application policy file is not set up correctly, the application may fail to run.
Use Domain Qualified User IDs	☐	ⓘ When true, user names returned by methods such as getUserPrincipal() will be qualified with the security domain in which they reside.
Cache Timeout	∗ 600	ⓘ Timeout value for security cache in seconds.
Issue Permission Warning	☑	ⓘ When enabled, a warning will be issued during application installation, if an application requires a Java 2 Permission that normally should not be granted to an application.
Active Protocol	CSI and SAS ▾	ⓘ Specifies the active security authentication protocol when security is enabled. Possible values are CSI (CSIv2), or CSI and SAS.
Active Authentication Mechanism	LTPA	ⓘ Specifies the active authentication mechanism when security is enabled.
Active User Registry	Local OS ▾	ⓘ Specifies the active user registry when security is enabled.
Use FIPS	☐	ⓘ This will enable the use of FIPS (Federal Information Processing Standard) approved cryptographic algorithms. Note that setting this flag does not automatically change the existing JSSE provider in the Secure Socket Layer configuration. Also note that a FIPS approved JSSE provider only allows TLS as the protocol. Moreover, the FIPS approved LTPA authentication mechanism is not backward compatible with the non-FIPS approved LTPA implementation that is used in all prior versions of WebSphere Application Server products.

Figure 4.20
Global Security configuration task.

If a valid server user ID and password have not already been entered using the user registry configuration task for the registry type being used (e.g., Local OS or LDAP), after trying to enable security and submitting the changes the console will display an error message and the user registry configuration task asking the administrator to supply a valid user ID and password to use before continuing. This user ID is the user id that the server will run as, and must match the user ID and password for a user configured within the underlying user registry.

If LTPA is being used as the authentication mechanism, and a password has not previously been configured using the LTPA configuration task, the console displays an error message indicating that the LTPA password has not yet been specified and displays the LTPA configuration task. A password must be entered and verified on the LTPA configuration page before security can be enabled. Once the password has been verified, the administrator should go back to the Global Security task and ensure that the Enabled field is still checked.

It is very important that the administrator review all informational and warning messages displayed after enabling security for the cell, as there might be special considerations regarding application requirements for Java2 security policies or user access to applications, depending on the security settings used.

Once the server credentials have been supplied using the appropriate user registry, a password has been supplied for LTPA encryption/decryption purposes, and security has been enabled, the administrator should synchronize the local changes to the master configuration repository, making sure to then synchronize all nodes with the master configuration repository and finally restart all management agents and servers defined in the cell so that they run in secure mode. Restarting the Deployment Manager (Network Deployment) or restarting the default server (Base) will require restarting the console, so the administrator should first shut down all servers not running the console, then shut down the servers and agents running the console. Use the `startManager` or `startServer` commands to restart the server running the console from a shell prompt.

Manage Other Environment Elements

In WebSphere Network Deployment, once the Deployment Manager and all node agents have restarted using the `startManager` and `startNode` commands from a shell prompt, the administrator can log into the console using the secure login page (see Figure 4.11) and then use the Administrative Console to start the remaining Application Servers and messaging servers.

Update Web Service Plug-in

When using an external Web server (e.g., IHS, IIS, etc.) rather than the HTTP server built into every WebSphere Application Server, it is necessary to generate a configuration file that will be used by the WebSphere plug-in for the externally connected Web server every time nodes, servers, and Web application configurations are updated. Use the Update Web Server Plug-in task under the Environment category to regenerate the plugin.xml file, which must then be manually transferred to the Web server machine. If you are running a browser on the machine where the external Web server is installed, and have firewall access to be able to use the console from within the DMZ, you can download the generated plugin.xml file using your browser and save it into the proper location in your Web server's configuration.

Virtual Hosts

The Virtual Hosts task can be used to configure the hostname and ports connections to be used by Web applications deployed into Application Servers. During application installation (and in the Map Web Modules to Virtual Hosts subtask), you can change the virtual host with which each Web module is associated. For each virtual host, you can supply a list of hostname patterns and ports that will match to the virtual host, as well as MIME type entries to be used for resources on those hosts. There is considerable information already available in the WebSphere InfoCenter on using and configuration of virtual hosts.

WebSphere Variables

In WebSphere configurations, variables are used to reduce or eliminate the presence of absolute path prefixes in configuration documents. The Variables task is used to add, remove, and edit the variables defined in the server, node, or cell scopes. Like resource scoping, variables in server scope take precedence over variables defined at the node or cell scopes with the same name. Most fields that take file system paths in configuration tasks can use variable name substitutions, such as `${varname}/relativePath/filename`. Check the field-level documentation to determine if there are special usage restrictions or limitations for the format of the path string. In general, it is a best practice to always use variable substitution in lieu of absolute path names in WebSphere configurations. Also, variable substitution is recursive, so a variable's value can contain variables as well as paths. The variables are resolved within the server run time during initialization.

Shared Libraries

If you have many applications, and those applications are known to share the same exact versions of libraries (jars) between the applications, the libraries can be placed in a common file system location so that there are not multiple copies of the binaries that need to be duplicated and transferred out to nodes.

To configure shared libraries using the console, select the Shared Libraries task in the navigation area. Next, select the scope at which the shared library entries will be relevant. If the shared libraries are in common with applications or modules that will only be running on the same server, use the server scope. If the shared libraries are only required between applications deployed into the servers on a single node, then specify node scope. If the shared libraries are required by applications that are clustered, define the shared library entries at cell scope. Note that WebSphere systems management will not automatically distribute your shared library binaries to nodes, even if cell scope is selected. You will need to choose a relative file system location that is available from every node that needs use of the shared libraries, and ensure that the binaries are copied to the relative file system location yourself prior to trying to use the libraries.

For each shared library, provide a name for the shared library (it's a good practice to include vendor name and library version in the name, such as Apache Commons JXPath 1.0). Also, provide a classpath that includes the relative location of all jars related to the library (possibly relative to a path variable), as well as the location of any native code (typically .so's or .dll's) required by the library. Libraries that make use of native code might have usage restrictions within a heterogeneous cell having different operating systems. Make sure that all native code is supplied for the appropriate scope that the shared library will be used.

To use one or more shared libraries within your applications, go to the Libraries subtask using the Enterprise Applications task for the applications (or individual modules) needing to access the shared library. The shared libraries you configured in the Shared Libraries task should appear in the list of available library names for use by your applications (or individual modules).

Manage Systems Administration

The Systems Administration group of tasks allow configuring and controlling the properties of the cell, the management agents and communications settings related to them, and the console application itself.

Cell

The Cell task provides configuration settings related to how WebSphere management agents discover themselves. It also provides a simple topology view for viewing the nodes that have been added to the cell.

Deployment Manager

The Deployment Manager task allows configuring settings of the DMgr management agent, which itself is a kind of server in the cell. In WebSphere Network Deployment, there can be only one DMgr in a cell, so unlike the other server management views there is not a list of

Deployment Managers. Instead the subtasks related to configuring the Deployment Manager itself are displayed. All of the tasks, with the exception of the Administration Services, offer basically the same configuration settings as tasks with the same name in the Application Server configuration task. In the Administration Services subtask, there are additional tasks for configuring the repository service that controls the WebSphere configuration repository, as well as other miscellaneous administrative connection settings that are rarely used.

Nodes

The Nodes task (see Figure 4.21) displays a filterable list of all nodes in the cell. For each node, a topology view is provided that allows viewing the servers defined on the node. The Nodes task is important when you need to determine the synchronization state of nodes with the master configuration repository. Whether a node is already in sync with or is out of sync with the master repository, the synchronization status can be determined quickly using this view. Move the mouse cursor over the status icon displayed to see a legend describing each sync state.

Nodes

A list of nodes in this cell. You can add new nodes into the cell by clicking on "Add Node" and specifying a remote, running WebSphere Application Server instance. ⓘ

Total: 1				
⊞ Filter				
⊞ Preferences				
Add Node	Remove Node	Synchronize	Full Resynchronize	Stop
☐ Name ⇕			Status ⇕ ⟳	
☐ DeploymentManager			⊕	

Figure 4.21
The Nodes task.

Node Agents

In WebSphere Network Deployment, before you can manage servers on any given node you need to ensure that a node agent is running on that node. Servers will run independently of whether a node agent is running on the same node; however, the DMgr cannot control the server (start, stop, terminate) unless there is a node agent running. The node agents also provide configuration synchronization services for the servers on the node, as well as basic file transfer services to and from the node for use by other management agents or tools. Use the Node Agents task to browse and find node agents in the cell and to quickly determine whether agents are running on various nodes.

Similar to the DMgr agent, which has some common services that can be configured on it (e.g., the ORB), node agents include settings for the configuration synchronization and file transfer services that are hosted by the node agent.

In production environments, you might want to disable the automatic synchronization of configuration changes between the master repository and one or more nodes and manually force the configuration synchronization to occur at predefined maintenance periods. To disable the configuration synchronization for a node, use the File Synchronization subtask and disable the Automatic synchronization check box. From this subtask, you can also specify other criteria for synchronization, such as whether to check for new configuration updates each time the node agent is started, or to exclude certain files from being transferred from the master repository to the node.

The File Transfer subtask is also unique to node agent servers. There are a few settings provided to control timeouts that might need to be changed under rare circumstances, such as when extremely large application binaries or configurations are being copied to multiple nodes.

Console Users

Use the Console Users task to configure administrative users with access to the console. From this task, you can add a new user (whose user ID must reside within the user registry configured for the cell). You can also associate users with any combination of the four administrative user roles. The users list is searchable and can be used to determine which users are currently logged into the console.

Console Groups

The Console Groups task can be used to configure groups of administrative users. From this task, you can create new groups (whose group ID must already reside within the user registry configured for the cell) for use by the console and assign administrative users to the groups. Like Console Users, groups can be associated with any combination of the four administrative user roles.

PROBLEM DETERMINATION USING THE ADMINISTRATIVE CONSOLE

When troubleshooting problems through the console, the first place to look for an indication of problems should be the console's status tray and event logs. From the status tray, you can find summaries of recent configuration problems as well as important run-time events from the server environment. If there is a problem trying to control the servers using command-line or console tooling, you might want to check general connectivity of the DMgr to its node agents and servers, making sure that the appropriate node agents are running.

If a server or application fails to start or stops suddenly, you will need to check the JVM error and output logs for the servers hosting the application. Finally, if all else fails, you might need to deal with lower level tracing of the server components with the assistance of an expert. This section discusses the console tasks provided for use in these problem situations.

Status Tray

In WebSphere Base and Network Deployment, the console status (see Figure 4.22) tray displays either configuration problems or run-time events for the cell being managed. To switch between the configuration and run-time events categories of data, use the Next and Previous links in the status tray. There is a user preference for the status tray that allows the view to switch periodically between configuration problems and run-time events (or other types of information). Other WebSphere product extensions can add additional categories of information to the status tray. Each status view contains summaries of events of different type or priority. Clicking on the total number of events in a category will bring up the event browser, showing all of the detailed events making up that category (see Figure 4.23).

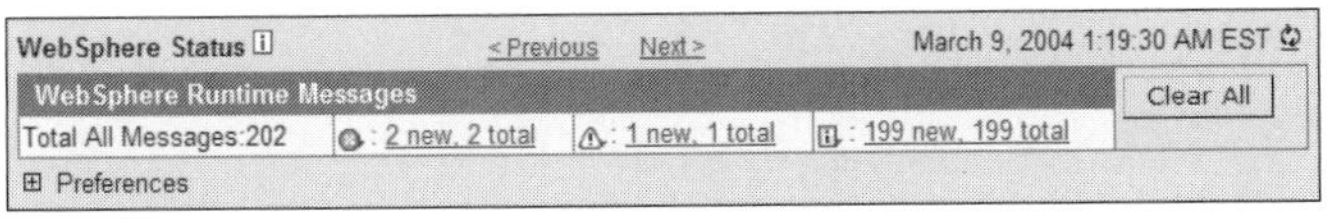

Figure 4.22
The console's status tray.

Use the event browser to find recent events and view each individual event's detail. The event detail views can provide additional information on further steps to take to try to resolve the problem.

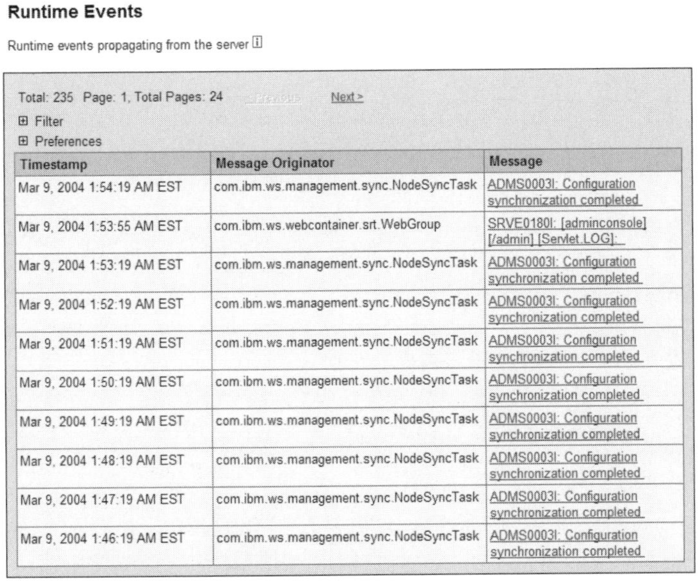

Runtime Events

Runtime events propagating from the server

Total: 235 Page: 1, Total Pages: 24 < Previous Next >

Filter

Preferences

Timestamp	Message Originator	Message
Mar 9, 2004 1:54:19 AM EST	com.ibm.ws.management.sync.NodeSyncTask	ADMS0003I: Configuration synchronization completed
Mar 9, 2004 1:53:55 AM EST	com.ibm.ws.webcontainer.srt.WebGroup	SRVE0180I: [adminconsole] [/admin] [Servlet.LOG]:
Mar 9, 2004 1:53:19 AM EST	com.ibm.ws.management.sync.NodeSyncTask	ADMS0003I: Configuration synchronization completed
Mar 9, 2004 1:52:19 AM EST	com.ibm.ws.management.sync.NodeSyncTask	ADMS0003I: Configuration synchronization completed
Mar 9, 2004 1:51:19 AM EST	com.ibm.ws.management.sync.NodeSyncTask	ADMS0003I: Configuration synchronization completed
Mar 9, 2004 1:50:19 AM EST	com.ibm.ws.management.sync.NodeSyncTask	ADMS0003I: Configuration synchronization completed
Mar 9, 2004 1:49:19 AM EST	com.ibm.ws.management.sync.NodeSyncTask	ADMS0003I: Configuration synchronization completed
Mar 9, 2004 1:48:19 AM EST	com.ibm.ws.management.sync.NodeSyncTask	ADMS0003I: Configuration synchronization completed
Mar 9, 2004 1:47:19 AM EST	com.ibm.ws.management.sync.NodeSyncTask	ADMS0003I: Configuration synchronization completed
Mar 9, 2004 1:46:19 AM EST	com.ibm.ws.management.sync.NodeSyncTask	ADMS0003I: Configuration synchronization completed

Figure 4.23
Event browser showing informational events that have occurred in the cell.

Troubleshooting Tasks

In the Navigation area under the Troubleshooting category there are tasks that can be useful when troubleshooting problems through the console.

Unavailable Server Status

In WebSphere Network Deployment, if you have only started the DMgr and have logged into the console, all tasks having lists displaying servers with their status in the console will show a Not Available icon for their status. This means that the DMgr is unable to contact the servers to determine their running status. Sometimes, this can mean that the node agent has not been started on one or more of the nodes in the cell. You can check the status of the node agents using the Node Agents task under the System Administration category, or by looking at all servers' status (not just Application Servers) in the Logs and Trace task under the Troubleshooting category. If the node agents have status as unavailable, run the `startNode` command on each unavailable node so that the DMgr can begin managing the application servers residing on those nodes.

Logs and Trace

The Logs and Trace task provides access to additional tasks related to logging and trace settings for the servers in the cell. On selecting the Logs and Trace task, you will first need to select a target server with which to begin working. Next, the console displays subtasks related to logging and tracing. Notice that the logging and tracing subtasks are also available from the server detail page if you are configuring or managing a server from that page already.

However, you will probably use the JVM Logs subtask frequently. Use the JVM Logs task to control and view logs for any servers in the cell (including the node agents and Deployment Manager). The console's basic log viewer can be used to view the various standard error and standard output logs of each server. To open the log viewer for a server, select the Runtime tab of the JVM Logs page, and then select the View button for either the SystemErr log or SystemOut log of the server. The console displays the log viewer page (see Figure 4.24).

To view logs from the console, the Deployment Manager coordinates with the node agent controlling the server and retrieves a user-defined portion of the log. When using the basic log viewer in the console, keep in mind that logs can potentially be many megabytes in size, and the portion of the log being viewed must be transferred from the node agent to the Deployment Manager to the browser. By default, the viewer only retrieves the "head" (250 lines) of the selected log. The log viewer displays the total number of lines available in the log for viewing, as well as the starting line and ending line of the log that is being displayed. To see the "tail" (last n lines) of the log for a server, enter a range in the Receive Lines field as follows: `|total - n| '-' total`.

Logging and Tracing > server1 > JVM Logs >
Log File

Display the contents of the given file.

Total: 704, Filtered total: 250

Retrieve Lines (eg. 250-600) [＿＿＿＿＿] [Refresh]

Log File

```
WebSphere Platform 5.1 [BASE 5.1.0 cf10406.04]  running with process name 2373-96uxppro\2373-96uxppro\server1 and p
Host Operating System is Windows XP, version 5.1
Java version = J2RE 1.4.1 IBM Windows 32 build cn1411-20031011 (JIT enabled: jitc), Java Compiler = jitc, Java VM n
was.install.root = C:\dev\rels\5.1.0\cf10406.04\WebSphere\AppServer
user.install.root = C:\dev\rels\5.1.0\cf10406.04\WebSphere\AppServer
Java Home = C:\dev\rels\5.1.0\cf10406.04\WebSphere\AppServer\java\jre
ws.ext.dirs = C:\dev\rels\5.1.0\cf10406.04\WebSphere\AppServer\java\lib;C:\dev\rels\5.1.0\cf10406.04\WebSphere\AppS
Classpath = C:\dev\rels\5.1.0\cf10406.04\WebSphere\AppServer/properties;C:\dev\rels\5.1.0\cf10406.04\WebSphere\AppS
Java Library path = C:\dev\rels\5.1.0\cf10406.04\WebSphere\AppServer\java\bin;.;C:\WINDOWS\System32;C:\WINDOWS;C:\d
************* End Display Current Environment *************
[2/28/04 20:30:53:080 EST] 7c3e1be0 ManagerAdmin   I TRAS0017I: The startup trace state is *=all=disabled.
[2/28/04 20:30:54:262 EST] 7c3e1be0 AdminInitiali  A ADMN0015I: AdminService initialized
[2/28/04 20:30:56:214 EST] 7c3e1be0 Configuration  A SECJ0215I: Successfully set JAAS login provider configuration c
[2/28/04 20:30:56:335 EST] 7c3e1be0 SecurityDM     I SECJ0231I: The Security component's FFDC Diagnostic Module com.
[2/28/04 20:30:56:905 EST] 7c3e1be0 SecurityCompo  I SECJ0309I: Java 2 Security is disabled.
[2/28/04 20:30:56:986 EST] 7c3e1be0 SecurityCompo  I SECJ0212I: WCCM JAAS configuration information successfully pus
[2/28/04 20:30:57:036 EST] 7c3e1be0 SecurityCompo  I SECJ0240I: Security service initialization completed successful
[2/28/04 20:30:57:066 EST] 7c3e1be0 JMSRegistrati  A MSGS0601I: WebSphere Embedded Messaging has not been installed
[2/28/04 20:31:04:176 EST] 7c3e1be0 ResourceMgrIm  I WSVR0049I: Binding PlantsByWebSphere Mail Session as mail/Plant
[2/28/04 20:31:04:607 EST] 7c3e1be0 ResourceMgrIm  I WSVR0049I: Binding Default Datasource as DefaultDatasource
[2/28/04 20:31:04:617 EST] 7c3e1be0 WASQueueConne  E WMSG0901E: The Embedded JMS Binders have been disabled as the E
[2/28/04 20:31:04:647 EST] 7c3e1be0 ResourceMgrIm  I WSVR0049I: Binding Default_CF as eis/DefaultDatasource_CMP
[2/28/04 20:31:04:647 EST] 7c3e1be0 ResourceMgrIm  I WSVR0049I: Binding TechSamp_CF as eis/WSsamples/TechSampDatasou
[2/28/04 20:31:04:657 EST] 7c3e1be0 ResourceMgrIm  I WSVR0049I: Binding PLANTSDB_CF as eis/jdbc/PlantsByWebSphereDat
```

Figure 4.24

For example, to retrieve the last 100 lines in a sample log file:

```
Total lines in log = 9867 n = 100
Retrieve Lines: 9667–9867
```

Use of either Diagnostic Trace or Service Logs subtasks with a server is typically done in conjunction with IBM support organization assistance, and can be used to debug inner workings of the server components. For this reason, these tasks are not described further.

It is possible for a node agent to launch and command non-Java processes. It is also possible for the start and stop commands used during the launching of a Java process to include redirects of native stderr and stdout process logs. When managing processes in these situations, the Process Logs subtask can be used to retrieve the native logs similar to the JVM log viewer. In typical scenarios, however, this subtask is not used.

Configuration Problems

The Configuration Problems tasks are where you can find configuration problems that Web-Sphere systems management agents have found in the console workspace or master configuration repository. Validating configurations of large cells can be a performance-intensive process, and there are various ways of controlling the scope within which the validation process occurs. You will want to try different settings within your management environment. In a production environment, where configuration changes are infrequent and monitored closely, it might be possible to disable validation completely. In a QA or test cell, it might be worthwhile to enable maximum or stronger validation so that a more thorough set of potential configuration problems can be caught.

Most configuration validation checks provided by WebSphere systems management are localized to a given server, an application, or a resource, and typically will not span between a server and an application or an application and resources. The Cross Validation option engages additional validation checks that can cross configurations of nodes and applications. In larger cells, these validation checks consume additional processor cycles and memory in the Deployment Manager node to be useful. For this reason, it is not a good idea to enable cross-validation in production cells. Limit the use of Cross Validation to QA or test cells or single nodes.

## CHAPTER 5

Administrative Scripting

This chapter covers the scripting command-line tool called *wsadmin* that comes with the WebSphere Application Server. Scripting provides a nongraphical alternative to manage and control the WebSphere Application Server. The wsadmin tool provides the ability to execute scripts. It supports a full range of administrative activities.

WSADMIN SCRIPTING ENVIRONMENT

The wsadmin scripting tool provides facilities to customize the scripting environment. You can use wsadmin tool options or properties to specify properties files to read, profiles to run, connector settings to connect to the server, and JVM parameters like classpath or heap size.

Wsadmin Overview

The wsadmin scripting client is a command-line tool used to manage and control the WebSphere installation. This tool uses Bean Scripting Framework (BSF), which supports a variety of scripting languages. The initial version of wsadmin supports only the Jacl scripting language. This tool makes Java objects available through language-specific interfaces. There are four available management objects, namely AdminApp, AdminConfig, AdminControl, and Help. Scripts use these objects for application management, configuration, and operation control to communicate with MBeans running in WebSphere server processes. Scripting commands can be run interactively, as individual commands, in a file, or in a profile. You can use options in the wsadmin tool to control how to run the scripting commands. Some of the options can also be specified in a wsadmin properties file.

JYTHON SUPPORT

Jython scripting language support is added to wsadmin tool starting with WebSphere
Application Server Version 5.1.

There is a default properties file named *wsadmin.properties* shipped with the WebSphere
install. This properties file is located in the properties directory. It provides initial setup for
the scripting client environment, including the specification of the connection type, the host
and port used when attempting a connection, the location where trace and logging output is
directed, the trace specification, profiles to load, and so on. You can edit this properties file
to suit your environment, or you can provide your own scripting properties file. There are
four levels of properties files recognized by the scripting client. This default properties file
shipped with WebSphere is loaded first, followed by a user default wsadmin.properties file
pointed to by the user.home property. The third level is the properties file pointed to by the
WSADMIN_PROPERTIES environment property. Last, the properties file specified on the
wsadmin command line is loaded.

If you have WebSphere Application Server install, you use wsadmin to connect to an application server process to configure and control your server environment. In a Network
Deployment install, there are three types of server processes to which wsadmin can connect: Deployment Manager, node agent, and application server. The default connection is to
the Deployment Manager process where the master configuration repository for the cell is
stored. You can override this default connection by providing wsadmin options or properties
to specify a host name and port to connect to a node agent or an application server. The
availability of scripting commands and the MBeans visible to the scripting client vary
depending on the server process connected to. When connected to a deployment manger, all
the scripting commands and all MBeans in all the server processes on that cell are accessible. When connected to a node agent, configuration commands are not available and only
MBeans in all server processes on that node are accessible. When connected to an application server, configuration commands are not available and only the MBeans running in that
server process are visible.

You can start the scripting client with or without a running server. When the scripting client
is started without connecting to a running server, it is operated in local mode. In local mode,
all the commands dealing with live run-time objects are not available, but most of the configuration commands are available. If a server is currently running, it is not recommended
that you run the wsadmin tool in local mode. Any configuration update made in local mode
is not captured by the running server and could cause potential loss of configuration data if
the same data is updated by both the running server and in local mode.

Invoking Wsadmin Tool

The wsadmin scripting client tool is located in the bin directory of your WebSphere install. To invoke a scripting client process, use wsadmin.bat for a Windows system, and use wsadmin.sh for a UNIX system. Wsadmin launcher accepts options to specify scripting language, scripting commands to run, connection type, and so on. If no scripting commands or script is specified, interactive mode is entered, displaying a wsadmin> prompt waiting for input. The syntax for running wsadmin tool is as follows:

In a Windows system:

```
wsadmin [options] [script_parameters]
```

In a UNIX system:

```
wsadmin.sh [options] [script_parameters]
```

where

script_parameters represents arguments to be passed to the script file. Any unrecognized option is passed to the script as parameter.

Options:

–?, -h(elp)

> Provide syntax help

–c *command*

> Provide a single scripting command to execute. A save is performed by default if the specified command results in configuration changes. Multiple –c options can exist on the command line. They are executed in the order in which you supply them. If multiple –c options are specified and result in configuration changes, a configuration save is performed after the last command is executed.

–conntype *type*

> Specify the type of connection to use to connect to the server process. Possible connection types include SOAP, RMI, and NONE. If a SOAP or RMI connection type is used, additional options including host, port, user, and password are available. Use the –conntype NONE option to run in local mode. The result is that the scripting client is not connected to any running server. The default *wsadmin.properties* file provides SOAP as the value of the connection type property if this option is not specified. If this option is specified on the command line, it overrides the value set in the com.ibm.ws.scripting.connectionType property.

-f *script_file*

> Provide a script to execute. If the script includes commands to change configuration, an explicit command to save the configuration must be included in your script. Otherwise, the configuration changes are not saved. Only one –f can exist on the command line. You can not specify both –c and –f options on the same command invocation.

-host *host_name*

> Specify a host name to which wsadmin should attempt to connect. The default *wsadmin.properties* file provides localhost as the value of the host property if this option is not specified. To connect to a different server, use this option to override the value in the property file. The specified host name should be the same as the value you provide during your WebSphere install.

-javaoption[1] *java_option*

> Specify a valid Java standard or nonstandard option. Multiple –javaoption can exist on the command line.

-lang *lang*

> Specify the language of script file, command, or interactive mode. The default *wsadmin.properties* file provides JACL as the value of the scripting language property if this option is not specified. If this option is specified on the command line, it overrides the value set in the com.ibm.ws.scripting.defaultLang property.

-p *property_file*

> Specify a Java property file to be loaded. Multiple –p can exist on the command line. They are loaded in the order in which you supply them. There is a default *wsadmin.properties* file provided with your WebSphere install. This default property file is loaded before any properties files specified with this option.

-password *password*

> Specify a password to be used by the connector to connect to the server if security is enabled in the server.

-port *port*

> Specify a port to be used by the connector. The default *wsadmin.properties* file provides a value in the port property to connect to your local server. To connect to a different server, use this option to override the value specified in the properties file.

---

1.   The –javaoption is available starting with WebSphere Application Server Version 5.0.2.

–profile *profile_file*

> Specify a profile script. The profile script runs before other commands or scripts. If you specify –c on the same command-line invocation, the profile is executed before the command is executed. If you specify –f on the same command-line invocation, the profile is executed before the script is run. Multiple –profile can exist on the command line. They are invoked in the order in which you supply them.
>
> The default *wsadmin.properties* file provides two security profiles in the profile property. If this option is specified on the command line, the profiles specified on the command line are executed before the profiles in the properties file.

–user *userid*

> Specify a user name to be used by the connector to connect to the server if security is enabled in the server.

–wsadmin_classpath *classpath_string*

> Specify additional paths to be added to the classpath used by the wsadmin scripting process. If there are additional classes needed by your script, this is how to make them available in the wsadmin scripting environment. Only one –wsadmin_classpath option can exist on the command line. To provide multiple classpath strings with this option, separate each classpath string with a semicolon (;).
>
> ```
> -wsadmin_classpath c:/test.jar;c:/test2.jar
> ```
>
> You can specify this option as a property in a properties file. The property is com.ibm.ws.scripting.classpath. However, if this option is specified on the command line, it overrides the value set in the properties. The classpath property and the command-line option are not concatenated.

The following syntax examples show the usage of various options.

- Run scripting client interactively

  ```
  wsadmin
  ```

- Run scripting commands as individual command.
  - In a Windows system,;

    ```
    wsadmin -c "$AdminApp uninstall myApp"
    ```
  - In a UNIX system;

    ```
    wsadmin.sh -c "\$AdminApp uninstall myApp"
    ```

- Run scripting commands in a script

  ```
  wsadmin -f /scripts/myScript.jacl
  ```

- Run scripting commands in a profile

  ```
  wsadmin -p /scripts/myProfile.jacl -f /scripts/myScript.jacl
  ```

- Use SOAP connection to a remote server

  ```
  wsadmin -conntype SOAP -host myRemoteHost -port 8881 -f
  /scripts/myScript.jacl
  ```

- Use RMI connection with security on

  ```
  wsadmin -conntype RMI -user myUser -password myPassword -f
  /scripts/myScript.jacl
  ```

- Use local mode to install an application
  - In a Windows system;

    ```
    wsadmin -conntype NONE -c "$AdminApp install
    /myInstallableApps/myApp.ear"
    ```

  - In a UNIX system;

    ```
    wsadmin.sh -conntype NONE -c "\$AdminApp install
    /myInstallableApps/myApp.ear"
    ```

- Specify initial and maximum Java heap size

  ```
  wsadmin -javaoption -Xms128m -javaoption² -Xmx256m -f
  myscript.jacl
  ```

- Add paths to classpath

  ```
  wsadmin -wsadmin_classpath /myClasses/myClass.jar;/myClasses/
  myClass2.jar -f /scripts/myScript2.jacl
  ```

- Use Jython scripting language

  ```
  wsadmin -lang jython³ -f /scripts/myScript.py
  ```

Properties

Much of the information entered in the command line when invoking wsadmin can also be specified in the properties file. As explained earlier, the scripting client loads the following levels of properties files:

- The properties in the properties/wsadmin.properties file located in the WebSphere install.
- The properties in the wsadmin.properties file pointed to by the Java user.home property.

---

2. The –javaoption is available starting with WebSphere Application Server Version 5.0.2.
3. Jython support is added in WebSphere Application Server Version 5.1.

- The properties in the file indicated by the WSADMIN_PROPERTIES environment variable.
- Any properties files specified on the wsadmin command-line option.

The properties files are loaded in that order. The properties file loaded last takes precedence over the one loaded before it. Table 5.1 describes the Java properties used by the scripting client.

Table 5.1   Quick Reference for Java Properties Used by Scripting Client

Property Name	Description
com.ibm.ws.scripting.classpath	Additional paths to append to the list of paths to search for classes and resources. This is no default value. The wsadmin.properties file does not provide a value for this property. The value specified in this property is overridden by the -wsadmin_classpath wsadmin option if specified.
com.ibm.ws.scripting.connectionType	Determines the connector to use. Valid values are SOAP, RMI, and NONE. The wsadmin.properties file specifies SOAP as the connector. The value in this property is overridden by the -conntype wsadmin option if specified.
com.ibm.ws.scripting.crossDocumentValidationEnabled	Determines whether the validation mechanism examines other documents when changes are made to one document. Valid values are true and false. The default value is true. The wsadmin.properties file does not provide a value for this property.
com.ibm.ws.scripting.defaultLang	Specifies the language to be used when executing script. Valid values are Jacl and Jython.* There is no default value. The wsadmin.properties file specifies Jacl as the scripting language. This property value is overridden by the -lang wsadmin option if specified.
com.ibm.ws.scripting.emitWarningForCustomSecurityPolicy	Controls whether message WASX7207W is emitted when custom permissions are found. Valid values are true and false. The default value is true. The wsadmin.properties file does not provide a value for this property.

Table 5.1   Quick Reference for Java Properties Used by Scripting Client (Continued)

Property Name	Description
com.ibm.ws.scripting.host	Determines the host to use when attempting to connect to a server process. The wsadmin.properties file specifies localhost as the host. This property value is overridden by the -host wsadmin option if specified.
com.ibm.ws.scripting.profiles	Specifies a list of profiles to run before running user commands, script, or entering interactive mode. The list should consist of path names separated by a ";". The wsadmin.properties file specifies securityProcs.jacl and LTPA_LDAPSecurityProcs.jacl as the profiles to run. If the -profiles wsadmin option is specified, the profiles specified on the command line are executed before the profiles in this property.
com.ibm.ws.scripting.tempdir	Determines the directory to use to create a copy of the provided application file to be installed and the temporary file to use to upload to the Deployment Manager during application install. The default is java.io.temp property. The wsadmin.properties file does not provide a value for this property.
com.ibm.ws.scripting.traceFile	Determines where trace and log output are directed. The wsadmin.properties file specifies logs/wsadmin.traceout located in the WebSphere install directory as the value of this property. If multiple users work with the wsadmin tool simultaneously, use the user properties file to set this property to point to a different output file. If the file name contains Double Byte Character Set (DBCS) characters, use Unicode format such as \xxxx, where xxxx is a number.
com.ibm.ws.scripting.traceString	Turns on tracing for the scripting client process. The default is to turn off tracing. The wsadmin.properties file does not provide a value for this property.

Table 5.1   Quick Reference for Java Properties Used by Scripting Client (Continued)

Property Name	Description
com.ibm.ws.scripting.validationLevel	Determines the level of validation to use when configuration changes are made. Valid values are NONE, LOW, MEDIUM, HIGH, and HIGHEST. The default is HIGHEST. The wsadmin.properties file does not provide a value for this property.
com.ibm.ws.scripting.validationOutput	Determines where the validation outputs are directed. The default is the logs/wsadmin.valout file located in the WebSphere install directory. The wsadmin.properties file does not provide a value for this property.

*Jython is supported starting with WebSphere Application Server Version 5.1.

The following is a sample default wsadmin.properties file created by WebSphere Application Server Version 5 install:

```
#---------------------------------------------------------------------
# Properties file for scripting client
#   Base App Server version
#---------------------------------------------------------------------
#
#---------------------------------------------------------------------
# The connectionType determines what connector is used.
# It can be SOAP or RMI.
# The default is SOAP.
#---------------------------------------------------------------------
com.ibm.ws.scripting.connectionType=SOAP
#com.ibm.ws.scripting.connectionType=RMI


#---------------------------------------------------------------------
# The port property determines what port is used when attempting
# a connection.
# The default SOAP port for a single-server installation is 8880
#---------------------------------------------------------------------
com.ibm.ws.scripting.port=8880


#---------------------------------------------------------------------
# The host property determines what host is used when attempting
# a connection.
# The default value is localhost.
```

```
#----------------------------------------------------------------------------
com.ibm.ws.scripting.host=localhost

#----------------------------------------------------------------------------
# The defaultLang property determines what scripting language to use.
# Supported values are jacl and jython.
# The default value is jacl.
#----------------------------------------------------------------------------
com.ibm.ws.scripting.defaultLang=jacl

#----------------------------------------------------------------------------
# The traceFile property determines where trace and logging
# output are directed.  If more than one user will be using
# wsadmin simultaneously, different traceFile properties should
# be set in user properties files.
# The default is that all tracing and logging go to the console;
# it is recommended that a value be specified here.
# If the file name contains DBCS characters, use unicode format such as
\uxxxx, where xxxx is a number
#----------------------------------------------------------------------------
com.ibm.ws.scripting.traceFile=C:/WebSphere/AppServer/logs/wsadmin.traceout

#----------------------------------------------------------------------------
# The validationOutput property determines where validation
# reports are directed.  If more than one user will be using
# wsadmin simultaneously, different validationOutput properties should
# be set in user properties files.
# The default is wsadmin.valout in the current directory.
# If the file name contains DBCS characters, use unicode format such as
\uxxxx,
# where xxxx is a number
#----------------------------------------------------------------------------
#com.ibm.ws.scripting.validationOutput=

#----------------------------------------------------------------------------
# The traceString property governs the trace in effect for
# the scripting client process.
# The default is no tracing.
#----------------------------------------------------------------------------
#com.ibm.ws.scripting.traceString=com.ibm.ws.*=all=disabled

#----------------------------------------------------------------------------
# The profiles property is a list of profiles to be run before
# running user commands, scripts, or an interactive shell.
# securityProcs is included here by default to make security
# configuration easier.
#----------------------------------------------------------------------------
```

```
com.ibm.ws.scripting.profiles=C:/WebSphere/AppServer/bin/
securtyProcs.jacl;C:/WebSphere/AppServer/bin/LTPA_LDAPSecurityProcs.jacl

#----------------------------------------------------------------------
# The emitWarningForCustomSecurityPolicy property controls whether
# message WASX7207W is emitted when custom permissions are found.
# Possible values are: true, false
# The default is "true"
#----------------------------------------------------------------------
#com.ibm.ws.scripting.emitWarningForCustomSecurityPolicy=true


#----------------------------------------------------------------------
# The tempdir property determines what directory to use for temporary
# files when installing applications.
# The default is that the JVM decides -- this is java.io.tmpdir
#----------------------------------------------------------------------
#com.ibm.ws.scripting.tempdir=


#----------------------------------------------------------------------
# The validationLevel property determines what level of validation to
# use when configuration changes are made from the scripting interface.
# Possible values are: NONE, LOW, MEDIUM, HIGH, HIGHEST
# The default is HIGHEST
#----------------------------------------------------------------------
#com.ibm.ws.scripting.validationLevel=


#----------------------------------------------------------------------
# The crossDocumentValidationEnabled property determines whether the
validation
# mechanism examines other documents when changes are made to one document.
# Possible values are: true, false
# The default is true
#----------------------------------------------------------------------
#com.ibm.ws.scripting.crossDocumentValidationEnabled=


#----------------------------------------------------------------------
# The classpath property is appended to the list of paths to search for
# classes and resources.
# There is no default value.
#----------------------------------------------------------------------
#com.ibm.ws.scripting.classpath=
```

Managing Configuration with Wsadmin

The AdminConfig object is one of the four scripting objects available for use in your scripts. The AdminConfig object is used to manage the configuration information stored in the repository. It communicates with the WebSphere configuration service component to make configuration inquires and changes. It allows you to query existing configuration objects, create configuration objects, modify existing objects, remove configuration objects, and obtain help. Updates to configuration through a scripting client are kept in a private tempo-rary area called *workspace* and are not copied to the master configuration repository until a save command is run. Workspace is a temporary repository of configuration information that administrative clients including WebSphere Administrative Console use. Workspace is kept in the wstemp subdirectory in your WebSphere install. The use of workspace allows multiple clients to access the master configuration. However, it is still possible that updates made by a scripting client cannot be saved if the same update is made by more than one cli-ent, causing conflict. If this happens, none of the updates will be saved in the configuration unless you have changed the default save policy with the `setSaveMode` command.

AdminConfig commands are available in both connected and local modes. If a server is cur-rently running, it is not recommended that you invoke the scripting client in local mode as the configuration changes made in the local mode are not reflected in the running server configuration and vice versa. In connnected mode, AdminConfig command availability depends on the type of server to which a scripting client is connected in a WebSphere Net-work Deployment install. AdminConfig commands are available only if a scripting client is connected to a Deployment Manager. When connected to a node agent or an application server, AdminConfig commands are not available, as the configurations for these server pro-cesses are just copies of the master configuration residing in the Deployment Manager. The copies are created in a node machine when configuration synchronization takes place between the Deployment Manager and the node agent. Any configuration changes to these server processes should be made by connecting a scripting client to a Deployment Manager. For this reason, you should not run a scripting client in local mode on a node machine to change the configuration because it is not a supported configuration.

Table 5.2 provides a quick reference to all the AdminConfig commands. For a current list of available AdminConfig commands related to the version of your WebSphere install, use the `help` command.

Table 5.2   Quick Reference for AdminConfig Commands

Command Name	Description
attributes	Shows attributes for a given configuration object type.
checkin	Checks a file into the configuration repository. Because this command works in the configuration repository level, changes are permanent. No configuration save is required to perform.
convertToCluster	Converts an existing server to be the first member of a new server cluster.

Table 5.2   Quick Reference for AdminConfig Commands (Continued)

Command Name	Description
create	Creates a configuration object with the given type, parent, and attributes.
createClusterMember	Creates a new server to be a new member of an existing cluster.
createDocument	Creates a new document in the configuration repository. Because this command works in the configuration repository level, changes are permanent. No configuration save is required to perform.
createUsingTemplate	Creates an object using a given template type.
defaults	Displays default values for attributes of a given configuration type.
deleteDocument	Deletes a document from the configuration repository. Because this command works in the configuration repository level, changes are permanent. No configuration save is required to perform.
existsDocument	Tests for existence of a document in the configuration repository.
Extract	Extracts a file from the configuration repository.
getCrossDocumentValidationEnabled	Returns true if cross-document validation is enabled.
getid	Returns the configuration ID of an object, given its containment path.
getObjectName	Returns a string version of the ObjectName for the running MBean that corresponds to a given configuration object name.
getSaveMode	Returns the mode used when a save is performed.
getValidationLevel	Returns the validation level used when files are extracted from the configuration repository.
getValidationSeverityResult	Returns the number of messages for a given severity from the most recent validation.
hasChanges	Returns true if unsaved configuration changes exist.
help	Shows general help information for this scripting object.
installResourceAdapter	Creates a J2C resource adapter with a given RAR file, node, and an option string.
list	Lists all configuration objects of a given configuration type.
listTemplates	Lists all configuration templates available for a given configuration type.

Table 5.2   Quick Reference for AdminConfig Commands (Continued)

Command Name	Description
modify	Updates specified configuration attributes of a given configuration object.
parents	Shows the configuration object type(s) that contain a given configuration type.
queryChanges	Returns a list of unsaved files.
remove	Removes a given configuration object.
require	Displays the required attributes of a given configuration type.
reset	Discards unsaved configuration changes.
save	Commits unsaved changes to configuration repository.
setCrossDocumentValidationEnabled	Sets the cross-document validation enabled mode. Possible values are true or false. Default value is true.
setSaveMode	Sets the mode to use when save is performed. Possible values are rollbackOnConflict and overwriteOnConflict. Default value is rollbackOnConflict.
setValidationLevel	Sets the validation level to use when files are extracted from the configuration repository. Possible values are none, low, medium, high, or highest. Default value is highest.
show	Shows the attributes of a given configuration object.
showall	Recursively shows the attributes of a given configuration object including all the configuration objects contained within each attribute.
showAttribute	Displays the value of a given attribute.
types	Displays all the supported configuration types.
validate	Invokes validation.

The following steps provide a common procedure to configure, including creating or updating a configuration object:

1. Identify a configuration type and its attributes.
2. Query an existing configuration object to obtain a configuration ID to be used for subsequent manipulation.
3. Create a new configuration object or modify an existing configuration object.
4. Save configuration changes.

Identify Configuration Object Types and Attributes

The first step in working with configuration using a scripting client is to understand the WebSphere configuration model. Without an understanding of the configuration model, it is rather hard to know what to look for in the WebSphere configuration. Appendix C provides information on the WebSphere configuration model. There are several helpful AdminConfig commands you can use to work with configuration object types described in the configuration model.

- Use the `types` command to get a list of configuration object types supported by your version of WebSphere install. This is an example of running this command in Jacl:

  ```
  $AdminConfig types
  ```

  Here is an example of running this command in Jython:

  ```
  print AdminConfig.types()
  ```

  The returned list is sorted in alphabetical order and contains the short names for each supported type. With such a long list with no explanation for each type, it might be hard to locate the configuration object type you are looking for. To help users get a better understanding of each configuration object type, there is documentation on the WebSphere configuration model shipped with your WebSphere Application Server install. The documents are located in the `web/configDocs` subdirectory of your WebSphere Application Server install. The WebSphere configuration model is also documented in Appendix C. Once you have identified the configuration object type you are going to work with, use the next three commands to look at its attributes.

- Use the `attributes` command to display the attributes and types for a configuration object type. An example of running this command displaying attributes for Server configuration object type in Jacl is shown here:

  ```
  $AdminConfig attributes Server
  ```

  The same example is shown here in Jython:

  ```
  print AdminConfig.attributes('Server')
  ```

  Depending on what configuration object type you are examining, it might contain the following types of attribute:

  - **Simple attribute containing string including ENUM, integer, or boolean.** Examples:
    ```
    "attr1 String"
    "attr2 int"
    "attr3 boolean"
    "attr4 ENUM(START, STOP)"
    ```

- **Nested attribute containing another configuration object.** Examples:

```
"attr5 ExampleType1"
"attr6 ExampleType2"
```

- **Nested attribute representing a list of objects of some type.** The * character is used to distinguish this type of attribute. Examples:

```
"attr7 String*"
"attr8 int*"
"attr9 ExampleType1*"
```

- **Reference attribute containing a reference to another object.** The @ sign is used to distinguish this type of attribute. Examples:

```
"attr10 ExampleType1@"
"attr11 ExampleType2@
```

- **Generic attribute containing configuration object of one of the possible listed subtypes.** Example:

```
"attr12 ExampleTypes(ExampleType1, ExampleType2)"
```

In this example, the `attr12` attribute represents an object of the generic type ExampleTypes. This generic type is associated with two specific subtypes, namely ExampleType1 and ExampleType2. The `attr12` attribute can have a value of ExampleType1, ExampleType2, or even ExampleTypes.

As attribute can contain an object of another configuration type, you might want to use another `attributes` command to see the attributes of the nested type. The `attributes` command displays attributes directly contained within the given configuration object type. It does not recursively display the attributes of nested types.

- Use the `required` command to display the required attributes for a configuration object type. This is an example of running this command looking for required attributes for the Server configuration object type in Jacl:

```
$AdminConfig required Server
```

The same example is shown here in Jython:

```
print AdminConfig.required('Server')
```

- Use the `defaults` command to see the default attribute values for a configuration object type. An example of running this command looking for default values for the Server configuration object type in Jacl is shown here:

```
$AdminConfig defaults Server
```

The same example is shown here in Jython:

```
print AdminConfig.defaults('Server')
```

Query Configuration Objects

Once you have identified the configuration object type and its attributes, the next step in working with a configuration object is to identify its configuration object name. To create a configuration object, you need to locate the configuration object name of a parent. To modify an existing configuration object, you need to identify its configuration object name.

Configuration object name is composed of two parts. The display name comes first, followed by the configuration data ID in parentheses. An example of such a configuration object name is the following:

```
Db2JdbcProvider(cells/testcell/nodes/testnode/resources.xml
#JDBCProvider_1)
```

For configuration data that do not have display names, the name of the object simply consists of the configuration data ID in parentheses. An example of such a name is the following:

```
(cells/testcell/nodes/testnode/resources.xml#J2CSecurityPermission_1)
```

Because the configuration data ID part of the name is completely unambiguous, you can always use it without the prepended display name in any command that requires a configuration object name.

There are two commands available to perform queries on configuration objects:

- Use the `getid` command to return configuration object names by specifying a fragment of the hierarchical containment path of the configuration object. The syntax of providing a containment path is /*type*:*name*/ where type is a configuration object type and name is the display name of a configuration object. The name part is optional. If you specify the type in the containment path without a name, include the colon. You can specify multiple /*type*:*name*/ pairs in the containment path string. The containment path must be a path containing the correct hierarchical order. An example of running this command looking for all Server type configuration objects in Jacl is shown here:

  ```
  set servers [$AdminConfig getid /Server:/]
  ```

  The same example is shown here in Jython:

  ```
  servers = AdminConfig.getid('/Server:/')
  ```

  The command returns a list of configuration object names for the Server configuration type. The list returned is assigned to the servers variable. You can narrow the configuration objects returned by specifying a more refined containment path. To look for a Server type configuration object in testNode of testCell, the command in Jacl is the following:

```
set servers [$AdminConfig getid /Cell:testCell/Node:testNode/
Server:/]
```

The same example is shown here in Jython:

```
servers = AdminCofig.getid('/Cell:testCell/Node:testNode/
Server:/')
```

- Use the list command to list configuration objects of a configuration object type. An example of running this command looking for all Server type configuration objects in Jacl is shown here:

```
set servers [$AdminConfig list Server]
```

This is the same example in Jython:

```
servers = AdminConfig.list('Server')
```

The command returns a list of configuration object names for the Server configuration type. The list returned is assigned to the servers variable. You can narrow the configuration objects returned by providing a scope. To look for a Server type configuration object in testNode of testCell, the command in Jacl is the following:

```
set node [$AdminConfig getid /Cell:testCell/Node:testNode/]
set servers [$AdminConfig list Server $node]
```

The same example is shown here in Jython:

```
node = AdminConfig.getid('/Cell:testCell/Node:testNode/')
servers = AdminConfig.list('Server', node)
```

If there is more than one configuration object name returned by the getid or list command, the configuration object names are returned in a list syntax in Jacl but a string syntax with each configuration object name separated by a line separator in Jython. For Jacl, you can use the lindex command to retrieve a single element from the list. For Jython, you can use the split method to format the returned string into a list from which a single element is retrieved. The following example retrieves the first configuration object name from the servers variable:

Using Jacl:

```
set aServer [lindex $servers 0]
```

Using Jython:

```
import java
lineSep = java.lang.System.getProperty('line.separator')
aServer = servers.split(lineSep)[0]
```

You can now use the configuration object name for any AdminConfig commands that require configuration object name as a parameter.

Create Configuration Objects

Once you have identified the configuration object type to create, its attributes, and the configuration object name of its parent, you are ready to create a configuration object by using the create or createUsingTemplate commands. With the create command, if there is a default template for the configuration object type, this template is used to provide values for attributes of a new object. Attribute values provided in the create command are applied on top of the template values. If there is no default template, then a new object is created using the attribute values provided in the command. The createUsingTemplate command allows you to specify a template to use to provide values for a new object. The createUsingTemplate command allows you to override the default template if there is one available for the configuration type to be created or to specify a template for a configuration object type that does not have a default template. A set of templates are provided in the config/templates subdirectory of your WebSphere install. You can use the listTemplates command to obtain the configuration object name for a template.

An example of using the create command to create a DataSource configuration object with JDBCProvider as the parent is shown here.

In Jacl:

```
set parent [$AdminConfig getid    /Node:testNode/
JDBCProvider:testJDBCProvider/]
$AdminConfig create DataSource $parent {{name testDataSource}}
```

In Jython:

```
parent = AdminConfig.getid('/Node:testNode/
JDBCProvider:testJDBCProvider/')
AdminConfig.create('DataSource', parent, [['name', 'testDataSource']])
```

The same example using the createUsingTemplate command but with a Sybase template is shown here.

In Jacl:

```
# look for templates for Sybase and use the first one.
set template [lindex [$AdminConfig listTemplates DataSource Sybase] 0]
set parent [$AdminConfig getid /Node:testNode/
JDBCProvider:testJDBCProvider]
$AdminConfig createUsingTemplate DataSource $parent {{name
testDataSource}} $template
```

In Jython:

```
import java
lineSep = java.lang.System.getProperty('line.separator')
# look for templates for Sybase, split the returned string
# into a Jython list using line separator, and use the
# first available template.
templates = AdminConfig.listTemplates('DataSource', 'Sybase')
aTemplate = templates.split(lineSep)[0]
parent = AdminConfig.getid('/Node:testNode/
JDBCProvider:testJDBCProvider/')
AdminConfig.createUsingTemplate('DataSource', parent, [['name',
'testDataSource']], aTemplate)
```

Both commands require attributes to be one of its input arguments. As described earlier, there are different types of attributes. The syntax of setting each attribute type follows the same general form but each is slightly different from the other one. Examples of how to set up each attribute type are described next.

- **Simple attributes**

  They contain the basic attribute types including string, integer, and boolean. Using the following as attributes of ExampleType1 configuration object type

  ```
  "name String"
  "attr2 int"
  "attr3 boolean"
  "attr4 ENUM(START, STOP)"
  ```

  the create command to set these attributes is provided in example here.

  In Jacl:

  ```
  $AdminConfig create ExampleType1 $parent {{name testType1} {attr2
  100} {attr3 true} {attr4 START}}
  ```

  In Jython:

  ```
  AdminConfig.create('ExampleType1', parent, [['name',
  'testType1'], ['attr2', 100], ['attr3', 'true'], ['attr4',
  'START']])
  ```

- **Nested attributes containing another configuration object**

  They represent attributes that contain a single configuration object. Using the following as attributes of ExampleType2 configuration object type

  ```
  "attr5 ExampleType1"
  "name String"
  ```

and assuming the same attributes exist for ExampleType1 as described earlier, there are two ways to create the ExampleType1 object that is contained inside an object of ExampleType2—directly, or as a nested attribute of its containing object. The following codes provide the commands to create an ExampleType1 object directly:

In Jacl:

```
set type2 [$AdminConfig create ExampleType2 $parent {{name
testType2}}]
$AdminConfig create ExampleType1 $type2 {{name test2Type1} {attr2
100} {attr3 true} {attr4 START}}
```

In Jython:

```
type2 = AdminConfig.create('ExampleType2', parent, [['name',
'testType2']])
AdminConfig.create('ExampleType1', type2, [['name',
'test2Type1'], ['attr2', 100], ['attr3', 'true'], ['attr4',
'START']])
```

Because there is only one attribute with ExampleType1 as its type in ExampleType2 object, the `create` command recognizes this and automatically creates an ExampleType1 object as a value of the `attr5` attribute. If there is more than one attribute containing the same object type as given in the `create` command, then you have to provide a fourth parameter with the `create` command to specify the attribute in the parent where this object should be created.

To create ExampleType1 as a nested attribute, examples in both Jacl and Jython are provided here.

In Jacl:

```
$AdminConfig create ExampleType2 $parent {{attr5 {{name test3Type1}
{attr2 100} {attr3 true} {attr4 START}}} {name test2Type2}}
```

In Jython:

```
AdminConfig.create('ExampleType2', parent, [['attr5',
[['name', 'test3Type1'], ['attr2', 100], ['attr3', 'true'],
['attr4', 'START']]], ['name', 'test2Type2']])
```

- **Nested list attributes**

  They represent attributes that contain a list of objects. Using the following as attributes of ExampleType3 configuration object type

```
"attr7 ExampleType1*"
"attr8 boolean"
```

and assuming the same attributes exist for ExampleType1 as described earlier, the following codes provide the commands to create an ExampleType1 object as nested attribute.

In Jacl:

```
set type3 [$AdminConfig create ExampleType3 $parent {{attr7
{{{name test4Type1} {attr2 100} {attr3 true} {attr4 START}}
{{name test5Type1} {attr2 200} {attr3 false} {attr4 STOP}}}}
{attr8 false}}]
```

In Jython:

```
type3 = AdminConfig.create('ExampleType3', parent, [['attr7',
[[['name', 'test4Type1'], ['attr2', 100], ['attr3', 'true'],
['attr4', 'START']], [['name', 'test5Type1'], ['attr2', 200],
['attr3', 'false'], ['attr4', 'STOP']]]], ['attr8', false]])
```

In the preceding example, the attr7 attribute contains a list of two ExampleType1 objects. {{name test4Type1} {attr2 100} {attr3 true} {attr4 START}} represent one object of ExampleType1, and {{name test5Type1} {attr2 200} {attr3 false} {attr4 STOP}} represent a second object.

You can also use the create command to create an ExampleType1 object directly. However, you can only create one object at a time. You cannot specify multiple objects as in the case with nested attributes. If there is an existing object in the list, the new object is added to the list. Following the same example codes resulting in saving an ExampleType3 configuration object in type3 variable, creating an ExampleType1 object with type3 as the parent will add a third ExampleType1 object to the attr7 attribute.

In Jacl:

```
$AdminConfig create ExampleType1 $type3 {{name test6Type1} {attr2
300} {attr3 true} {attr4 START}}
```

In Jython:

```
AdminConfig.create('ExampleType1', type3, [['name',
'test6Type1'], ['attr2', 300], ['attr3', 'true'], ['attr4',
'START']])
```

If an attribute represents a list of string (i.e., String*), the syntax to set a string list is different. The values of such a list are just strings, and not a list of attribute name–value pairs. The strings should be separated by a semicolon regardless of the platform. Using attr11 String* as an example attribute, the attribute string to set this attribute is as follows:

In Jacl:

```
{{attr11 c:/db2/db2.jar;c:/db2/java/db2java.jar}}
```

In Jython:

```
[['attr11', 'c:/db2/db2.jar;c:/db2java/db2java.jar']]
```

- **Reference attributes**

  They represent attributes that reference another object. The values of these attributes are configuration object names of the reference object. Using the following as attributes of ExampleType4 configuration object type

  ```
  "attr9 ExampleType1@"
  "attr10 String"
  ```

  and assuming the same attributes exist for ExampleType1 as described earlier, the following example shows the create command to set this reference attribute:

  In Jacl:

  ```
  set type1 [$AdminConfig getid /ExampleType1:testType1/]

  $AdminConfig create ExampleType4 $parent [subst {{attr9 $type1}
  {attr10 testType4}}]
  ```

  In Jython:

  ```
  type1 = AdminConfig.getid('/ExampleType1:testType1')

  AdminConfig.create('ExampleType4', parent, [['attr9', type1],
  ['attr10', 'testType4']])
  ```

  This example sets the configuration object name for testType1 as value of the `attr9` attribute. The `subst` command is needed in the Jacl example because Jacl will not perform automatic variable substitution inside a list. The `subst` command forces the configuration object name saved in the type1 variable to be used.

- **Generic attributes**

  They represent attributes that can have value of a generic type or its specific subtypes. Using the following as attributes of ExampleType5 configuration object type

  ```
  "attr11 ExampleTypes(ExampleType1, ExampleType4)"
  ```

  and assuming the same attributes exist for ExampleType1 and ExampleType4 as described earlier, to create an object of ExampleType1 as a value of the `attr11` attribute:

In Jacl:

```
$AdminConfig create ExampleType5 $parent {{attr11:ExampleType1
{{name test7Type1} {attr2 700} {attr3 true} {attr4 START}}}}
```

In Jython:

```
AdminConfig.create('ExampleType5', parent,
[['attr11:ExampleType1', [['name', 'test7Type1'], ['attr2',
700], ['attr3', 'true'], ['attr4', 'START']]]])
```

To create an ExampleType4 object as a value of the `attr11` attribute, use `attr11:ExampleType4` as the attribute. If you do not include the specific subtype in your `create` command, a generic ExampleTypes object is created.

If you have WebSphere Application Server Network Deployment installed, you can use `convertToCluster` and `createClusterMember` to configure an application server to be a member of a cluster. Use `convertToCluster` to convert an existing application server as the first member of a new cluster. Use `createClusterMember` to create a new application server as a new member of an existing cluster.

Modify Configuration Objects

Once you have identified the configuration object name of an existing object and its attributes as described in sections Identify Configuration Object Types and Attributes and Query Configuration Objects, you can modify an existing configuration object. The following example changes the description attribute of a DataSource configuration object.

In Jacl:

```
set myds [$AdminConfig getid /DataSource:testDataSource/]
$AdminConfig modify $myds {{description "This is a new description"}}
```

In Jython:

```
myds = AdminConfig.getid('/DataSource:testDataSource/')
AdminConfig.modify(myds, [['description', 'This is a new
description']])
```

The syntax to provide different attribute type values is the same as described using the `create` command in section Create Configuration Objects. There is an important behavior to remember when modifying a list attribute. The `modify` command results in adding new objects to the existing list. To replace the existing list, you have to use two `modify` commands. The first one is to reset the list to empty, and the second one is to add the new list. For example:

In Jacl:

```
set jdbcProvider [$AdminConfig  getid /JDBCProvider:testProvider/]
$AdminConfig modify $jdbcProvider {{classpath {}}}
$AdminConfig modify $jdbcProvider {{classpath c:/db2/db2.jar;c:/db2/
java/db2java.jar}}
```

In Jython:

```
jdbcProvider = AdminConfig.getid('/JDBCProvider:testProvider/')
AdminConfig.modify(jdbcProvider, [['classpath', ""]])
AdminConfig.modify(jdbcProvider, [['classpath', 'c:/db2/db2.jar;c:/
db2/java/db2java.jar']])
```

In this example, classpath is an attribute with string* as the type. This example sets the classpath attribute to c:/db2/db2.jar;c:/db2/java/db2java.jar. Without the first modify command, the new value is appended to the existing classpath list.

Save Configuration

Because a scripting client uses workspace to keep configuration changes, it is important that you save your configuration to transfer the updates to the master configuration repository.

In Jacl:

```
$AdminConfig save
```

In Jython:

```
AdminConfig.save()
```

If you want to undo changes made to your configuration since your last save, use the reset command. If a scripting process ends and a save has not been performed, any configuration changes since the last save are discarded except in interactive mode and the –c option is used in wsadmin. In interactive mode, the user is prompted if unsaved changes are about to be lost. If a command is provided by using the –c option in wsadmin, a save is automatically performed if configuration changes are made.

Managing Applications with Wsadmin

The AdminApp scripting object is used to manage applications in your WebSphere install. It communicates with the WebSphere run-time application management object to make application inquiries and changes. This includes installing and uninstalling applications, listing applications, editing applications or modules, exporting, and more. Because applications are part of configuration data, any changes made to an application are kept in the workspace just like the other configuration data. It is important that you save your application changes to transfer the data from the workspace to the master repository.

The current postapplication install support in the AdminApp object limits updates to application metadata, maps virtual hosts to Web modules, and maps servers to modules. Any other postconfiguration changes, such as specifying the library to be used by the application and setting session management configuration properties, have to be performed using AdminConfig commands.

Like AdminConfig commands, you can run AdminApp commands in local mode. Again like configuration, if a server is currently running, it is not recommended that you run a scripting client without connecting to a server. The same concern documented in section Managing Configuration with Wsadmin applies here.

Table 5.3 provides a quick reference to all the AdminApp commands. For a current list of available AdminApp commands pertaining to the version of your WebSphere install, use the `help` command.

Table 5.3   Quick Reference for AdminApp Commands

Command Name	Description
deleteUserAndGroupEntries	Deletes users or groups for all roles, and deletes userIDs and passwords for all RunAs roles defined in the given application.
edit	Edits an application or module.
editInteractive	Edits an application or module in interactive mode.
export	Exports an application to a file.
exportDDL	Exports Data Definition Language (DDL) from an application to a directory.
help	Shows general help or help for an AdminApp command or install option.
install	Installs or updates an application.
installInteractive	Installs or updates an application in interactive mode.
list	Lists applications installed in the configuration.
listModules	Lists the modules in an application.
options	Shows a list of valid installation options for an application file.
publishWSDL[a]	Publishes Web Services Description Language (WSDL) files to a file.
taskInfo	Provides information about a particular task option for an application file.
uninstall	Uninstalls an application.

Table 5.3 Quick Reference for AdminApp Commands

Command Name	Description
updateAccessIDs	Updates the access ID information for users and groups assigned to various roles defined in an application.
view[b]	View an installed application.

a. PublishWSDL command is available starting with WebSphere Application Server Version 5.02.
b. View command is available starting with WebSphere Application Server Version 5.1.

The following list outlines the common procedure to manage the cycle of an application:

1. Install an application.

2. Edit an application.

3. Update an application.

4. Uninstall an application.

Install Applications

The first step in managing an application is to install the application. This can be accomplished either in batch or interactive mode. Use the `install` command to install an application in batch mode. Use the `installInteractive` command to prompt you through a series of installation tasks to provide information to install your application. The input file must be an archive ending with .ear, .jar, or .war. If the file is a .jar or .war, it will be automatically wrapped as an .ear file. An example of installing an application named *myApp1* on server *testServer* residing on node *testNode* in batch mode follows:

In Jacl:

```
$AdminApp install c:/myApp/myApp1.ear {-appname myApp1 -node testNode
-server testServer}
$AdminConfig save
```

In Jython:

```
AdminApp.install('c:/myApp/myApp1.ear', "[-appname myApp1 -node
testNode -server testServer]")
AdminConfig.save()
```

Because installing an application changes the configuration, it is important that the configuration is saved. Appname, node, and server are just a few of the installation options. There are many possible options for the install and installInteractive command. Each option consists of a dash followed by the option name, followed optionally by the option value. Some options take no values:

```
-nopreCompileJSPs
```

Others take simple values:

```
-node testNode
```

Still other options (called *task options*) correspond to install tasks and take lists of values. The number of values for each task option varies and depends on the installation task itself. Each member of the list corresponds to data to one entry of the install task, for example:

```
-MapWebModToVH {{"JavaMail Sample WebApp" mtcomps.war,WEB-INF/web.xml
newVH}}
```

This particular example is a Jacl list containing a single instance of the MapWebModToVH data, consisting of three fields:

```
"JavaMail Sample WebApp"
mtcomps.war,WEB-INF/web.xml
NewVH
```

Use the `taskInfo` command to obtain install task information about the data needed for your application. You only need to provide data for rows or entries that are missing information or those where you want to update existing data. Table 5.4 provides a quick reference to the available install options.

Table 5.4   Quick Reference for Installation Options

Option Name	Description
allowPermInFilterPolicy*	Specifies to continue with the application deployment process even when the application contains policy permissions that are in the filter policy. This option does not require a value. The default setting is noallowPermInFilterPolicy.
appname	Specifies the name of the application. The default is the display name of the application.
BackendIdSelection	Specifies the back-end ID for the enterprise bean jar modules that have container managed persistence (CMP) beans.
BindJndiForEJBMessageBinding	Binds enterprise beans to listener port names.
BindJndiForEJBNonMessageBinding	Binds enterprise beans to Java Naming and Directory Interface (JNDI) names.
cell	Specifies the cell name where the application is installed.

Table 5.4   Quick Reference for Installation Options (Continued)

Option Name	Description
cluster	Specifies the cluster name where the application is installed. This option applies only to a network deployment configuration.
contextroot	Specifies the context root for installing a stand-alone WAR file.
CorrectOracleIsolationLevel	Specifies the isolation level for the Oracle type provider. Valid isolation level values are 2 or 4.
CorrectUseSystemIdentity	Replaces RunAs System or RunAs roles.
CeateMBeansForResources	Specifies that MBeans are created for all the resources defined in an application when the application is started on a deployment target. The default is nocreatMBeansForResources.
DataSourceFor10CMPBeans	Specifies optional data sources for 1.x CMP beans.
DataSourceFor20CMPBeans	Specifies optional data sources for 2.x CMP beans. Valid values for resource authorization field are per connection factory or container.
DataSourceFor10EJBModules	Specifies the default data source for the enterprise bean module that contains 1.x CMP beans.
DataSourceFor20EJBModules	Specifies the default data source for an enterprise bean module that contains 2.x CMP beans. Valid values for resource authorization field are per connection factory or container.
defaultbinding.cf.jndi	Specifies the default JNDI name for a connection factory. This option applies only if you specify the usedefaultbindings option.
defaultbinding.datasource.jndi	Specifies the default JNDI name for a data source. This option applies only if you specify the usedefaultbindings option.
defaultbinding.datasource.password	Specifies the default password for a data source. This option applies only if you specify the usedefaultbindings option.
defaultbinding.datasource.password	Specifies the default user name for a data source. This option applies only if you specify the usedefaultbindings option.
defaultbinding.ejbjndi.prefix	Specifies the default prefix to use for the enterprise bean JNDI name. This option applies only if you specify the usedefaultbindings option.
defaultbinding.force	Specifies that the default bindings should override any existing current bindings. This option applies only if you specify the usedefaultbindings option.
defaultbinding.strategy.file	Specifies a custom default bindings strategy file. This option applies only if you specify the usedefaultbindings option.
defaultbinding.virtual.host	Specifies the default name for a virtual host. This option applies only if you specify the usedefaultbindings option.

Table 5.4   Quick Reference for Installation Options (Continued)

Option Name	Description
deployejb	Specifies to run EJBDeploy during installation. This option does not require a value. If an application is predeployed, then the default value is nodeployejb. Otherwise, the default value is deployejb.
deployejb.classpath	Specifies extra classpath for EJBDeploy.
deployejb.dbschema	Specifies the database schema for EJBDeploy.
deployejb.dbtype	Specifies the database type for EJBDeploy. For a list of supported database vendor types pertaining to your WebSphere install, run ejbdeploy -?.
deployejb.rmic	Specifies extra RMIC options to use for EJBDeploy.
deployws	Specifies to deploy WebServices. This option does not have a value. The default value is nodeployws.
deployws.classpath	Specifies extra classpath to deploy WebServices.
deployws.jardirs	Specifies extra extension directories to deploy WebServices.
distributeApp	Specifies to distribute application binaries. This option does not require a value. This is the default setting.
EnsureMethodProtectionFor10EJB	Selects method protections for unprotected 1.x enterprise bean methods. Specify to leave the method as unprotected, or assign protection that denies all access with a value of methodProtection.denyAllPermission
EnsureMethodProectionFor20EJB	Selects method protections for unprotected 2.x enterprise bean methods. Valid values include: methodProtection.exclude (include the method to the exclude list), methodProection.uncheck (mark the method as unchecked), or a list of security roles separated by commas.
installdir	Specifies the directory in which to place the application binaries.
MapModulesToServers	Specifies the application server where you want to install modules contained in your application. You can install modules to the same server, disperse them among several servers, or to a cluster for a Network Deployment configuration.
MapEJBRefToEJB	Maps enterprise Java references to enterprise beans.
MapResEnvRefToRes	Maps resource environment references to resources.
MapResRefToEJB	Maps resource references to resources.
MapRolesToUsers	Maps users to roles. You can specify multiple users or groups for a single role by separating them with a |.

Table 5.4   Quick Reference for Installation Options (Continued)

Option Name	Description
MapRunAsRolesToUsers	Maps RunAs roles to users.
MapWebModToVH	Specifies the virtual host where you want to install the Web modules contained in your application. You can install Web modules on the same virtual host or disperse them among several hosts.
noallowPermInFilterPolicy*	Specifies not to continue with the application deployment process when the application contains policy permissions that are in the filter policy. This option does not require a value. This is the default setting.
nocreateMBeansForResources	Specifies that MBeans are not created for all the resources defined in an application when the application is started on a deployment target. This is the default setting.
nodeployejb	Specifies not to run EJBDeploy. This option does not require a value. If an application is predeployed, then the default value is nodeployejb. Otherwise, the default value is deployejb.
nodeployws	Specifies not to deploy WebServices. This option does not require a value. This value is the default setting.
nodistributeApp	Specifies not to distribute application binaries. This option does not require a value. The default setting is distributeApp.
nopreCompileJSPs	Specifies not to precompile JavaServer Pages files. This option does not require a value. This is the default setting.
noreloadEnabled	Specifies not to enable class reloading. The default is reloadEnabled.
nouseMetaDataFromBinary	Specifies that the metadata used at run time comes from the configuration repository. This option does not require a value. This is the default setting. Use useMetaDataFromBinary to indicate that the metadata used at run time should come from the EAR file.
nousedefaultbindings	Specifies not to use default bindings. This option does not require a value. This is the default setting.
preCompileJSPs	Specifies to precompile JavaServer Pages files. This option does not require a value. The default is nopreCompileJSPs.
reloadEnabled	Specifies to enable class reloading. This is the default setting.
reloadInterval	Specifies the time period (in seconds) in which the application's filesystem will be scanned for updated files. The default setting is three seconds.
server	Specifies the server name where to install the application.

Table 5.4   Quick Reference for Installation Options (Continued)

Option Name	Description
update	Updates the installed application with a new version of the EAR file. This option does not require a value. This option requires the specification of the appname option to indicate the installed application to be updated. The update action merges bindings from the new version with the bindings from the old version, uninstalls the old version, and installs the new version. The binding information from the new version of the EAR file is preferred over the corresponding one from the old version. If any element of binding is missing in the new version, the corresponding element from the old version is used.
update.ignore.old	Specifies that during the update action, bindings from the installed version of the application are ignored. This option does not require a value. This option applies only if you specify the update option.
update.ignore.new	Specifies that during the update action, bindings from the new version of the application are ignored. This option does not require a value. This option applies only if you specify the update option.
useMetaDataFromBinary	Specifies that the metadata used at run time comes from the EAR file. This option does not require a value. The default value is nouseMetaDataFromBinary to get metadata from the configuration repository.
usedefaultbindings	Specifies to use default bindings. This option does not require a value. The default setting is nousedefaultbindings
verbose	Causes additional messages to display. This option does not require a value.

*These options are available starting with WebSphere Application Server Version 5.1.

Edit Applications

You can edit an installed application to change its metadata by using the `edit` or `editInteractive` command. Use the `edit` command with options in batch mode processing. Use the `editInteractive` command to be prompted for a series of tasks to provide data to update the application. You can edit the entire application or a module contained in your application. To specify a module, use the return from the `listModules` command as the module name; for example, `ivtApp#ivtEJB.jar+META-INF/ejb-jar.xml`. The following `edit` command specifies to not distribute the application binaries.

In Jacl:

```
$AdminApp edit myApp1 {-nodistributeApp}
$AdminConfig save
```

In Jython:

```
AdminApp.edit('myApp1', '[-nodistributeApp]')
AdminConfig.save()
```

As with application installation, it is important that you save the configuration after editing an installed application.

Most of the installation options are supported by the edit or editInteractive commands. However, the following list of options does not apply when editing an installed application:

```
appname
BackendIdSelection
cell cluster
EnsureMethodProtectionFor10EJB
EnsureMethodProtectionFor20EJB
installdir
node server
All the defaultbinding related options
All the deployejb related options
All the deployws related options
All the preCompileJSPs related options
All the update related options
```

Update Applications

You can update an installed application with a new version of the application EAR file. Update is performed by specifying the update option with the install command. There are three update actions:

- Merge the new bindings with the old bindings

  This is the default action. If both the old and new versions of the application have binding elements with different data, the new binding information is preferred over the old binding information. If any element of binding is missing in the new version, the corresponding one from the old version is used.

- Use new bindings

  This action ignores bindings set in the installed version of the application. Only bindings in the new version are used.

- Use old bindings

This action ignores bindings in the new version of the application. Only bindings in the installed version are used.

Regardless of which action you use for your application update, after the bindings are taken care of, the installed application is uninstalled before a new version is installed. The followings are examples of an application update using a different update action:

- Update an installed application named myApp1 using the default merge action.

  In Jacl:

  ```
  $AdminApp install myApp1New.ear {-appname myApp1 —update}
  $AdminConfig save
  ```

  In Jython:

  ```
  AdminApp.install('myApp1New.ear', '[-appname myApp1 —update]')
  AdminConfig.save()
  ```

- Update an installed application named myApp1 using bindings from the new application.

  In Jacl:

  ```
  $AdminApp install myApp1New.ear {-appname myApp1 —update
  —update.ignore.old}
  $AdminConfig save
  ```

  In Jython:

  ```
  AdminApp.install('myApp1New.ear', '[-appname myApp1 —update
  —update.ignore.old]')
  AdminConfig.save()
  ```

- Update an installed application named myApp1 using bindings from the installed application.

  In Jacl:

  ```
  $AdminApp install myApp1New.ear {-appname myApp1 —update
  —update.ignore.new}
  $AdminConfig save
  ```

  In Jython:

  ```
  AdminApp.install('myApp1New.ear', '[-appname myApp1 —update
  —update.ignore.new]')
  AdminConfig.save()
  ```

As with application install, it is important that you save the configuration after updating an installed application.

Uninstall Applications

Use the `uninstall` command to uninstall an existing application. The `uninstall` command removes the application from the configuration. Like other AdminApp commands that change the configuration, you have to save the configuration to complete the uninstall. The following example uninstalls an application named myApp1.

In Jacl:

```
$AdminApp uninstall myApp1
$AdminConfig save
```

In Jython:

```
AdminApp.uninstall('myApp1')
AdminConfig.save()
```

Managing Live Run-time Components with Wsadmin

The AdminControl scripting object is used for operational control. It communicates with MBeans that represent live objects running in a WebSphere server process. It includes commands to query existing running objects and their attributes and invoke operation on the running objects. In addition to the operational commands, the AdminControl object supports commands to query information on the connected server, convenient commands for client tracing, reconnecting to a server, and starting and stopping the server for a Network Deployment environment.

Many of the operational commands have two sets of signatures so that they can either invoke using string-based parameters or using JMX objects as parameters. For more information on JMX MBeans representing WebSphere live running objects, refer to Appendix B. Depending on the server process to which a scripting client is connected, the number and type of MBeans available varies. If a scripting client is connected to a deployment manager, then all MBeans in all server processes are visible. If a scripting client is connected to a node agent, all MBeans in all server processes on that node are accessible. When connected to an application server, only MBeans running in that application server are visible.

Table 5.5 provides a quick reference to all the AdminControl commands. For a current list of available AdminControl commands pertaining to the version of your WebSphere install, use the `help` command.

Table 5.5   Quick Reference for AdminControl Commands

Command Name	Description
completeObjectName	Returns a string representation of a running object complete object name based on a fragment.
getAttribute	Displays value of a given attribute.
getAttribute_jmx	Displays value of a given attribute.
getAttributes	Displays attribute values in name–value pairs.
getAttributes_jmx	Displays attribute values in name–value pairs.
getCell	Displays the name of the connected cell.
getConfigId	Returns a configuration object name corresponding to the given string version of an MBean object name.
getDefaultDomain	Returns the default domain name from the connected server.
getDomainName	Returns the domain name from the connected server.
getHost	Returns the name of the connected host.
getMBeanCount	Returns the number of MBeans registered with the server.
getMBeanInfo_jmx	Returns the JMX MBeanInfo structure that corresponds to a given ObjectName.
getNode	Displays the name of the connected node.
getPort	Displays the port used by the connected host.
getType	Displays the connection type.
help	Displays general and individual command help.
invoke	Invokes a method on a given MBean with optional parameters and signatures.
invoke_jmx	Invokes a method on a given MBean.
isRegistered_jmx	Returns true if the ObjectName value is a member of the given class.
isRegistered	Returns true if string version of an object name is registered in the connected server.
makeObjectName	Creates an ObjectName based on the input string.
queryNames	Returns string representation of all object names that match a given name template.
queryNames_jmx	Returns a set of ObjectName objects based on the given ObjectName and QueryExp.
reconnect	Reconnects to the server and clears out local cache.
setAttribute	Sets the given single attribute value.
setAttribute_jmx	Sets the given single attribute value.

Table 5.5   Quick Reference for AdminControl Commands (Continued)

Command Name	Description
setAttributes	Sets the given attribute values.
setAttributes_jmx	Sets the given attribute values.
startServer	Starts the given application server by locating it in the configuration. This command is valid in the deployment manager environment.
stopServer	Stops the given application server.
testConnection	Communicates with the DataSourceCfgHelper MBean to test the given DataSource connection.
trace	Sets the trace specification for the scripting process to the given value.

The following steps provide a common procedure to work with a running MBean:

1. Identify a running MBean to obtain an object name string to be used for subsequent manipulation.
2. List attributes and operations of a running MBean.
3. Invoke the operations on a running MBean.
4. Modify the attributes on a running MBean.

Query Running MBeans

To work with WebSphere running objects in a scripting client, an understanding of WebSphere run-time MBeans is a plus. Appendix B includes information on WebSphere run-time MBeans. There are two AdminControl commands you can use to query running MBeans residing in the connected server process.

- Use the `QueryNames` command to return running object names by specifying an object name template. An object name template is a string containing a segment of the object name to be matched. The template has the same format as a JMX ObjectName with the following pattern:

      [*domain:*]*property=value*[,*property=value*]*

An object name string consists of the following:

- The domain name WebSphere
- Several key properties, for example:
  - **type**—indicates the type of object accessible through this MBean, for example, ApplicationServer, EJBContainer. Refer to Appendix B for a list of running MBean types to use in your query.
  - **name**—represents the display name of the object; for example, myServer.

- **node**—represents the name of the node on which the object runs.
- **process**—represents the name of the server process in which the object runs.
- **mbeanIdentifier**—correlates the MBean instance with the corresponding configuration data.

An example of object name template is

```
WebSphere:type=Server,name=myServer,*
```

The asterisk is a wildcard character for matching any other properties in the object name. Without this character, you have to specify all the properties to get a match. An example of using queryNames command with this template is shown here:

In Jacl:

```
set myServers [$AdminControl queryNames
WebSphere:type=Server,name=myServer,*]
```

In Jython:

```
myServers =
AdminControl.queryNames('WebSphere:type=Server,name=myServer,*
')
```

The command returns matching object names to the myServers variable. If there are multiple running MBeans matching this query, they are returned in a list syntax in Jacl but a string syntax with each object name string separated by a line separator in Jython. For Jacl, you can use the lindex command to retrieve a single element from the list. For Jython, you can use the split method to format the returned string into a list from which a single element is retrieved. The following example retrieves the first object name from the myServers variable.

Using Jacl:

```
set aServer [lindex $myServers 0]
```

Using Jython:

```
import java
lineSep = java.lang.System.getProperty('line.separator')
aServer = myServers.split(lineSep)[0]
```

- Use the completeObjectName command to return a single object name. This command has the exact syntax as the queryNames command except that if there are multiple MBeans matching the template, only the first matched object name is returned. To look for a Server type MBean for running server named myServer, use the following example.

In Jacl:

```
set aServer [$AdminControl completeObjectName
WebSphere:type=Server,name=myServer,*]
```

In Jython:

```
aServer =
AdminControl.CompleteObjectName('WebSphere:type=Server,name=my
Server,*')
```

You can now use the MBean object name for any AdminControl or Help commands that require object name as a parameter.

List Attributes and Operations of Running MBeans

Once you obtain an object name of a running MBean, you can examine its contents such as attributes and operations. Use the `attributes` and `operations` commands of the Help scripting object to display information about the attributes and operations of this MBean. There are other Help commands to display other kinds of information for a running MBean. Such commands include `description`, `classname`, `constructors`, and `notifications`. Examples of using `attributes` and `operations` commands follow.

In Jacl:

```
set aServer [$AdminControl completeObjectName
WebSphere:type=Server,name=myServer,*]
$Help attributes $aServer
$Help operations $aServer
```

In Jython:

```
aServer =
AdminControl.CompleteObjectName('WebSphere:type=Server,name=myServer,*')
print Help.attributes(aServer)
print Help.operations(aServer)
```

Perform Operations on Running MBeans

Once you have identified a running MBean and examine the operations supported by this MBean, you can use the `invoke` command to invoke an operation on the identified MBean. The `invoke` command is provided to support operations that allow parameters to be specified as string. Wsadmin provides conversion from or to a string for the following Java classes:

- java.lang.Boolean
- java.lang.Byte
- java.lang.Character

- java.lang.Double
- java.lang.Float
- java.lang.Integer
- java.lang.Long
- java.lang.Short
- java.lang.String
- java.net.URL
- java.util.Properties
- javax.management.ObjectName

If an operation contains only one or more of these Java classes as its input arguments, then you can use the `invoke` command. Otherwise, you have to use the `invoke_jmx` command to provide Java objects as inputs. There are three command signatures for the `invoke` command. Examples of using `invoke` commands with different number of arguments are given here.

- The first variety of the `invoke` command expects two parameters and is used for MBean operations that take no argument. You need to specify the MBean on which you want to issue an operation and the name of an operation. This example invokes the stop operation on a server MBean.

  In Jacl:

  ```
  set aServerObject [$AdminControl completeObjectName
  type=Server,name=myServer,*]
  $AdminControl invoke $aServerObject stop
  ```

  In Jython:

  ```
  aServerObject =
  AdminControl.completeObjectName('type=Server,name=myServer,*')
  AdminControl.invoke(aServerObject, 'stop')
  ```

- The second variety takes three parameters. The third parameter is to specify a string that contains all the arguments for the operation. This example invokes the appendTraceString operation to enable trace to all com.ibm packages on a TraceService MBean.

  In Jacl:

  ```
  set aTraceServiceObject [$AdminControl completeObjectName
  type=TraceService,name=myServer,*]
  $AdminControl invoke $aTraceServiceObject appendTraceString
  com.ibm.*=all=enabled
  ```

In Jython:

```
aTraceServiceObject =
AdminControl.completeObjectName('type=TraceService,name=
myServer,*')
AdminControl.invoke(aTraceServiceObject, 'appendTraceString',
'com.ibm.*=all=enabled')
```

This example contains an argument string that has a single argument. If there are multiple arguments for the operation, the arguments need to be separated by a space, as shown here.

In Jacl:

```
set aSecurityAdminObject [$AdminControl completeObjectName
type=SecurityAdmin,name=myServer,*]
$AdminControl invoke $aSecurityAdminObject checkPassword
{myUserid myPassword ""}
```

In Jython:

```
aSecurityAdminObject =
AdminControl.completeObjectName('type=SecurityAdmin,name=
myServer,*')
AdminControl.invoke(aSecurityAdminObject, 'checkPassword',
'myUserid myPassword ""')
```

- The third variety takes four parameters with the fourth parameter being a string providing a list of argument types for the invoked operation. This variety should be used only if the MBean operation has signatures that are ambiguous. This example invokes the appendTraceString operation again but passing in the fourth parameter.

In Jacl:

```
set aTraceServiceObject [$AdminControl completeObjectName
type=TraceService,name=myServer,*]
$AdminControl invoke $aTraceServiceObject appendTraceString
com.ibm.*=all=enabled java.lang.String
```

In Jython:

```
aTraceServiceObject =
AdminControl.completeObjectName('type=TraceService,name=
myServer,*')
AdminControl.invoke(aTraceServiceObject, 'appendTraceString',
'com.ibm.*=all=enabled', 'java.lang.String')
```

If you have to use the invoke_jmx command, this command takes four parameters as the one in the invoke command. However, except for the operation name, the other parameters are expecting Java objects. The same example for the appendTraceString operation is invoked by using the invoke_jmx command.

In Jacl:

```
set aTraceServiceObjectStr [$AdminControl completeObjectName
type=TraceService,name=myServer,*]
set aTraceServiceObject [$AdminControl makeObjectName
$aTraceServiceObjectStr]
set parms [java::new {java.lang.Object[]} 1 com.ibm.*=all=enabled]
set signature [java::new {java.lang.String[]} 1 java.lang.String]
$AdminControl invoke $aTraceServiceObject appendTraceString $parms
$signature
```

In Jython:

```
aTraceServiceObjectStr =
AdminControl.completeObjectName('type=TraceService,name=myServer,*')
aTraceServiceObject =
AdminControl.makeObjectName(aTraceServiceObjectStr)
parms = ['com.ibm.*=all=enabled']
signature = ['java.lang.String']
AdminControl.invoke($aTraceServiceObject, 'appendTraceString',
parms, signature)
```

Modify Attributes on Running MBeans

Once you have identified a running MBean and the attributes supported by this MBean, you can use the getAttribute/getAttributes and setAttribute/setAttributes commands to work with run-time attributes. The following example show how to use these commands to display and change run-time attributes for a TraceService type MBean:

In Jacl:

```
set aTraceServiceObject [$AdminControl completeObjectName
type=TraceService,name=myServer,*]
$AdminControl getAttribute $aTraceServiceObject traceSpecification
$AdminControl getAttributes $aTraceServiceObject {traceSpecification
traceFileName}
$AdminControl setAttribute $aTraceServiceObject traceSpecification
com.ibm.*=all=enabled
$AdminControl setAttributes $aTraceServiceObject {{traceSpecification
com.ibm.*=all=disabled} {ringBufferSize 10}}
```

In Jython:

```
aTraceServiceObject =
AdminControl.completeObjectName('type=TraceService,name=myServer,*')
print AdminControl.getAttribute(aTraceServiceObject,
'traceSpecification')
```

```
print AdminControl.getAttributes(aTraceServiceObject,
'traceSpecification traceFileName')
AdminControl.setAttribute(aTraceServiceObject, 'traceSpecification',
'com.ibm*=all=enabled')
AdminControl.setAttributes(aTraceServiceObject, [['traceSpecification',
'com.ibm.*=all=disabled'], ['ringBufferSize',   10]])
```

The syntax for providing attribute value is the same name–value pair as in a configuration object. It is important to point out that any update in attribute values belonging to an MBean does not have any effect on the persistent configuration object that represents this MBean. In fact, the attributes supported for manipulation by an MBean are generally different from those supported by the corresponding configuration. The configuration is likely to contain more attributes that cannot be queried or set by the live running object.

There are also JMX signature-based commands to get and set run-time attributes. They are the getAttribute_jmx, getAttributes_jmx, setAttribute_jmx, and setAttributes _jmx commands. An example of using setAttributes_jmx is given here.

In Jacl:

```
set aTraceServiceObjectStr [$AdminControl completeObjectName
WebSphere:type=TraceService,name=myServer,*]
set aTraceServiceObject [$AdminControl makeObjectName
$aTraceServiceObjectStr]
set attr [java::new javax.management.Attribute traceSpecification
com.ibm.ws.*=all=enabled]
set alist [java::new javax.management.AttributeList]
$alist add $attr
$AdminControl setAttributes_jmx $aTraceServiceObject $alist
```

In Jython:

```
aTraceServiceObjectStr =
AdminControl.completeObjectName('type=TraceService,name=myServer,*')
aTraceServiceObject =
AdminControl.makeObjectName(aTraceServiceObjectStr)
import javax.management as mgmt
attr = mgmt.Attribute('traceSpecification', 'com.ibm.ws.*=all=enabled')
alist = mgmt.AttributeList()
alist.add(attr)
AdminControl.setAttributes_jmx(aTraceServiceObject, alist)
```

TASK REFERENCE

Example Jacl scripts are provided in this section. They are presented in the same grouping and order as the topology provided in the navigation tree of the Administrative Console. There are scripts providing configuration tasks, scripts for accessing and invoking methods of live run-time objects, and scripts for managing applications. The scripts are provided to show what probable objects and attributes to work with for each task. They do not mean to cover all the scenarios. They should be used as references when developing your own scripts. For configuration objects, always use the `attributes` command to find out what other attributes are available.

Manage Servers

This section covers administrative servers and other types of servers such as JMS servers.

Manage Application Servers

Get a List of Application Servers   Example 5.1 shows a Jacl script to list all application servers configured in the cell. The application servers are displayed using their configuration object names.

Example 5.1   Listing application servers

```
set servers [$AdminConfig list Server]
puts "There are [llength $servers] application servers:"
foreach aServer $servers {
   puts $aServer
}
```

Start Application Servers   Example 5.2 shows a Jacl script to start all the application servers configured in the node myNode. This script works in a Network Deployment environment only.

Example 5.2   Starting application servers

```
set servers [$AdminConfig getid /Node:myNode/Server:/]
foreach aServer $servers {
   # identify server name
   set serverName [$AdminConfig showAttribute $aServer name]
   $AdminControl startServer $serverName myNode
}
```

Stop Application Servers   Example 5.3 shows a Jacl script to stop all running application servers for the node myNode.

Example 5.3   Stopping application servers

```
set runningServers [$AdminControl queryNames type=Server,node=myNode,*]
foreach aRunningServer $runningServers {
```

Example 5.3 Stopping application servers (Continued)

```
    set serverName [$AdminControl getAttribute $aRunningServer name]
    $AdminControl stopServer $serverName myNode
}
```

Create a New Application Server Definition Example 5.4 shows a Jacl script to create a new application server named newServer using the default application server template for server1. The new server is created on node myNode. A configuration save is performed to transfer configuration changes from workspace to the master repository.

Example 5.4 Creating an application server

```
set aParent [$AdminConfig getid /Node:myNode/]
set aTemplate [$AdminConfig listTemplates Server server1]
set nameAttr [list name newServer]
set attrs [list $nameAttr]
$AdminConfig createUsingTemplate Server $aParent $attrs $aTemplate
$AdminConfig save
```

Delete an Application Server Definition Example 5.5 shows a Jacl script to delete an application server named newServer. Because the delete action changes the existing configuration, a configuration save is performed at the end of the script.

Example 5.5 Deleting an application server

```
set aServer [$AdminConfig getid /Node:myNode/Server:newServer/]
$AdminConfig remove $aServer
$AdminConfig save
```

Modify the Configuraton of an Application Server This section provides task scripts to configure various properties of an application server including transaction service, Web container, EJB container, message listener service, ORB service, custom service, performance monitoring service, administration service, debugging service, and so on. For logging and tracing properties including IBM service logs, refer to section Logs and Traces for scripting examples.

Example 5.6 is a Jacl task script to configure the transaction properties of an application server. The timeout values specified in lines 3 and 4 are in number of seconds.

Example 5.6 Configuring properties of transaction service

```
 1  set aServer [$AdminConfig getid /Node:myNode/Server:newServer/]
 2  set aTransService [$AdminConfig list TransactionService $aServer]
 3  set totTrantimeoutAttr [list totalTranLifetimeTimeout 500]
 4  set inactTimeoutAttr [list clientInactivityTimeout 50]
 5  set logDirAttr [list transactionLogDirectory c:/newServer/logs/
    transaction.log]
 6  set attrs [list $totTrantimeoutAttr $inactTimeoutAttr $logDirAttr]
 7  $AdminConfig modify $aTransService $attrs
 8  $AdminConfig save
```

Examples 5.7, 5.8, and 5.9 are Jacl scripts to configure Web container of an application
server. Example 5.7 configures general and thread pool properties for a Web container. Lines
5–11 modify the general properties. Lines 13–19 set up the thread pool properties. Lines 25–
35 create a thread pool if the Web container does not have a configured thread pool; otherwise the existing thread pool properties are modified. Line 37 saves the configuration.

Example 5.7 Configuring thread pool properties for Web container

```
 1  set aServer [$AdminConfig getid /Node:myNode/Server:newServer/]
 2  # get the WebContainer config object name for the above server
 3  set aWC [$AdminConfig list WebContainer $aServer]
 4
 5  # setting up virtualHost and servletCaching attributes
 6  set virtualHostAttr [list defaultVirtualHostName admin_host]
 7  set servletCachingAttr [list enableServletCaching true]
 8  # modifying virtualHost and servletCaching attributes
 9  puts "Modifying general properties"
10  set attrs [list $virtualHostAttr $servletCachingAttr]
11  $AdminConfig modify $aWC $attrs
12
13  # setting up ThreadPool attributes
14  # inactivity time out is in number of milliseconds
15  set inactivityTimeoutAttr [list inactivityTimeout 1000]
16  set isGrowableAttr [list isGrowable true]
17  set maxSzAttr [list maximumSize 20]
18  set minSzAttr [list minimumSize 5]
19  set threadPoolAttrs [list $inactivityTimeoutAttr $isGrowableAttr
    $maxSzAttr $minSzAttr]
20
21  # get ThreadPool config object name for the WebContainer
```

Example 5.7   Configuring thread pool properties for Web container (Continued)

```
22  set threadPool [$AdminConfig showAttribute $aWC threadPool]
23
24  # check if there is existing thread pool
25  if {[llength $threadPool] != 0} {
26  # modifying ThreadPool attribute
27    puts "Modifying ThreadPool properties"
28    $AdminConfig modify $threadPool $threadPoolAttrs
29    puts [$AdminConfig showall $threadPool]
30  } else {
31    # create a thread pool
32    puts "Creating a new ThreadPool"
33    set threadPool [$AdminConfig create ThreadPool $aWC $threadPoolAttrs]
34    puts [$AdminConfig showall $threadPool]
35  }
36
37  $AdminConfig save
```

Example 5.8 is a Jacl task script to configure HTTP transports for communication requests
to the Web container. Lines 4–15 modify existing transports to use a different host and port.
Lines 17–27 create a new transport with Secure Sockets Layer enabled. Line 29 saves the
configuration.

Example 5.8   Configuring HTTP transport for Web container

```
 1  set aServer [$AdminConfig getid /Node:myNode/Server:newServer/]
 2  set aWC [$AdminConfig list WebContainer $aServer]
 3  set transports [lindex [$AdminConfig showAttribute $aWC transports] 0]
 4  foreach aTransport $transports {
 5    puts "Modify existing HTTP transports"
 6    # modify existing transports to change host name from oldHost to
      newHost
 7    set address [$AdminConfig showAttribute $aTransport address]
 8    if {[$AdminConfig showAttribute $address host] == "oldHost"} {
 9      $AdminConfig modify $address {{host newHost}}
10    }
11    # modify existing transports to change port from 9082 to 9083
12    if {[$AdminConfig showAttribute $address port] == 9082} {
13      $AdminConfig modify $address {{port 9083}}
14  }
15  }
```

Example 5.8   Configuring HTTP transport for Web container (Continued)

```
16
17  # create a HTTP transport
18  puts "Create a new HTTP transport"
19  set hostAttr [list host ibm.com]
20  set portAttr [list port 5555]
21  set addressAttr [list address [list $hostAttr $portAttr]]
22  set externalAttr [list external true]
23  set sslEnableAttr [list sslEnabled true]
24  # assuming a SSL with the name myCell/DefaultSSLSettings are
    configured in the cell
25  set sslConfigAttr [list sslConfig myCell/DefaultSSLSettings]
26  set httpAttrs [list $addressAttr $externalAttr $sslEnableAttr
    $sslConfigAttr]
27  $AdminConfig create HTTPTransport $aWC $httpAttrs
28
29  $AdminConfig save
```

Example 5.9 shows a Jacl task script to configure session management of a Web container.
Lines 3–8 enable session serialization access to allow a servlet to gain access to the session
and continue execution even if the session is still locked by another servlet. Lines 10–18
configure tracking a session with cookies as the session tracking mechanism to pass the session ID between the browser and the servlet, and to use the database to save a session in a
distributed environment. Lines 20–27 set up cookie properties. Lines 33–36 modify existing
cookie properties. Lines 38–41 create a cookie configuration. Lines 44–61 configure session database persistence. Line 46 requires the JNDI name of an existing data source. If
you have not defined a data source to point to an existing database, you have to define one
first. Lines 63–89 configure tuning parameters. Line 91 saves the configuration.

Example 5.9   Configuring session manager for Web container

```
1   set aServer [$AdminConfig getid /Node:myNode/Server:newServer/]
2   set aSessionMgr [$AdminConfig list SessionManager $aServer]
3   puts "Configure session serialization access"
4   set serialAccessAttr [list allowSerializedSessionAccess true]
5   set waitTimeAttr [list maxWaitTime 125000]
6   set timeoutAttr [list accessSessionOnTimeout true]
7   set attrs [list $serialAccessAttr $waitTimeAttr $timeoutAttr]
8   $AdminConfig modify $aSessionMgr $attrs
9
10  puts "Configure to track session with cookies"
```

Example 5.9   Configuring session manager for Web container (Continued)

```
11  set cookieAttr [list enableCookies true]
12  set protocolAttr [list enableProtocolSwitchRewriting false]
13  set urlAttr [list enableUrlRewriting false]
14  set sslAttr [list enableSSLTracking false]
15  # valid session persistence mode values are NONE, DATABASE, and
    DATA_REPLICATION]
16  set sessionPersistenceAttr [list sessionPersistenceMode DATABASE]
17  set attrs [list $cookieAttr $urlAttr $sslAttr $protocolAttr]
18  $AdminConfig modify $aSessionMgr $attrs
19
20  # setting up Cookie attributes
21  set domainAttr [list domain myDomain]
22  # set cookie maximum age to use current browser session
23  set maxAgeAttr [list maximumAge -1]
24  set nameAttr [list name myCookie]
25  set pathAttr [list path "/"]
26  set secureAttr [list secure true]
27  set cookieAttrs [list $domainAttr $maxAgeAttr $nameAttr $pathAttr
    $secureAttr]
28
29  # get the cookie config object name for the above SessionManager
30  set cookie [$AdminConfig showAttribute $aSessionMgr
    defaultCookieSettings]
31  # check if there is existing cookie properties
32  if {[llength $cookie] != 0} {
33    # modifying existing cookie
34    puts "Modify existing cookie"
35    $AdminConfig modify $cookie $cookieAttrs
36    puts [$AdminConfig showall $cookie]
37  } else {
38    # create a cookie
39    puts "Create a cookie"
40    set cookie [$AdminConfig create Cookie $aSessionMgr $cookieAttrs]
41    puts [$AdminConfig showall $cookie]
42  }
43
44  # setting up database session persistence
45  puts "Configure for database session persistence"
46  set dsJndiAttr [list datasourceJNDIName jdbc/mySession]
47  set userAttr [list userId myUser]
```

Example 5.9   Configuring session manager for Web container (Continued)

```
48  set pwdAttr [list password myPassword]
49  set sessionDbPersAttrs [list $dsJndiAttr $userAttr $pwdAttr]
50
51  # get session database persistence config object name
52  set aSessionDbPers [$AdminConfig showAttribute $aSessionMgr
    sessionDatabasePersistence]
53  if {[llength $aSessionDbPers] != 0} {
54    puts "Modify existing session database persistence"
55    $AdminConfig modify $aSessionDbPers $sessionDbPersAttrs
56    puts [$AdminConfig showall $aSessionDbPers]
57  } else {
58    puts "Create a session database persistence object"
59    set aSessionDbPers [$AdminConfig create
      SessionDatabasePersistence $aSessionMgr $sessionDbPersAttrs]
60    puts [$AdminConfig showall $aSessionDbPers]
61  }
62
63  # setting up attributes for TuningParams
64  set aofAttr [list allowOverflow true]
65  set isAttr [list invalidationSchedule [list [list firstHour 2]
    [list secondHour 5]]]
66  set itAttr [list invalidationTimeout 10]
67  set mimscAttr [list maxInMemorySessionCount 5]
68  set siAttr [list scheduleInvalidation true]
69  set umrsAttr [list usingMultiRowSchema true]
70  set wcAttr [list writeContents ONLY_UPDATED_ATTRIBUTES]
71  set wfAttr [list writeFrequency END_OF_SERVLET_SERVICE]
72  set wiAttr [list writeInterval 5]
73  set tuningParamAttrs [list $aofAttr $isAttr $itAttr $mimscAttr
    $siAttr $umrsAttr $wcAttr $wfAttr $wiAttr]
74
75  # get tuning params config object name
76  set tp [$AdminConfig showAttribute $aSessionMgr tuningParams]
77
78  # check if there is existing tuning params
79  if {[llength $tp] != 0} {
80    # modifying TuningParams attributes
81    puts "Modify existing tuning params"
82    $AdminConfig modify $tp $tuningParamAttrs
83    puts [$AdminConfig showall $tp]
```

Example 5.9   Configuring session manager for Web container (Continued)

```
84  } else {
85    # create a turning params object
86    puts "Create a tuning params object"
87    set tp [$AdminConfig create TuningParams $aSessionMgr
         $tuningParamAttrs]
88    puts [$AdminConfig showall $tp]
89  }
90
91  $AdminConfig save
```

Example 5.10 shows a Jacl script to configure an EJB container. Lines 4–13 set up EJB container properties. Lines 17–20 modify existing EJB container properties. Lines 22–25 create a new EJB container object if there is no EJB container configured for the application server. Line 28 saves the configuration.

Example 5.10   Configuring EJB container

```
1   set aServer [$AdminConfig getid /Node:myNode/Server:newServer/]
2   set aEJB [$AdminConfig list EJBContainer $aServer]
3
4   # setting up EJBContainer properties
5   # cleanup interval is specified in milliseconds
6   set ejbCacheAttr [list cacheSettings [list [list cacheSize 4000]
     [list cleanupInterval 5000]]]
7   # specify the JNDI name for an existing data source
8   set dsJNDIAttr [list defaultDatasourceJNDIName ds/myds]
9   set ipciAttr [list inactivePoolCleanupInterval 20000]
10  set nameAttr [list name MyEJB]
11  set pdAttr [list passivationDirectory /temp/mydir]
12  set initStateAttr [list stateManagement [list [list initialState
     STOP]]]
13  set EJBContainerAttrs [list $ejbCacheAttr $dsJNDIAttr $ipciAttr
     $nameAttr $pdAttr $initStateAttr]
14
15  # check if there is existing EJB container
16  if {[llength $aEJB] != 0} {
17    # modifying existing EJB container
18    puts "Modifying existing EJB container"
19    $AdminConfig modify $aEJB $EJBContainerAttrs
20    puts [$AdminConfig showall $aEJB]
21  } else {
```

Example 5.10   Configuring EJB container (Continued)

```
22    # create an EJB container object
23    puts "Create a EJB container"
24    set aEJB [$AdminConfig create EJBContainer $aServer
      $EJBContainerAttrs]
25    puts [$AdminConfig showall $aEJB]
26    }
27
28  $AdminConfig save
```

Example 5.11 shows a Jacl script to configure dynamic cache service of an application server. Lines 4–11 set up dynamic cache properties. Lines 15–18 modify existing dynamic cache properties. Lines 20–23 create a dynamic cache service if there is no dynamic cache service configured for the application server. Lines 26–31 set up external cache group properties. Lines 32–47 configure a new external cache group named myECG if one does not exist.

Example 5.11   Configuring dynamic cache

```
 1    set aServer [$AdminConfig getid /Node:myNode/Server:newServer/]
 2    set aDynamicCache [$AdminConfig list DynamicCache $aServer]
 3
 4    # setting up DynamicCache attributes
 5    set cSizeAttr [list cacheSize 2000]
 6    set dpAttr [list defaultPriority 2]
 7    set dolAttr [list diskOffloadLocation /myLoc]
 8    set enableAttr [list enable true]
 9    set enableDOLAttr [list enableDiskOffload true]
10    set repTypeAttr [list replicationType NONE]
11    set dynamicCacheAttrs [list $cSizeAttr $dpAttr $dolAttr $enableAttr
      $enableDOLAttr $repTypeAttr]
12
13    # check if there is existing dynamic cache
14    if {[llength $aDynamicCache] != 0}} {
15      # modify dynamic cache properties
16      puts "Modify existing dynamic cache properties"
17      $AdminConfig modify $aDynamicCache $dynamicCacheAttrs
18      puts [$AdminConfig showall $aDynamicCache]
19    } else {
20      # create a dynamic cache object
21      puts "Create a new dynamic cache object"
```

Example 5.11   Configuring dynamic cache (Continued)

```
22    set aDynamicCache [$AdminConfig create DynamicCache $aServer
      $dynamicCacheAttrs]
23    puts [$AdminConfig showall $aDynamicCache]
24  }
25
26  # setting up external cache group
27  set memberAttr [list members [list [list [list adapterBeanName
    myAdapterBeanName] [list address myAddress]]]]
28  set nameAttr [list name myECG]
29  set typeAttr [list type SHARED]
30  set externalCacheGroupAttrs [list $memberAttr $nameAttr $typeAttr]
31
32  set extCacheGps [lindex [$AdminConfig showAttribute
    $aDynamicCache cacheGroups] 0]
33  # check if there is existing external cache group named myECG
34  set found false
35  foreach aExtCacheGp $extCacheGps {
36    if {[$AdminConfig showAttribute $aExtCacheGp name] == "myECG"} {
37      set found true
38      break
39    }
40  }
41
42  if {$found == "false"} {
43    # create an external cache group
44    puts "Create a new external cache group"
45    set newExtCacheGp [$AdminConfig create ExternalCacheGroup
      $aDynamicCache $externalCacheGroupAttrs
46    puts [$AdminConfig showall $newExtCacheGp]
47  }
48
49  $AdminConfig show
```

Example 5.12 shows a Jacl task script to configure message listener ports of an application server. Lines 5–14 create a new listenerPort if a port is not configured. Lines 16–21 change the existing properties of listener ports. Lines 23–45 configure thread pool properties. Lines 47–53 configure a new property. Line 55 saves the configuration.

Example 5.12   Configuring message listener service

```
 1   set aServer [$AdminConfig getid /Node:myNode/Server:newServer/]
 2   set aMLService [$AdminConfig list MessageListenerService $aServer]
 3   set alPorts [$AdminConfig showAttribute $aMLService listenerPorts]
 4   if {[llength $alPorts] == 0} {
 5     puts "Create a new listener port"
 6     set nameAttr [list name myListenerPort]
 7     set cfJNDIAttr [list connectionFactoryJNDIName jms/
       connectionFactory]
 8     set destJNDIAttr [list destinationJNDIName jms/destination]
 9     set retriesAttr [list maxRetries 2]
10     set sessionAttr [list maxSessions 2]
11     set stateAttr [list stateManagement [list [list initialState
       START]]]
12     set attrs [list $nameAttr $cfJNDIAttr $destJNDIAttr $retriesAttr
       $sessionAttr $stateAttr]
13     set newListenerPort [$AdminConfig create ListenerPort
       $aMLService $attrs]
14     puts [$AdminConfig showall $newListenerPort]
15   } else {
16     puts "Modify existing listener ports to configure number of
       times to deliver the messages"
17     foreach alPort $alPorts {
18       $AdminConfig modify $alPort {{maxRetries 2}}
19       puts [$AdminConfig showall $alPort]
20     }
21   }
22
23   # setting up ThreadPool attributes
24   # inactivity time out is in number of milliseconds
25   set inactivityTimeoutAttr [list inactivityTimeout 1000]
26   set isGrowableAttr [list isGrowable true]
27   set maxSzAttr [list maximumSize 20]
28   set minSzAttr [list minimumSize 5]
29   set threadPoolAttrs [list $inactivityTimeoutAttr $isGrowableAttr
     $maxSzAttr $minSzAttr]
30
31   # get ThreadPool config object name
32   set threadPool [$AdminConfig showAttribute $aMLService threadPool]
33
34   # check if there is existing thread pool
35   if {[llength $threadPool] != 0} {
```

Example 5.12   Configuring message listener service (Continued)

```
36    # modifying ThreadPool attribute
37    puts "Modify ThreadPool attributes"
38    $AdminConfig modify $threadPool $threadPoolAttrs
39  puts [$AdminConfig showall $threadPool]
40  } else {
41    # create a thread pool
42    puts "Create a new ThreadPool"
43    set threadPool [$AdminConfig create ThreadPool $aMLService
      $threadPoolAttrs]
44    puts [$AdminConfig showall $threadPool]
45  }
46
47  # create a new property
48  puts "Create a new property"
49  set nameAttr [list name property1]
50  set valueAttr [list value property1Value]
51  set attrs [list $nameAttr $valueAttr]
52  set prop [$AdminConfig create Property $aMLService $attrs
53  puts [$AdminConfig showall $prop]
54
55  $AdminConfig save
```

Example 5.13 shows a Jacl task script to configure the Java Object Request Broker (ORB) service. Lines 3–6 change the ORB configuration to enable pass by reference and use 252 as the maximum number of connections allowed to stay in the connection cache. Lines 7–18 configure the thread pool setting, which is a nested attribute. Lines 9–14 configure a new thread pool if there is no existing thread pool configuration. The new thread pool setting includes setting the maximum and minimum number of threads allowed, and the thread inactivity timeout in number of milliseconds. A configuration save is performed in line 19.

Example 5.13   Configuring Object Request Broker service

```
 1  set aServer [$AdminConfig getid /Node:myNode/Server:newServer/]
 2  set aORB [$AdminConfig list ObjectRequestBroker $aServer]
 3  set connectionCacheMaxAttr [list connectionCacheMaximum 252]
 4  set localCopiesAttr [list noLocalCopies true]
 5  set attrs [list $connectionCacheMaxAttr $localCopiesAttr]
 6  $AdminConfig modify $aORB $attrs
 7  set aThreadPool [$AdminConfig showAttribute $aORB threadPool]
 8  if {[llength $aThreadPool] == 0} {
 9    puts "Create a new thread pool as one does not exist"
```

Example 5.13   Configuring Object Request Broker service (Continued)

```
10    set maxSizeAttr [list maximumSize 45]
11    set minSizeAttr [list minimumSize 5]
12    set inactTimeoutAttr [list inactivityTimeout 2500]
13    set attrs [list $maxSizeAttr $minSizeAttr $inactTimeoutAttr]
14    $AdminConfig create ThreadPool $aORB $attrs
15  } else {
16    puts "Modify isGrowable attribute in existing thread pool"
17    $AdminConfig modify $aThreadPool {{isGrowable true}}
18  }
19  $AdminConfig save
```

Example 5.14 shows a Jacl script to configure custom properties of an application server.
Lines 6–11 list all existing properties. Lines 14–20 check if there is an existing property
named property1. Lines 23–30 create a new property named property1 if such a property is
not found. Line 32 saves the configuration.

Example 5.14   Configuring custom properties

```
1   set aServer [$AdminConfig getid /Node:myNode/Server:newServer/]
2   set aAppServer [$AdminConfig list ApplicationServer $aServer]
3   set props [lindex [$AdminConfig showAttribute
    $aAppServer properties] 0]

4
5   # list all properties
6   if {[llength $props] != 0} {
7     puts "Existing properties:"
8     foreach aProp $props {
9       puts [$AdminConfig showall $aProp]
10    }
11  }
12
13  # look for property named property1
14  set found false
15  foreach aProp $props {
16    if {[$AdminConfig showAttribute $aProp name] == "property1"} {
17      set found $aProp
18      break
19    }
20  }
21
```

Example 5.14 Configuring custom properties (Continued)

```
22  # if property1 is not found, create one
23  if {$found == "false"} {
24    puts "Create a new property"
25    set nameAttr [list name property1]
26    set valueAttr [list value property1Value]
27    set attrs [list $nameAttr $valueAttr]
28    set prop [$AdminConfig create Property $aAppServer $attrs]
29    puts [$AdminConfig showall $prop]
30  }
31
32  $AdminConfig save
```

Example 5.15 shows a Jacl script to configure administration service. Lines 10–16 display all the connectors for the associated application server. Line 17 sets up an RMI connector as the preferred connector. Line 20 modifies the general properties. Line 25 disables the auditing of repository updates in the log file. Line 27 saves the configuration.

Example 5.15 Configuring administration service

```
 1  set aServer [$AdminConfig getid /Node:myNode/Server:newServer/]
 2  set aAdminService [$AdminConfig list AdminService $aServer]
 3
 4  # configure general properties
 5  # set standalone to false if the application server participates
    in the network deployment system
 6  set standaloneAttr [list standalone true]
 7  # change preferred connector to RMI
 8  set connectors [lindex [$AdminConfig showAttribute $aAdminService
    connectors]]
 9  set rmiConnector false
10  puts "List all connectors:"
11  foreach aConnector $connectors {
12    puts [$AdminConfig showall $aConnector]
13    if {[regexp RMIConnector $aConnector] == 1} {
14      set rmiConnector $aConnector
15    }
16  }
17  set perfConnAttr [list preferredConnector $rmiConnector]
18  set attrs [list $standaloneAttr $perfConnAttr]
19  puts "Modify general properties"
```

Example 5.15 Configuring administration service (Continued)

```
20   $AdminConfig modify $aAdminService $attrs
21   puts [$AdminConfig show $aAdminService]
22
23   puts "Modify repository service"
24   set configRepo [$AdminConfig showAttribute $aAdminService
     configRepository]
25   $AdminConfig modify $configRepo [list [list auditEnabled false]]
26
27   $AdminConfig save
```

Example 5.16 shows a Jacl script to configure trace service. Lines 5–8 modify trace specification to enable trace. Lines 11–17 configure memory buffer as the trace output type. Line 19 saves the configuration.

Example 5.16 Configuring trace service

```
 I   set aServer [$AdminConfig getid /Node:myNode/Server:newServer/]
 2   set aTraceService [$AdminConfig list TraceService $aServer]
 3
 4   # Modify trace specification to enable trace
 5   puts "Modify trace specification"
 6   set traceSpecAttr [list startupTraceSpecification
     com.ibm.websphere.management.*=all=enabled]
 7   $AdminConfig modify $aTraceService [list $traceSpecAttr]
 8   puts [$AdminConfig show $aTraceService]
 9
10   # modify to use memory buffer as the trace output. Valid values are
     SPECIFIED_FILE or MEMORY_BUFFER
11   puts "Modify trace output type and size"
12   set typeAttr [list traceOutputType MEMORY_BUFFER]
13   # memory buffer size is specified in number of thousand entries
14   set sizeAttr [list memoryBufferSize 10]
15   set attrs [list $typeAttr $sizeAttr]
16   $AdminConfig modify $aTraceService $attrs
17   puts [$AdminConfig show $aTraceService]
18
19   $AdminConfig save
```

Example 5.17 shows a Jacl script to configure debugging for the JVM of an application server. Line 3 configures startup of this debug service when the server starts. Line 4 configures the debug argument. Line 7 saves the configuration.

Example 5.17   Configuring debugging service

```
1  set aServer [$AdminConfig getid /Node:myNode/Server:newServer/]
2  set aJVM [$AdminConfig list JavaVirtualMachine $aServer]
3  set debugAttr [list debugMode true]
4  set debugArgAttr [list debugArgs "-Djava.compiler=NONE -Xdebug
   -Xnoagent -Xrunjdwp:transport=dt_socket,server=y,suspend=n,
   address=7777"]
5  set attrs [list $debugAttr $debugArgAttr]
6  $AdminConfig modify $aJVM $attrs
7  $AdminConfig save
```

Example 5.18 shows a Jacl script to configure a custom service. Lines 3–11 set up properties for a new custom service. Line 14 creates a new custom service for newServer. Lines 18–23 create a custom property for the newly created custom service. Line 25 saves the configuration.

Example 5.18   Configuring custom service

```
1   set aServer [$AdminConfig getid /Node:myNode/Server:newServer/]
2
3   # setting up properties for a new custom service
4   puts "Set up properties for a new custom service"
5   set nameAttr [list displayName myCustomService]
6   set classnameAttr [list classname com.my.custom.myCustomService]
7   set classpathAttr [list classpath /mylib/myCustomService.jar]
8   set descAttr [list description "my custom service"]
9   # enable start up of this service when the application server starts
10  set enableAttr [list enable true]
11  set attrs [list $nameAttr $classnameAttr $classpathAttr $descAttr
    $enableAttr]
12
13  puts "Create a new custom service"
14  set newCustomService [$AdminConfig create CustomService $aServer
    $attrs]
15  puts [$AdminConfig show $newCustomService]
16
17  # create a new custom property
18  puts "Create a new custom property for the created custom service"
```

Example 5.18   Configuring custom service (Continued)

```
19  set nameAttr [list name customServiceProperty1]
20  set valueAttr [list value customServiceValue1]
21  set propertyAttrs [list $nameAttr $valueAttr]
22  set property [$AdminConfig create Property $newCustomService
    $propertyAttrs]
23  puts [$AdminConfig show $property]
24
25  $AdminConfig save
```

Example 5.19 shows a Jacl script to configure process definition. Lines 3–26 set up properties to be modified. Lines 28–50 perform several modifications. Line 52 saves the configuration. For logs and tracing, refer to section Logs and Traces, for scripting examples.

Example 5.19   Configuring process definition

```
1   set aServer [$AdminConfig getid /Node:myNode/Server:newServer/]
2   set aProcessDef [$AdminConfig showAttribute $aServer
    processDefinition]
3   puts "Set up various properties"
4   # setting up working directory property
5   set workingDirAttr [list workingDirecotry \${WAS_HOME}]
6
7   # setting up JVM heap size properties in number of megabytes
8   set initHeapAttr [list initialHeapSize 80]
9   set maxHeapAttr [list maximumHeapSize 512]
10  set jvmAttrs [list $initHeapAttr $maxHeapAttr]
11
12  # setting up process execution priority
13  set priorityAttr [list processPriority 10]
14  set processExeAttrs [list $priorityAttr]
15
16  # setting up a new environment entry
17  set nameAttr [list name envEntry1]
18  set valueAttr [list value value1]
19  set descAttr [list description "A dummy environment entry"]
20  set envAttrs [list $nameAttr $valueAttr $descAttr]
21
22  # setting up monitoring policy
23  set maxStartupAttr [list maximumStartupAttempts 4]
24  # ping interval is specified in number of seconds
25  set pingIntervalAttr [list pingInterval 50]
```

Example 5.19 Configuring process definition (Continued)

```
26  set monitorPolicyAttrs [list $maxStartupAttr $pingIntervalAttr]
27
28  # Modify process definition with the above setup
29  puts "Modify general properties of process definition"
30  $AdminConfig modify $aProcessDef [list $workingDirAttr]
31
32  puts "Modify JVM properties"
33  set jvms [lindex [$AdminConfig showAttribute $aProcessDef
    jvmEntries] 0]
34  foreach $aJVM $jvms {
35    $AdminConfig modify $aJVM $jvmAttrs
36    puts [$AdminConfig show $aJVM]
37  }
38
39  puts "Modify process execution properties"
40  set execution [$AdminConfig showAttribute $aProcessDef execution]
41  $AdminConfig modify $execution $processExeAttrs
42  puts [$AdminConfig show $execution]
43
44  puts "Add an environment entry"
45  puts [$AdminConfig create Property $aProcessDef $envAttrs]
46
47  puts "Modify monitoring policy"
48  set monitorPolicy [$AdminConfig showAttribute $aProcessDef
    monitoringPolicy]
49  $AdminConfig modify $monitorPolicy $monitorPolicyAttrs
50  puts [$AdminConfig show $monitorPolicy]
51
52  $AdminConfig save
```

Example 5.20 shows a Jacl task script to configure performance monitoring (PMI) service for an application server. Line 3 enables the server to start the PMI service when the server starts. Line 4 specifies the specification levels for all components in the server. Levels N, L, M, H, and X represent None, Low, Medium, High, and Maximum, respectively. Configuration changes are saved in line 7.

Example 5.20 Configuring performance monitoring service

```
1  set aServer [$AdminConfig getid /Node:myNode/Server:newServer/]
2  set aPMIService [$AdminConfig list PMIService $aServer]
```

Example 5.20   Configuring performance monitoring service (Continued)

```
3   set enableAttr [list enable true]
4   set specAttr [list initialSpecLevel
    beanModule=H:cacheModule=H:connectionPoolModule=H:j2cModule=H:
    jvmRuntimeModule=H:orbPerfModule=H:servletSessionsModule=H:
    systemModule=H:threadPoolModule=H:transactionModule=H:
    webAppModule=H:webServicesModule=H:wlmModule=H:wsgwModule=H]
5   set attrs [list $enableAttr $specAttr]
6   $AdminConfig modify $aPMIService $attrs
7   $AdminConfig save
```

Example 5.21 shows a Jacl task script to modify various end points used by an application server.

Example 5.21   Configuring end points

```
 1   set aServerEntry [$AdminConfig getid /ServerEntry:newServer/]
 2   set endpoints [lindex [$AdminConfig showAttribute $aServerEntry
     specialEndpoints] 0]
 3
 4   # list all configured end points
 5   puts "List of configured end points:"
 6   foreach aEndpoint $endpoints {
 7      puts [$AdminConfig showall $aEndpoint]
 8   }
 9
10   # modify existing end points
11   puts "Modify existing end points"
12   foreach aEndpoint $endpoints {
13      if {[$AdminConfig showAttribute $aEndpoint endPointName] ==
         "BOOTSTRAP_ADDRESS"} {
14         puts "Modify BOOTSTRAP_ADDRESS"
15         $AdminConfig modify $aEndpoint [list [list port 2810] [list
            host newHost]]
16      } else if {[$AdminConfig showAttribute $aEndpoint endPointName]
         == "SOAP_CONNECTOR_ADDRESS"} {
17         puts "Modify SOAP_CONNECTOR_ADDRESS"
18         $AdminConfig modify $aEndpoint [list [list port 8881] [list
            host newHost]]
19      } else if {[$AdminConfig showAttribute $aEndpoint endPointName]
         == "DRS_CLIENT_ADDRESS"} {
20         puts "Modify DRS_CLIENT_ADDRESS"
```

Example 5.21 Configuring end points (Continued)

```
21        $AdminConfig modify $aEndpoint [list [list port 7874] [list
          host newHost]]
22      } else if {[$AdminConfig showAttribute $aEndpoint endPointName]
        == "SAS_SSL_SERVERAUTH_LISTENER_ADDRESS"} {
23        puts "Modify SAS_SSL_SERVERAUTH_LISTENER_ADDRESS"
24        $AdminConfig modify $aEndpoint [list [list port 1005] [list
          host newHost]]
25      } else if {[$AdminConfig showAttribute $aEndpoint endPointName]
        == "CSIV2_SSL_SERVERAUTH_LISTENER_ADDRESS"} {
26        puts "Modify CSIV2_SSL_SERVERAUTH_LISTENER_ADDRESS"
27        $AdminConfig modify $aEndpoint [list [list port 1007] [list
          host newHost]]
28      } else if {[$AdminConfig showAttribute $aEndpoint endPointName]
        == "CSIV2_SSL_MUTUALAUTH_LISTENER_ADDRESS"} {
29        puts "Modify CSIV2_SSL_MUTUALAUTH_LISTENER_ADDRESS"
30        $AdminConfig modify $aEndpoint [list [list port 1009] [list
          host newHost]]
31      }
32    }
33
34  $AdminConfig save
```

Example 5.22 shows a Jacl task script to configure classloader. Lines 4–10 configure an application class application loader policy to use a single classloader for all applications and loading mode to search in the parent classloader first to load a class. Lines 15–24 create a classloader and library reference for a shared library to be used. It is assumed that a library with the name mySharedLibrary exists in the configuration. For a scripting example of how to create a shared library, refer to section Shared Libraries.

Example 5.22 Configuring classloader

```
1   set aServer [$AdminConfig getid /Node:myNode/Server:newServer/]
2   set aAppServer [$AdminConfig list ApplicationServer $aServer]
3   # configure general properties
4   # valid values for applicationClassLoaderPolicy property are
    MULTIPLE and SINGLE
5   set policyAttr [list applicationClassLoaderPolicy SINGLE]
6   # valid values for applicationClassLoadingMode property are
    PARENT_FIRST and PARENT_LAST
7   set modeAttr [list applicationClassLoadingMode PARENT_FIRST]
8   set attrs [list $policyAttr $modeAttr]
```

Example 5.22   Configuring classloader (Continued)

```
 9   puts "Modify classloader policy and mode property"
10   $AdminConfig modify $aAppServer $attrs
11
12   # check if there is existing class loader
13   set classloaders [lindex [$AdminConfig showAttribute $aAppServer
     classloaders] 0]
14   if {[llength $classloaders] == 0} {
15       puts "Create a new class loader"
16       set aClassloader [$AdminConfig create Classloader $aAppServer
         [list [list mode PARENT_FIRST]]]
17       puts [$AdminConfig showall $aClassloader]
18
19       puts "Associate an existing shared library with this
         application server"
20       set nameAttr [list libraryName mySharedLibrary]
21       set sharedAttr [list sharedClassloader true]
22       set libraryRefAttr [list $nameAttr $sharedAttr]
23       $AdminConfig create LibraryRef $aClassloader $libraryRefAttr
24       puts [$AdminConfig showall $aClassloader]
25   }
26
27   $AdminConfig save
```

View and Modify the Application Server Run Time   This section contains example scripts to identify various Mbeans; view product information, process ID, transaction service; and start a listener port.

Example 5.23 shows a Jacl task script to query for various MBeans belonging to application server myServer.

Example 5.23   Querying MBeans

```
1   puts "All the MBeans belonging to myServer:"
2   $AdminControl queryNames process=myServer,cell=myCell,
    node=myNode,*
3
4   puts "\nmyServer Server MBean:"
5   $AdminControl queryNames type=Server,process=myServer,
    cell=myCell,node=myNode,*
6
7   puts "\nmyServer TransactionService MBean:"
```

Example 5.23 Querying MBeans (Continued)

```
 8  $AdminControl queryNames
    type=TransactionService,process=myServer,cell=myCell,node=myNode,*

 9

10  puts "\nmyServer TraceService MBean:"
11  $AdminControl queryNames
    type=TraceService,process=myServer,cell=myCell,node=myNode,*

12

13  puts "\nmyServer ApplicationManager MBean:"
14  $AdminControl queryNames
    type=ApplicationManager,process=myServer,cell=myCell,node=myNode,*

15

16  puts "\nmyServer AppManagement MBean:"
17  AdminControl queryNames
    type=AppManagement,process=myServer,cell=myCell,node=myNode,*

18

19  puts "\nmyServer SessionManager MBeans (one per application):"
20  $AdminControl queryNames
    type=SessionManager,process=myServer,cell=myCell,node=myNode,*

21

22  puts "\nmyServer JVM MBean:"
23  $AdminControl queryNames
    type=JVM,process=myServer,cell=myCell,node=myNode,*
```

Example 5.24 shows a Jacl script to view run-time read-only information. Line 2 displays the product information. Line 3 displays the process ID, cell name, node name, and process type information for application server myServer.

Example 5.24 Viewing product and process information

```
 1  set aRunningServer [$AdminControl queryNames
    type=Server,name=myServer,cell=myCell,node=myNode,*]
 2  $AdminControl getAttribute $aRunningServer serverVersion
 3  $AdminControl getAttributes $aRunningServer {pid cellName
    nodeName processType}
```

Example 5.25 shows a Jacl script to view and modify run-time properties of transaction service on application server myServer. Line 2 displays the runtime properties. Lines 3–6 modify two run-time properties of transaction service. The property values are in number of seconds. It is important to note that modification to the run-time properties of transaction service has no effect on the persistent configuration properties that represent this MBean.

Example 5.25 Configuring run-time transaction service

```
 1  set aRuntimeTranService [$AdminControl queryNames
    type=TransactionService,name=myServer,cell=myCell,node=myNode,*]
 2  $AdminControl getAttributes $aRuntimeTranService {
    transactionLogDirectory totalTranLifetimeTimeout
    clientInactivityTimeout}
 3  set lifetimeTimeoutAttr [list totalTranLifetimeTimeout 180]
 4  set inactTimeoutAttr [list clientInactivityTimeout 30]
 5  set attrs [list $lifetimeTimeoutAttr $inactTimeoutAttr]
 6  $AdminControl setAttributes $aRuntimeTranService $attrs
```

Example 5.26 shows a Jacl script to start all listener ports for the running server myServer.

Example 5.26 Starting listener ports

```
 1  set runningListenerPorts [$AdminControl queryNames
    type=ListenerPort,process=myServer,cell=myCell,node=myNode,*]
 2  if {[llength $runningListenerPorts] != 0}
 3     foreach aListenerPort $runningListenerPorts {
 4        if {[$AdminControl getAttribute $aListenerPort started]
           == "false"} {
 5           $AdminControl invoke $aListenerPort start
 6        }
 7     }
 8  }
```

Manage JMS Servers (WebSphere Application Server Network Deployment)

Get a List of JMS Servers Example 5.27 shows a Jacl script to list all the JMS servers configured in the cell. The JMS servers are displayed using their configuration object names.

Example 5.27 Listing JMS servers

```
set jmsServers [$AdminConfig list /Server:jmsserver/]
puts "There are [llength $jmsServers] JMS servers:"
foreach aJmsServer $jmsServers {
  puts $aJmsServer
}
```

Start JMS Servers   Example 5.28 shows a Jacl script to start all the JMS servers configured in the cell. Lines 6 and 7 are to identify the node where the JMS server is configured by using the configuration object name. Line 6 provides the pattern matching string.

Example 5.28   Starting JMS servers

```
1   set jmsServers [$AdminConfig getid /Server:jmsserver/]
2   foreach aJmsServer $jmsServers {
3       # identify server name
4       set serverName [$AdminConfig showAttribute $aJmsServer name]
5       # identify node name
6       set exp {(["A-Z_a-z0-9\(/ ]+)/nodes/(["A-Z_a-z0-9 ]+)/servers/
        ([A-Z_a-z0 -9\)/#: ]+)}
7       regexp $exp $aJmsServer junk junk2 nodeName
8       $AdminControl startServer $serverName $nodeName
9   }
```

Stop JMS Servers   Example 5.29 shows a Jacl script to stop all running JMS servers in the cell.

Example 5.29   Stopping JMS servers

```
1   set jmsServers [$AdminControl queryNames type=Server,name=
    jmsserver,*]
2   foreach aJmsServer $jmsServers {
3       # identify node name
4       set nodeName [$Admintrol getAttribute $aJmsServer nodeName]
5       $AdminControl stopServer jmsserver $nodeName
6   }
```

Modify the Configuraton of a JMS Server   This section provides task scripts to configure general properties of a JMS server and its security port end points. For other JMS server properties such as custom properties, administrative services, and end points, follow similar scripts provided in the section Manage Application Servers. For logging and tracing properties including IBM service logs, refer to section Logs and Traces for scripting examples.

Example 5.30 shows a Jacl script to modify the general properties of a JMS server. Line 1 obtains the configuration object name of a JMS server for server myServer. Lines 5–8 set up the attributes to be modified. Line 9 modifies the attributes. Line 12 saves the configuration.

Example 5.30   Configuring general properties of a JMS server

```
 I   set aJmsServer [$AdminConfig getid /Node:myNode/Server:myServer/
     JMSServer:/]
 2   if {[llength $aJmsServer] != 0} {
 3       # modify general properties
 4       puts "Modify general properties of JMS server $aJmsServer'
 5       set descAttr [list description "JMSServer description"]
 6       set numThreadAttr [list numThreads 8]
 7       set qNamesAttr [list queueNames {JMSQueue1;JMSQueue2}]
 8       set attrs [list $descAttr $numThreadAttr $qNamesAttr]
 9       $AdminConfig modify $aJmsServer $attrs
10       puts [$AdminConfig show $aJmsServer]
11
12       $AdminConfig save
13   }
```

Example 5.31 shows a Jacl script to modify the security port end point properties of a JMS server. Line 1 obtains the configuration object name of a JMS server for server myServer. Line 4 gets the configuration object name for security port end point. Line 7 displays the current value of end point. Lines 9–11 set up the attributes to be modified. Line 12 modifies the attributes. Line 13 displays the new value of end point. Line 15 saves the configuration.

Example 5.31   Configuring security port end point of a JMS server

```
 I   set aJmsServer [$AdminConfig getid /Node:myNode/Server:myServer/
     JMSServer:/]
 2   if {[llength $aJmsServer] != 0} {
 3       # get configuration object name for securityPort
 4       set secPort [$AdminConfig showAttribute $aJmsServer
         securityPort]
 5       # modify the endpoint
 6       puts "Modify security port endpoint"
 7       puts "existing values: [$AdminConfig show $secPort]"
 8
 9       set hostAttr [list host myhost]
10       set portAttr [list port 5555]
11       set attrs [list $hostAttr $portAttr]
12       $AdminConfig modify $secPort $attrs
13       puts "new values: [$AdminConfig show $secPort]"
14
15       $AdminConfig save
16   }
```

View and Modify the JMS Server Run time   For a task to view run-time read-only information of a JMS server, refer to Example 5.24. You can modify this example to obtain the run-time object name of a JMS server.

Manage Clusters (WebSphere Application Server Network Deployment)

Clusters are sets of application servers that are managed together and participate in the workload management. The following tasks show how to get a list of existing clusters, start and stop a cluster, and create and delete a cluster.

Get a List of Clusters   Example 5.32 shows a Jacl script to list all configured clusters. The clusters are displayed in their configuration object name.

Example 5.32   Listing clusters

```
set clusters [$AdminConfig list ServerCluster]
puts "There are [llength $clusters] clusters:"
foreach aCluster $clusters {
   puts $aCluster
}
```

Start a Cluster   Example 5.33 shows a Jacl script to start nonrunning clusters. Line 1 obtains the cluster manager MBean. Line 2 requests the cluster manager MBean to retrieve all cluster configuration objects from the configuration. Line 3 gets hold of all the cluster MBeans. Lines 4–8 start each cluster that is not currently running. The start operation is asynchronous. If there are several nonrunning clusters in the cell, you might want to add codes to wait for a cluster to start successfully before starting another cluster.

Example 5.33   Starting clusters

```
1  set clusterMgr [$AdminControl queryNames cell=myCell,
   type=ClusterMgr,*]
2  $AdminControl invoke $clusterMgr retrieveClusters
3  set clusters [$AdminControl queryNames cell=myCell,
   type=Cluster,*]
4  foreach aCluster $clusters {
5     if {[$AdminControl getAttribute $aCluster state] ==
      "websphere.cluster.stopped"} {
6        $AdminControl invoke $aCluster start
7     }
8  }
```

Stop a Cluster   Example 5.34 shows a Jacl script to stop all running clusters.

Example 5.34   Stopping running clusters

```
1  set clusters [$AdminControl queryNames type=Cluster,cell=myCell,*]
2  foreach aCluster $clusters {
3    if {[$AdminControl getAttribute $aCluster state] ==
       "websphere.cluster.running"} {
4      $AdminControl invoke $aCluster stop
5    }
6  }
```

Ripple Start a Cluster   Example 5.35 shows a Jacl script to ripple start all running clusters. Like the start operation, the rippleStart is an asynchonrous operation.

Example 5.35   Ripple starting clusters

```
1  set clusters [$AdminControl queryNames type=Cluster,cell=myCell,*]
2  foreach aCluster $clusters {
3    if {[$AdminControl getAttribute $aCluster state] ==
       "websphere.cluster.running"} {
4      $AdminControl invoke $aCluster rippleStart
5    }
6  }
```

Immediate Stop a Cluster   Example 5.36 shows a Jacl script to immediate stop all running clusters.

Example 5.36   Immediate stopping clusters

```
1  set clusters [$AdminControl queryNames type=Cluster,cell=myCell,*]
2  foreach aCluster $clusters {
3    if {[$AdminControl getAttribute $aCluster state] ==
       "websphere.cluster.running"} {
4      $AdminControl invoke $aCluster stopImmediate
5    }
6  }
```

Create a New Cluster Definition   Example 5.37 shows a Jacl script to create a new cluster. Line 3 creates a new server. Line 4 converts the newly created server as the first member of the new cluster myCluster. Lines 6 and 7 create another cluster member using an existing template. Line 8 saves the configuration.

Example 5.37   Creating a new cluster

```
I  set aServerTemplate [$AdminConfig listTemplates Server]
2  set aNode [$AdminConfig getid /Node:myNode/]
3  set aNewServer [$AdminConfig createUsingTemplate Server $aNode
   {{name newClusterServer}} $aServerTemplate]
4  set aCluster [$AdminConfig convertToCluster $aNewServer
   myCluster]
5  set anotherNode [$AdminConfig getid /Node:anotherNode/]
6  set aClusterTemplate [$AdminConfig listTemplates ClusterMember]
7  $AdminConfig createClusterMember $aCluster $anotherNode
   {{memberName anotherClusterMember}} $aClusterTemplate
8  $AdminConfig save
```

Delete a Cluster Definition   Example 5.38 shows a Jacl script to remove a cluster. Lines 1–5 stop the cluster to be deleted if it is running. Line 6 gets the corresponding configuration object name for the running cluster MBean. Line 7 removes the cluster from the configuration. Line 8 saves the configuration.

Example 5.38   Deleting a cluster

```
I  set aRunningCluster [$AdminControl queryNames
   type=Cluster,cell=myCell,name=myCluster,*]
2  if {[$AdminControl getAttribute $aCluster state] ==
   "websphere.cluster.running"} {
4      $AdminControl invoke $aRunningCluster stop
5  }
6  set aConfigCluster [$AdminControl getConfigId $aRunningCluster]
7  $AdminConfig remove $aConfigCluster
8  $AdminConfig save
```

Manage Applications

Enterprise applications are applications that confirm to Java 2 Platform Enterprise Edition specification. The following tasks show how to manage an enterprise application including starting and stopping an application, installing and uninstalling an application, and postinstall configuration modification of an application.

Get a List of Installed Applications

To list all installed applications in the configuration, run the following command:

```
$AdminApp list
```

Start an Application

Example 5.39A shows a Jacl script to start an application on a deployed server target using an ApplicationManager MBean. If the application is installed in multiple server targets and you want the application to start in all server targets, repeat lines 3 and 4 for each server target on which the application is deployed. If the application is installed in a cluster, you have to start the application in each server of the cluster. Alternatively, if you have WebSphere Version 5.0.1 or later installed, you can invoke the startApplication operation in an App-Management MBean. The startApplication operation in an AppManagement MBean starts an application in all the deployed targets including single server and cluster. Example 5.39B shows a Jacl script to start an application using an AppManagement MBean. This example assumes the application to be started is saved in the configuration repository.

Example 5.39A   Starting an application on a single server

```
 I  set myRunningApp [$AdminControl queryNames
    type=Application,name=myApp,*]
 2  if {[llength $myRunningApp] == 0} {
 3     set appManager [$AdminControl queryNames cell=mycell,
          node=mynode,type=ApplicationManager,process=server1,*]
 4  }        $AdminControl invoke $appManager startApplication myApp
```

Example 5.39B   Starting an application on all deployed targets

```
 I  set myRunningApp [$AdminControl queryNames
    type=Application,name=myApp,*]
 2  if {[llength $myRunningApp] == 0} {
 3     set appManagement [$AdminControl queryNames
          cell=mycell,node=mynode,type=AppManagement,*]
 4     $AdminControl invoke $appManagement startApplication
       {myApp null null}
 5  }
```

Stop an Application

Example 5.40A shows a Jacl script to stop a running application on a single server target using an ApplicationManager MBean. If the application is running on multiple servers and you would like to stop the application on all servers, repeat lines 3 and 4 for each server on which the application is running. Alternatively, if you have WebSphere Version 5.0.1 or later installed, you can invoke the stopApplication operation in an AppManagement MBean. The stopApplication operation in an AppManagement MBean stops the application on all targets. Example 5.40B shows a Jacl script to stop an application using an AppManagement MBean.

Example 5.40A   Stopping an application on a single server

```
 I  set myRunningApp [$AdminControl queryNames
    type=Application,name=myApp,*]
 2  if {[llength $myRunningApp] != 0} {
 3      set appManager [$AdminControl queryNames
        cell=mycell,node=mynode,type=ApplicationManager,
        process=server1,*]
 4      $AdminControl invoke $appManager stopApplication myApp
 5  }
```

Example 5.40B   Stopping an application on all targets

```
 I  set myRunningApp [$AdminControl queryNames
    type=Application,name=myApp,*]
 2  if {[llength $myRunningApp] != 0} {
 3      set appManagement [$AdminControl queryNames
        cell=mycell,node=mynode,type=AppManagement,*]
 4      $AdminControl invoke $appManagement stopApplication {myApp
        null null}
 5  }
```

Install an Application

The following install examples show various Jacl scripts using different installation options to install an application. Example 5.41 shows the simplest form of application install using the appname option only. Example 5.42 shows the use of default binding options to populate bindings with specified default values. Example 5.43 uses server and node options to install all modules in the application to the same server. Example 5.44 uses cluster option to install all modules in the application to the same cluster. Cluster support is available in the WebSphere Application Server Network Deployment environment. Example 5.45 shows the use of MapModulesToServer task option to install a given module to two servers, whereas the other modules are installed to just one server. Examples 5.46 and 5.47 show the use of deployejb options. Example 5.48 demonstrates the use of various installation task and non-task options.

Example 5.41   Installing an application with appName option

```
 I  $AdminApp install /installableApps/myApp.ear {-appName myApp}
 2  $AdminConfig save
```

Example 5.42   Installing an application with default binding options

```
 I   set bindOpt [list -usedefaultbindings
                       -defaultbinding.datasource.jndi ds1
                       -defaultbinding.datasource.username user1
                       -defaultbinding.datasource.password pw1
                       -defaultbinding.cf.jndi ds1
                       -defaultbinding.ejbjndi.prefix ds2
                       -defaultbinding.virtual.host myvh]
 2   append opts " " $bindOpt
 3   lappend opts -name myApp2
 4   $AdminApp install /installableApps/myApp.ear $opts
 5   $AdminConfig save
```

Example 5.43   Installing an application with node and server options

```
 I   $AdminApp install /installableApps/myApp.ear {-appname myApp3
     -node myNode -server myServer}
 2   $AdminConfig save
```

Example 5.44   Installing an application with cluster option

```
 I   $AdminApp install /installableApps/myApp.ear {-appname myApp4
     -cluster myCluster}
 2   $AdminConfig save
```

Example 5.45   Installing an application with MapModulesToServers option

```
 I   set aServer WebSphere:cell=myCell,node=myNode,server=myServer
 2   set aServer2 WebSphere:cell=myCell,node=myNode,server=myServer2
 3   set mapping [list "Increment Enterprise Java Bean" Increment.jar,
     META-INF/ejb-jar.xml $aServer+$aServer2]
 4   set mapServerOpt [list -MapModulesToServers [list $mapping]]
 5   unset opts
 6   append opts " " $mapServerOpt
 7   lappend opts -appname myApp5
 8   lappend opts -server myServer
 9   lappend opts -node myNode
10   $AdminApp install /installableApps/myApp.ear $opts
11   $AdminConfig save
```

Example 5.46 Installing an application with nodeployejb option

```
 I  $AdminApp install /intallableApps/myApp.ear {-appname myApp6
    —nodeployejb}
 2  $AdminConfig save
```

Example 5.47 Installing an application with deploy ejb options

```
 I  $AdminApp install /installableApps/myApp.ear {-appname myApp7
    —deployejb —deployedb.dbtype DB2UDB_V72}
 2  $AdminConfig save
```

Example 5.48 Installing an application with various task and nontask options

```
 I  unset opts
 2  set nameOpt [list -appname app8]
 3  appends opts " " $nameOpt
 4  set mapping [list "Increment Enterprise Java Bean" Increment
    Increment.jar,META-INF/ejb-jar.xml Increment]
 5  set mapjndibindOpt [list -BindJndiForEJBNonMessageBinding [list
    $mapping]]
 6  append opts " " $mapjndibindOpt
 7  set mapping [list "Default Web Application" ""
    DefaultWebApplication.war,WEB-INF/web.xml Increment
    com.ibm.defaultapplication.Increment Increment]
 8  set mapejbrefOpt [list -MapEJBRefToEJB [list $mapping]]
 9  append opts " " $mapejbrefOpt
10  set mapping [list "Increment Enterprise Java Bean" Increment.jar,
    META-INF/ejb-jar.xml DefaultDatasource cmpBinding
    .perConnectionFactory]
11  set mapdsejbOpt [list -DataSourceFor20EJBModules [list $mapping]]
12  append opts " " $mapdsejbOpt
13  set mapping [list "Default Web Application"
    DefaultWebApplication.war,WEB-INF/web.xml default_host]
14  set mapVHOpt [list -MapWebModToVH [list $mapping]]
15  append opts " " $mapVHOpt
16  set miscOpts [list -nopreCompileJSPs -distributeApp
    -nouseMetaDataFromBinary]
17  append opts " " $miscOpts
18  $AdminApp install /installableapps/myApp.ear $opts
19  $AdminConfig save
```

Uninstall an Application

Example 5.49 shows a Jacl script to uninstall an application.

Example 5.49   Uninstalling an application

```
$AdminApp uninstall myApp
$AdminConfig save
```

Update an Application

The next three example Jacl scripts show the binding merge options available to update an existing application with a new version of an application file. Example 5.50 shows an update using merge action to merge bindings from the new application with the bindings from the old application. Example 5.51 shows an update using merge action to ignore bindings from the old application. Example 5.52 shows an update using merge action to ignore bindings from the new application.

Example 5.50   Updating an application using default merge

```
 1  append opts " " —update
 2  lappend opts -appname myApp
 3  $AdminApp install /installableApps/newMyApp.ear $opts
 4  $AdminConfig save
```

Example 5.51   Updating an application with update.ignore.old option

```
 5  unset opts
 6  append opts " " -update
 7  lappend opts —update.ignore.old
 8  lappend opts —appname myApp
 9  $AdminApp install /installableApps/newMyApp.ear $opts
10  $AdminConfig save
```

Example 5.52   Updating an application with update.ignore.new option

```
11  unset opts
12  append opts " " -update
13  lappend opts —update.ignore.new
14  lappend opts —appname myApp
15  $AdminApp install /installableApps/newMyApp.ear $opts
16  $AdminConfig save
```

Export an Application

Example 5.53 shows a Jacl script to export application data for each installed application.

Example 5.53   Exporting applications

```
I   set apps [$AdminApp list]
2   foreach app $apps {
3       $AdminApp export $app "/export/$app.ear"
4   }
```

Export DDL

Example 5.54 shows a Jacl script to export DDL data for each installed application.

Example 5.54   Export application DDL

```
I   set apps [$AdminApp list]
2   foreach app $apps {
3       $AdminApp exportDDL $app "/exportDDL/$app"
4   }
```

Modify the Configuration of an Application

The AdminApp object provides limited capability to modify the existing configuration beyond what is in the bindings. You can use the edit or editInteractive command to modify bindings, application configuration properties specific to applications binaries, metadata from binaries, reload, reload interval, create MBeans for resources, and modules to servers mappings. Beyond that, you have to use the AdminConfig object to perform post-configuration of an application.

Starting Weight   Example 5.55 shows a Jacl script to configure the starting weight of an application. Starting weight is used to specify the order in which modules are started during server startup. The module with the lowest starting weight is started first.

Example 5.55   Configuring starting weight for an application

```
I   set aDeployment [$AdminConfig getid /Deployment:myApp/]
2   set aAppDeploy [$AdminConfig showAttribute $aDeployment
    deployedObject]
3   $AdminConfig modify $aAppDeploy {{startingWeight 10}}
4   $AdminConfig save
```

Classloader Policy   Example 5.56 shows a Jacl script to configure classloader policy for WAR files. Valid values are SINGLE or MODULE. Line 3 specifies to use a single class-loader to load all WAR files in the application.

Example 5.56 Configuring classloader policy for an application

```
1  set aDeployment [$AdminConfig getid /Deployment:myApp/]
2  set aAppDeploy [$AdminConfig showAttribute $aDeployment
   deployedObject]
3  $AdminConfig modify $aAppDeploy {{warClassLoaderPolicy SINGLE}}
4  $AdminConfig save
```

Classloader Mode   Example 5.57 shows a Jacl script to configure classloader loading mode. Loading mode is used to specify whether the classloader searches in the parent classloader (PARENT_FIRST) before searching in the application classloader to load a class (PARENT_LAST). The default is PARENT_FIRST. Line 4 configures use of PARENT_LAST as the loading mode.

Example 5.57 Configuring classloader loading mode for an application

```
1  set aDeployment [$AdminConfig getid /Deployment:myApp/]
2  set aAppDeploy [$AdminConfig showAttribute $aDeployment
   deployedObject]
3  set aClassloader [$AdminConfig showAttribute $aAppDeploy
   classloader]
4  $AdminConfig modify $aClassloader {{mode PARENT_LAST}}
5  $AdminConfig save
```

Session Management   Example 5.58 shows a Jacl script to configure session management for an application. Lines 3–6 enable SSL ID tracking as the session tracking mechanism. Lines 7–9 configure serialize session access with 90 seconds as the maximum amount of time a servlet should wait on an HTTP session before continuing execution. Line 10 indicates session data to be discarded when the server shuts down. Lines 11–12 set the maximum number of sessions maintained in memory but allow the number of sessions to exceed this limit. Line 13 configures the amount of time in minutes a session can go unused before it is no longer valid. Lines 14–16 put together these properties, and line 17 creates a session management configuration for the application. Line 18 saves the configuration.

Example 5.58 Configuring session management for an application

```
1  set aDeployment [$AdminConfig getid /Deployment:myApp/]
2  set aAppDeploy [$AdminConfig showAttribute $aDeployment
   deployedObject]
3  set cookieAttr [list enableCookies false]
4  set protocolAttr [list enableProtocolSwitchRewriting false]
5  set urlAttr [list enableUrlRewriting false]
6  set sslAttr [list enableSSLTracking true]
7  set accessAttr [list allowSerializedSessionAccess true]
```

Example 5.58   Configuring session management for an application (Continued)

```
 8  set timeoutAttr [list accessSessionOnTimeout true]
 9  set waitTimeAttr [list maxWaitTime 90]
10  set modeAttr [list sessionPersistenceMode NONE]
11  set overflowAttr [list allowOverflow true]
12  set sessionCountAttr [list maxInMemorySessionCount 1500]
13  set invalidateTimeoutAttr [list invalidationTimeout 40]
14  set tuningParamsAttr [list tuningParams [list $overflowAttr
    $invalidateTimeoutAttr $sessionCountAttr]]
15  set enableAttr [list enable true]
16  set attrs [list $cookieAttr $urlAttr $sslAttr $protocolAttr
    $accessAttr $timeoutAttr $waitTimeAttr $modeAttr $enableAttr
    $tuningParamsAttr]
17  set sessionMgrAttr [list [list sessionManagement $attrs]]
18  $AdminConfig create ApplicationConfig $aAppDeploy $sessionMgrAttr
19  $AdminConfig save
```

Target Mappings   Example 5.59 shows a Jacl script to disable the loading of an application on each deployed target.

Example 5.59   Configuring application loading

```
1  set aDeployment [$AdminConfig getid /Deployment:myApp/]
2  set aAppDeploy [$AdminConfig showAttribute $aDeployment
   deployedObject]
3  set targetMappings [lindex [$AdminConfig showAttribute
   $aAppDeploy targetMappings] 0]
4  foreach aTargetMapping $targetMappings {
5      $AdminConfig modify $aTargetMapping {{enable false}}
6  }
7  $AdminConfig save
```

Libraries   Example 5.60 shows a Jacl script to configure the library reference that is used to specify the shared library to be used by an application. This script assumes that you have an existing shared library named mySharedLibrary. For a task script on how to create a shared library, refer to section Shared Libraries.

Example 5.60   Configuring library reference for an application

```
1  set aDeployment [$AdminConfig getid /Deployment:myApp/]
2  set aAppDeploy [$AdminConfig showAttribute $aDeployment
   deployedObject]
3  set aClassloader [$AdminConfig showAttribute $aAppDeploy classloader]
```

Example 5.60 Configuring library reference for an application

```
4  $AdminConfig create LibraryRef $aClassloader {{libraryName
   MyshareLibrary} {sharedClassloader true}}
5  $AdminConfig save
```

Map Modules to Application Servers Example 5.61 shows a Jacl script to modify application servers where you want to install modules contained in an application. Lines 1 and 2 set up two application server properties to be used in lines 3 and 4. Line 5 sets up the Map-ModulesToServers task option for two modules in the application. Line 9 runs the edit command to change the module to application server mapping. Line 10 saves the configuration.

Example 5.61 Mapping modules to application servers

```
 1  set aServer WebSphere:cell=myCell,node=myNode,server=myServer
 2  set aServer2 WebSphere:cell=myCell,node=myNode,server=myServer2
 3  set mapping1 [list "Increment Enterprise Java Bean" Increment.jar,
    META-INF/ejb-jar.xml $aServer]
 4  set mapping2 [list "Default Web Application"
    DefaultWebApplication.war,WEB-INF/web.xml $aServer2]
 5  set mapServerOpt [list -MapModulesToServers [list $mapping1
    $mapping2]]
 6  unset opts
 7  append opts " " $mapServerOpt
 8  lappend opts -appname myApp
 9  $AdminApp edit /installableApps/myApp.ear $opts
10  $AdminConfig save
```

EJB Modules Example 5.62 is a Jacl script to configure a deployed EJB module setting. Lines 1–3 obtain all the modules belonging to application myApp. Lines 4–12 locate all the EJB modules to modify their starting weights and disable the loading of each EJB module on its deployment targets. Line 13 saves the configuration.

Example 5.62 Configuring EJB modules of an application

```
 1  set aDeployment [$AdminConfig getid /Deployment:myApp/]
 2  set aAppDeploy [$AdminConfig showAttribute $aDeployment
    deployedObject]
 3  set modules [lindex [$AdminConfig showAttribute $aAppDeploy modules] 0]
 4  foreach aModule $modules {
 5      if {[regexp EJBModuleDeployment $aModule] == 1} {
 6          $AdminConfig modify $aModule {{startingWeight 1500}}
 7          set targetMappings [lindex [$AdminConfig showAttribute
            $aModule targetMappings] 0]
```

Example 5.62 Configuring EJB modules of an application (Continued)

```
 8          foreach aTargetMapping $targetMappings {
 9              $AdminConfig modify $aTargetMapping {{enable false}}
10          }
11      }
12  }
13  $AdminConfig save
```

Web Modules Example 5.63 is a Jacl script for Web module configuration. Lines 1–3 get hold of all the modules belonging to application myApp. Line 4 configures the starting order of the module during server startup. Line 5 specifies that the application classloader should be searched first to load a class. Lines 6 and 7 configure the name and description of the Web module configuration. Lines 8–10 allow session management settings configured in a Web module to take precedence over those in the application level. Lines 12–19 create a new Web module configuration for any Web module that has not yet been configured. Line 20 saves the configuration changes to the master repository.

Example 5.63 Configuring Web modules of an application

```
 1  set aDeployment [$AdminConfig getid /Deployment:myApp/]
 2  set aAppDeploy [$AdminConfig showAttribute $aDeployment
    deployedObject]
 3  set modules [lindex [$AdminConfig showAttribute $aAppDeploy modules] 0]
 4  set weightAttr [list startingWeight 250]
 5  set loaderModeAttr [list classloaderMode PARENT_FIRST]
 6  set nameAttr [list name myWebModuleConfig]
 7  set descAttr [list description "Web Module config post create"]
 8  set enableAttr [list enable true]
 9  set sessionAttr [list $enableAttr]
10  set sessionMgrAttr [list sessionManagement $sessionAttr]
11  set webAttrs [list $nameAttr $descAttr $sessionMgrAttr]
12  foreach aModule $modules {
13    if {[regexp WebModuleDeployment $aModule] == 1} {
14      if {[llength [$AdminConfig showAttribute $aModule config]]
        == 0} {
15        $AdminConfig create WebModuleConfig $aModule $webAttrs
16        $AdminConfig modify $aModule [list $weighAttr
          $loaderModeAttr]
17      }
18    }
19  }
20  $AdminConfig save
```

Connector Modules   Example 5.64 shows a Jacl script to create a J2C connection factory for each connection module in an application. Lines 1–3 obtain all the modules belonging to application myApp. Lines 4–9 configure the J2C connection factory properties including using component-managed authentication and setting the connection timeout to be 150 seconds. Lines 11–16 create a new J2C connection factory with the settings defined in lines 4–9 for each connector module. A configuration save is performed at the end.

Example 5.64   Configuring connector modules of an application

```
 1   set aDeployment [$AdminConfig getid /Deployment:myApp/]
 2   set aAppDeploy [$AdminConfig showAttribute $aDeployment
     deployedObject]
 3   set modules [lindex [$AdminConfig showAttribute $aAppDeploy modules] 0]
 4   set nameAttr [list name myJ2CCF]
 5   set descAttr [list description "Connection Factory created in
     application post configuration"]
 6   set authDataAttr [list authDataAlias myNode/DefaultSSLSettings]
 7   set timeoutAttr [list connectionTimeout 150]
 8   set connectionPoolAttr [list connectionPool [list $timeoutAttr]]
 9   set attrs [list $nameAttr $descAttr $authDataAttr $connectionPoolAttr]
10
11   foreach aModule $modules {
12     if {[regexp ConnectorModuleDeployment $aModule] == 1} {
13         set aResAdapter [$AdminConfig showAttribute $aModule
           resourceAdapter]
14         $AdminConfig create J2CConnectionFactory $aResAdapter $attrs
15     }
16   }
17   $AdminConfig save
```

Manage Resources

Applications connect to various accessible resources such as databases, Enterprise Information System (EIS), or directory files on a machine in the network to get data for the applications. The following tasks show how to configure various supported resources in the node-level scope, except for resource environment provider, which is configured in the server scope. Because resources can be configured in the cell, node, or server scope, the tasks can be modified to configure a resource in a different scope.

JDBC Providers

Example 5.65 shows a Jacl script to configure a JDBC provider. Lines 3–10 create a new JDBC provider named myJDBCProvider in the node scope. Line 13 modifies the description property of the existing JDBC provider. Lines 16–24 create a new data source named myDataSource if one does not exist. Lines 26–37 create a new custom property. Line 39 saves the configuration. To configure a JDBCProvider in a different scope, three are three changes required in the example. For example, to use server scope with myServer as the server, lines 1 and 16 have to include Server type and the server name in the configuration object name hierarchy (i.e., `/Node:myNode/Server:myServer/JDBCProvide:myJDBC-Provider/`). Line 9 has to change to use a server configuration object as the parent, (i.e., `set aParent [$AdminConfig getid /Node:myNode/Server:myServer/]`).

Example 5.65 Configuring JDBC provider

```
 1  set aJDBC [$AdminConfig getid /Node:myNode/
    JDBCProvider:myJDBCProvider/]
 2  if {[llength $aJDBC] == 0} {
 3     # create a new JDBCProvider with required and optional attributes
 4     set nameAttr [list name myJDBCProvider]
 5     set implAttr [list implementationClassName
       com.ibm.db2j.jdbc.DB2jConnectionPoolDataSource]
 6     # use CLOUDSCAPE_JDBC_DRIVER_PATH WebSphere variable in
       setting up classpath
 7     set classpathAttr [list classpath
       "\${CLOUDSCAPE_JDBC_DRIVER_PATH}/db2j.jar"]
 8     set attrs [list $nameAttr $implAttr $classpathAttr]
 9     set aParent [$AdminConfig getid /Node:myNode/]
10     set aJDBC [$AdminConfig create JDBCProvider $aParent $attrs]
11  } else {
12     # modify existing description
13     $AdminConfig modify $aJDBC {{description "JDBC Provider with
       Cloudscape as the implementation class"}}
14  }
15
16  set aDataSource [$AdminConfig getid /Node:myNode/
    JDBCProvider:myJDBCProvider/DataSource:myDataSource/]
17  if {[llength $aDataSource] == 0} {
18     # create a new DataSource with required and optional attributes
19     set nameAttr [list name myDataSource]
20     # setup for container-managed authentication using existing
       alias names defined in security settings
21     set mappingModuleAttr [list mapping [list [list authDataAlias
       myNode/DefaultSSLSettings] [list mappingConfigAlias
       DefaultPrincipalMapping]]]
22     set attrs [list $nameAttr $mappingModuleAttr]
23     set aDataSource [$AdminConfig create DataSource $aJDBC $attrs]
```

Example 5.65 Configuring JDBC provider (Continued)

```
24  }
25
26  set aPropertySet [$AdminConfig showAttribute $aDataSource
    propertySet]
27  if {[llength $aPropertySet] == 0} {
28    # create a property set
29    set aPropertySet [$AdminConfig create J2EEResourcePropertySet
      $aDataSource {}]
30  }
31  # create a custom property
32  set nameAttr [list name newProperty1]
33  set valueAttr [list value property1Value]
34  set requireAttr [list required false]
35  set typeAttr [list type java.lang.String]
36  set attrs [list $nameAttr $valueAttr $requireAttr $typeAttr]
37  $AdminConfig create J2EEResourceProperty $aPropertySet $attrs
38  # repeat lines 32-37 to set additional custom property
39  $AdminConfig save
```

Generic JMS Providers

Example 5.66 shows a Jacl script to configure a generic JMS provider. Lines 1–10 create a new generic JMS provider named myJMSProvider if one is not configured. Lines 12–23 create a new generic JMS destination named myJMSDestination to configure a JMS queue destination. Lines 25–36 create a new generic JMS connection factory named myJMSCF to configure its property to create a connection to a generic JMS queue destination. Line 38 saves the configuration.

Example 5.66 Configuring generic JMS provider

```
 1  set aJMSProvider [$AdminConfig getid /Node:myNode/
    JMSProvider:myJMSProvider/]
 2  if {[[llength $aJMSProvider] == 0] {
 3    # create a JMSProvider
 4    set nameAttr [list name myJMSProvider]
 5    set contextAttr [list externalInitialContextFactory
      com.myCompany.jms.myJMSFactory]
 6    set urlAttr [list externalProviderURL http://myJMS]
 7    set attrs [list $nameAttr $contextAttr $urlAttr]
 8    set aNode [$AdminConfig getid /Node:myNode/]
 9    set aJMSProvider [$AdminConfig create JMSProvider $aNode $attrs]
10  }
```

Example 5.66   Configuring generic JMS provider (Continued)

```
11
12   set aJMSDestination [$AdminConfig getid /Node:myNode/
     JMSProvider:myJMSProvider/GenericJMSDestination:myJMSDestination/]
13   if {[llength $aJMSDestination] == 0} {
14      # create a JMS queue destination
15      set nameAttr [list name myJMSDestination]
16      set jndiAttr [list jndiName jms/JMSDestination]
17      set extJndiAttr [list externalJNDIName jms/externalJMSD]
18      # to configure a topic destination, add
19      # set typeAttr [list type TOPIC] and include
20      # this attribute to attrs.
21      set attrs [list $nameAttr $jndiAttr $extJndiAttr]
22      $AdminConfig create GenericJMSDestination $aJMSProvider $attrs
23   }
24
25   set aJMSCF [$AdminConfig getid /Node:myNode/JMSProvider:
     myJMSProvider/GenericJMSConnectionFactory:myJMSCF/]
26   if {[llength $aJMSCF] == 0} {
27      # create a JMS connection factory
28      set nameAttr [list name myJMSCF]
29      set jndiAttr [list jndiName jms/JMSCF]
30      set extJndiAttr [list externalJNDIName jms/externalJMSCF]
31      # to configure for a topic destination, add
32      # set typeAttr [list type TOPIC] and include
33      # this attribute to attrs.
34      set attrs [list $nameAttr $jndiAttr $extJndiAttr]
35      $AdminConfig create GenericJMSConnectionFactory $aJMSProvider
        $attrs]
36   }
37
38   $AdminConfig save
```

WebSphere JMS Providers

Example 5.67 shows a Jacl script to configure a WebSphere JMS provider. Lines 1–11 create a new WebSphere JMS queue connection factory named myWASQueueCF to create connections to the built-in WebSphere JMS provider for point-to-point messaging if one does not exist. Line 13 modifies its description. Lines 15–25 create a new WebSphere JMS topic connection factory named myWASTopicCF to create connections to the built-in WebSphere JMS provider for publish and subscribe messaging if one does not exist. Line 26 modifies its description. Lines 28–36 create a new WebSphere JMS queue destination named myWASQueue if one does not exist. Lines 37–48 create a new custom property for it. Lines 50–59 create a new WebSphere JMS topic destination named myWASTopic if one does not exist. Line 62 configures its persistence property. Line 64 saves the configuration.

Example 5.67   Configuring WebSphere JMS provider

```
 1  set aWASJMSProvider [$AdminConfig getid "/Node:myNode/
    JMSProvider:WebSphere JMS Provider/"]
 2  set aWASQueueCF [$AdminConfig getid "/Node:myNode/
    JMSProvider:WebSphere JMS Provider/
    WASQueueConnectionFactory:myWASQueueCF/"]
 3  if {[llength $aWASQueueCF] == 0} {
 4     # create a WAS queue connection factory
 5     set nameAttr [list name myWASQueueCF]
 6     set jndiAttr [list jndiName jms/WASQCF]
 7     # use component-managed authentication
 8     set aliasAttr [list authDataAlias myNode/DefaultSSLSettings]
 9     set nodeAttr [list node myNode]
10     set attrs [list $nameAttr $jndiAttr $aliasAttr $nodeAttr]
11     set aWASQueueCF [$AdminConfig create WASQueueConnectionFactory
       $aWASJMSProvider $attrs]
12  }
13  $AdminConfig modify $aWASQueueCF {{description "WAS Queue
    Connection Factory example"}}
14
15  set aWASTopicCF [$AdminConfig getid "/Node:myNode/
    JMSProvider:WebSphere JMS Provider/
    WASTopicConnectionFactory:myWASTopicCF/"]
16  if {[llength $aWASTopicCF] == 0} {
17     # create a WAS topic connection factory
18     set nameAttr [list name myWASTopicCF]
19     set jndiAttr [list jndiName jms/WASTCF]
20     # use container-managed authentication
21     set mappingModuleAttr [list mapping [list [list authDataAlias
       myNode/DefaultSSLSettings] [list mappingConfigAlias
       DefaultPrincipalMapping]]]
22     set nodeAttr [list node myNode]
23     set attrs [list $nameAttr $jndiAttr $mappingModuleAttr
       $nodeAttr]
24     set aWASTopicCF [$AdminConfig create WASTopicConnectionFactory
       $aWASJMSProvider $attrs]
25  }
```

Example 5.67   Configuring WebSphere JMS provider (Continued)

```
26  $AdminConfig modify $aWASTopicCF {{description "WAS Topic
    Connection Factory example"}}
27
28  set aWASQueueDest [$AdminConfig getid "/Node:myNode/
    JMSProvider:WebSphere JMS Provider/WASQueue:myWASQueue/"]
29  if {[llength $aWASQueueDest] == 0} {
30     # create a WAS queue destination
31     set nameAttr [list name myWASQueue]
32     set jndiAttr [list jndiName jms/WASQD]
33     set nodeAttr [list node myNode]
34     set attrs [list $nameAttr $jndiAttr $nodeAttr]
35     set aWASQueueDest [$AdminConfig create WASQueue
       $aWASJMSProvider $attrs]
36  }
37  set aPropertySet [$AdminConfig showAttribute $aWASQueueDest
    propertySet]
38  if {[llength $aPropertySet] == 0} {
39     # create a property set
40     set aPropertySet [$AdminConfig create J2EEResourcePropertySet
       $aWASQueueDest {}]
41  }
42  # create a custom property
43  set nameAttr [list name newProperty1]
44  set valueAttr [list value property1Value]
45  set requireAttr [list required false]
46  set typeAttr [list type java.lang.String]
47  set attrs [list $nameAttr $valueAttr $requireAttr $typeAttr]
48  $AdminConfig create J2EEResourceProperty $aPropertySet $attrs
49
50  set aWASTopicDest [$AdminConfig getid "/Node:myNode/
    JMSProvider:WebSphere JMS Provider/WASTopic:myWASTopic/"]
51  if {[llength $aWASTopicDest] == 0} {
52     # create a WAS topic destination
53     set nameAttr [list name myWASTopic]
54     set jndiAttr [list jndiName jms/WASTD]
55     set nodeAttr [list node myNode]
56     set topicAttr [list topic myWASTopic]
57     set attrs [list $nameAttr $jndiAttr $nodeAttr $topicAttr]
58     set aWASTopicDest [$AdminConfig create WASTopic
       $aWASJMSProvider $attrs]
```

Example 5.67   Configuring WebSphere JMS provider (Continued)

```
59  }

60

61  # modify persistence attribute to indicate messages sent to
    destination is not persistent

62  $AdminConfig modify $aWASTopicDest {{persistence NONPERSISTENT}}

63

64  $AdminConfig save
```

WebSphere MQ JMS Providers

Example 5.68 shows a Jacl script to configure a WebSphere MQ JMS provider. Lines 1–11 create a new WebSphere MQ queue connection factory named myMQQueueCF to create connections to the built-in WebSphere MQ JMS provider for point-to-point messaging if one does not exist. Line 13 modifies its description. Lines 15–24 create a new WebSphere MQ topic connection factory named myMQTopicCF to create connections to the built-in WebSphere MQ JMS provider for publish and subscribe messaging if one does not exist. Line 25 modifies its description. Lines 27–36 create a new WebSphere MQ queue destination named myMQQueue if one does not exist. Lines 37–48 create a new custom property for it. Lines 50–58 create a new WebSphere MQ topic destination named myMQTopic if one does not exist. Line 61 configures its persistence property. Line 63 saves the configuration.

Example 5.68   Configuring WebSphere MQ JMS provider

```
 1  set aMQJMSProvider [$AdminConfig getid "/Node:myNode/
    JMSProvider:WebSphere MQ JMS Provider/"]

 2  set aMQQueueCF [$AdminConfig getid "/Node:myNode/
    JMSProvider:WebSphere MQ JMS Provider/
    MQQueueConnectionFactory:myMQQueueCF/"]

 3  if {[llength $aMQQueueCF] == 0} {

 4      # create a MQ queue connection factory

 5      set nameAttr [list name myMQQueueCF]

 6      set jndiAttr [list jndiName jms/MQQCF]

 7      # use component-managed authentication

 8      set aliasAttr [list authDataAlias myNode/DefaultSSLSettings]

 9      set attrs [list $nameAttr $jndiAttr $aliasAttr]

10      set aMQQueueCF [$AdminConfig create MQQueueConnectionFactory
        $aMQJMSProvider $attrs]

11  }

12

13  $AdminConfig modify $aMQQueueCF {{description "MQ Queue Connection
    Factory example"}}
```

Example 5.68   Configuring WebSphere MQ JMS provider (Continued)

```
14
15  set aMQTopicCF [$AdminConfig getid "/Node:myNode/
    JMSProvider:WebSphere MQ JMS Provider/
    MQTopicConnectionFactory:myMQTopicCF/"]
16  if {[llength $aMQTopicCF] == 0} {
17      # create a MQ topic connection factory
18      set nameAttr [list name myMQTopicCF]
19      set jndiAttr [list jndiName jms/MQTCF]
20      # use container-managed authentication
21      set mappingModuleAttr [list mapping [list [list authDataAlias
        myNode/DefaultSSLSettings] [list mappingConfigAlias
        DefaultPrincipalMapping]]
22      set attrs [list $nameAttr $jndiAttr $mappingModuleAttr]
23      set aMQTopicCF [$AdminConfig create MQTopicConnectionFactory
        $aMQJMSProvider $attrs]
24  }
25  $AdminConfig modify $aMQTopicCF {{description "MQ Topic Connection
    Factory example"}}
26
27  set aMQQueueDest [$AdminConfig getid "/Node:myNode/
    JMSProvider:WebSphere MQ JMS Provider/MQQueue:myMQQueue/"]
28  if {[llength $aMQQueueDest] == 0} {
29      # create a MQ queue destination
30      set nameAttr [list name myMQQueue]
31      set jndiAttr [list jndiName jms/MQQD]
32      set queueAttr [list baseQueueName myMQQueue]
33      set queueManagerAttr [list baseQueueManagerName
        myMQQueueManager]
34      set attrs [list $nameAttr $jndiAttr $queueAttr
        $queueManagerAttr]
35      set aMQQueueDest [$AdminConfig create MQQueue $aMQJMSProvider
        $attrs]
36  }
37  set aPropertySet [$AdminConfig showAttribute $aMQQueueDest
    propertySet]
38  if {[llength $aPropertySet] == 0} {
39      # create a property set
40      set aPropertySet [$AdminConfig create J2EEResourcePropertySet
        $aMQQueueDest {}]
41  }
42  # create a custom property
43  set nameAttr [list name newProperty1]
```

Example 5.68   Configuring WebSphere MQ JMS provider (Continued)

```
44   set valueAttr [list value property1Value]
45   set requireAttr [list required false]
46   set typeAttr [list type java.lang.String]
47   set attrs [list $nameAttr $valueAttr $requireAttr $typeAttr]
48   $AdminConfig create J2EEResourceProperty $aPropertySet $attrs
49
50   set aMQTopicDest [$AdminConfig getid "/Node:myNode/
     JMSProvider:WebSphere MQ JMS Provider/MQTopic:myMQTopic/"]
51   if {[llength $aMQTopicDest] == 0} {
52      # create a MQ topic destination
53      set nameAttr [list name myMQTopic]
54      set jndiAttr [list jndiName jms/MQTD]
55      set topicAttr [list baseTopicName myMQTopic]
56      set attrs [list $nameAttr $jndiAttr $topicAttr]
57      set aMQTopicDest [$AdminConfig create MQTopic $aMQJMSProvider
        $attrs]
58   }
59
60   # modify persistence attribute to indicate messages sent to
     destination is not persistent
61   $AdminConfig modify $aMQTopicDest {{persistence NONPERSISTENT}}
62
63   $AdminConfig save
```

Mail Providers

Example 5.69 shows a Jacl script to configure a mail provider and its mail session. Lines 1–9 create a new mail provider named myMailProvider if one is not configured. Lines 11–22 create a custom property. Lines 24–32 create a new protocol provider named myProtocol-Provider if one does not exist. Lines 34–45 create a new mail session named myMailSession using myProtocolProvider as the transport protocol. Line 47 saves the configuration.

Example 5.69   Configuring mail provider

```
1   set aMailProvider [$AdminConfig getid /Node:myNode/
    MailProvider:myMailProvider/]
2   if {[llength $aMailProvider] == 0} {
3      # create a mail provider
4      set nameAttr [list name myMailProvider]
5      set descAttr [list description "Mail Provider example"]
6      set attrs [list $nameAttr $descAttr]
```

Example 5.69   Configuring mail provider (Continued)

```
 7    set aNodeParent [$AdminConfig getid /Node:myNode/]
 8    set aMailProvider [$AdminConfig create MailProvider
      $aNodeParent $attrs]
 9  }
10
11  set aPropertySet [$AdminConfig showAttribute $aMailProvider
    propertySet]
12  if {[llength $aPropertySet] == 0} {
13    # create a property set
14    set aPropertySet [$AdminConfig create J2EEResourcePropertySet
      $aMailProvider {}]
15  }
16  # create a custom property in the property set
17  set nameAttr [list name property1]
18  set valueAttr [list value property1Value]
19  set requireAttr [list required false]
20  set typeAttr [list type java.lang.String]
21  set attrs [list $nameAttr $valueAttr $requireAttr $typeAttr]
22  $AdminConfig create J2EEResourceProperty $aPropertySet $attrs
23
24  set aProtocolProvider [$AdminConfig getid /Node:myNode/
    MailProvider:myMailProvider/ProtocolProvider:myProtocolProvider/]
25  if {[llength $aProtocolProvider] == 0} {
26    # create a protocol provider
27    set protocolAttr [list protocol myProtocolProvider]
28    set classnameAttr [list classname
      com.my.mail.myProtocolProvider.MYPROTOCOLPROVIDERSTORE]
29    set typeAttr [list type STORE]
30    set attrs [list $protocolAttr $classnameAttr $typeAttr]
31    set aProtocolProvider [$AdminConfig create ProtocolProvider
      $aMailProvider $attrs]
32  }
33
34  set aMailSession [$AdminConfig getid /Node:myNode/
    MailProvider:myMailProvider/MailSession:myMailSession/]
35  if {[llength $aMailSession] == 0} {
36    # create a mail session
37    set nameAttr [list name myMailSession]
38    set jndiAttr [list jndiName mail/myMailSession]
39    set storeProtocolAttr [list mailStoreProtocol $aProtocolProvider]
```

Example 5.69   Configuring mail provider (Continued)

```
40    set storeHostAttr [list mailStoreHost myMailServer]
41    set storeUserAttr [list mailStoreUser myMailUser]
42    set storePasswordAttr [list mailStorePassword myMailPassword]
43    set attrs [list $nameAttr $jndiAttr $storeProtocolAttr
      $storeHostAttr $storeUserAttr $storePasswordAttr]
44    set aMailSession [$AdminConfig create MailSession
      $aMailProvider $attrs]
45  }
46
47  $AdminConfig save
```

Resource Environment Providers

Example 5.70 shows a Jacl script to configure a resource environment provider and its resource environment entry. Lines 1–9 create a new resource environment provider named myResEnvProvider if one is not configured. Line 10 configures the classpath property for the provider. Lines 11–22 create a new custom property. Lines 24–31 configure a referenceable named myRef if one does not exist. Lines 33–41 create a new resource environment entry using the referenceable myRef. Line 43 saves the configuration.

Example 5.70   Configuring resource environment provider

```
 1  set aResEnvProvider [$AdminConfig getid /Node:myNode/Server:
    myServer/ResourceEnvironmentProvider:myResEnvProvider/]
 2  if {[llength $aResEnvProvider] == 0} {
 3    # create a resource environment provider
 4    set nameAttr [list name myResEnvProvider]
 5    set descAttr [list description "Resource Environment Provider
      example"]
 6    set attrs [list $nameAttr $descAttr]
 7    set aServerParent [$AdminConfig getid /Node:myNode/
      Server:myServer/]
 8    set aResEnvProvider [$AdminConfig create
      ResourceEnvironmentProvider $aServerParent $attrs]
 9  }
10  $AdminConfig modify $aResEnvProvider {{classpath /Resource/
    myResource.jar}}
11  set aPropertySet [$AdminConfig showAttribute $aResEnvProvider
    propertySet]
12  if {[llength $aPropertySet] == 0} {
13    # create a property set
```

Example 5.70   Configuring resource environment provider (Continued)

```
14    set aPropertySet [$AdminConfig create J2EEResourcePropertySet
      $aResEnvProvider {}]
15  }
16  # create a custom property in the property set
17  set nameAttr [list name property1]
18  set valueAttr [list value property1Value]
19  set requireAttr [list required false]
20  set typeAttr [list type java.lang.String]
21  set attrs [list $nameAttr $valueAttr $requireAttr $typeAttr]
22  $AdminConfig create J2EEResourceProperty $aPropertySet $attrs
23
24    set aRef [$AdminConfig getid /Node:myNode/Server:myServer/
      ResourceEnvironmentProvider:myResEnvProvider/Referenceable
      :myRef/]
25  if {[llength $aRef] == 0} {
26      # create a referenceable
27      set factoryClassnameAttr [list factoryClassname
        com.my.resourceEnv.objectFactory]
28      set classnameAttr [list classname java.util.Properties]
29      set attrs [list $factoryClassnameAttr $classnameAttr]
30      set aRef [$AdminConfig create Referenceable $aResEnvProvider
        $attrs]
31  }
32
33  set aResEnvEntry [$AdminConfig getid /Node:myNode/Server
    :myServer/ResourceEnvironmentProvider:myResEnvProvider/
    ResourceEnvEntry:myResEnvEntry/]
34    if {[llength $aResEnvEntry] == 0} {
35      # create a resource environment entry
36      set nameAttr [list name myResEnvEntry]
37      set jndiAttr [list jndiName mail/myResEnv]
38      set refAttr [list referenceable $aRef]
39      set attrs [list $nameAttr $jndiAtr $refAttr]
40      set aResEnvEntry [$AdminConfig create ResourceEnvEntry
        $aResEnvProvider $attrs]
41  }
42
43  $AdminConfig save
```

URL Providers

Example 5.71 shows a Jacl script to configure a URL provider and its URL. Lines 1–10 create a new URL provider named myURLProvider if one is not configured. Line 12 modifies its description. Lines 14–25 create a new custom property for this URL provider. Lines 27–35 configure a new URL named myURL if one is not configured. Line 37 saves the configuration.

Example 5.71   Configuring URL provider

```
 1  set aURLrovider [$AdminConfig getid /Node:myNode/
    URLProvider:myURLProvider/]
 2  if {[llength $aURLProvider] == 0} {
 3    # create a URL provider
 4    set nameAttr [list name myURLProvider]
 5    set protocolAttr [list protocol ftp]
 6    set streamHandlerAttr [list streamHandlerClassName
      com.my.URL.streamHandler]
 7    set attrs [list $nameAttr $protocolAttr $streamHandlerAttr]
 8    set aNodeParent [$AdminConfig getid /Node:myNode/]
 9    set aURLProvider [$AdminConfig create URLProvider
      $aNodeParent $attrs]
10  }
11
12  $AdminConfig modify $aURLProvider {{description "URL Provider
    example"}}
13
14  set aPropertySet [$AdminConfig showAttribute $aURLProvider
    propertySet]
15  if {[llength $aPropertySet] == 0} {
16    # create a property set
17    set aPropertySet [$AdminConfig create J2EEResourcePropertySet
      $aURLProvider {}]
18  }
19  # create a custom property in the property set
20  set nameAttr [list name property1]
21  set valueAttr [list value property1Value]
22  set requireAttr [list required false]
23  set typeAttr [list type java.lang.String]
24  set attrs [list $nameAttr $valueAttr $requireAttr $typeAttr]
25  $AdminConfig create J2EEResourceProperty $aPropertySet $attrs
26
27  set aURL [$AdminConfig getid /Node:myNode/URLProvider:
    myURLProvider/URL:myURL/]
```

Example 5.71   Configuring URL provider (Continued)

```
28  if {[llength $aURL] == 0} {
29      # create a URL
30      set nameAttr [list name myURL]
31      set jndiAttr [list jndiName URL/myURL]
32      set specAttr [list spec mySpec]
33      set attrs [list $nameAttr $jndiAttr $specAttr]
34      set aURL [$AdminConfig create URL $aURLProvider $attrs]
35  }
36
37  $AdminConfig save
```

Resource Adapters

Example 5.72 shows a Jacl script to configure a J2C resource adapter and its connection factory. Lines 1–7 create a J2C resource adapter named myJ2CRA if one is not configured. Lines 9–14 display the custom properties for the installed resource adapter. Lines 16–24 create a J2C connection factory named myJ2CCF for the installed resource adapter if a connection factory with that name does not exist. The connection factory enables component-managed authentication using an existing J2C authentication data entry. To create a new authentication data entry, refer to section JAAS. Lines 26–33 configure the connection pool. Line 35 saves the configuration.

Example 5.72   Configuring resource adapter

```
 I  set aJ2CRA [$AdminConfig getid /Node:myNode/
    J2CResourceAdapter:myJ2CRA/]
 2  if {[llength $aJ2CRA] == 0} {
 3      # create a J2C resource adapter
 4      set options [list —rar.name myJ2CRA —rar.description "This is
        a J2C resource adapter example"]
 5      set rarFile /installable/myra.rar
 6      set aJ2CRA [$AdminConfig installResourceAdapter $rarFile
        $options]
 7  }
 8
 9  set aPropertySet [$AdminConfig showAttribute $aJ2CRA propertySet]
10  if {[llength $aPropertySet] != 0} {
11      puts [$AdminConfig showall $aPropertySet]
12  } else {
13      puts "There is no custom properties for this resource adapter."
14  }
```

Example 5.72 Configuring resource adapter (Continued)

```
15
16   set aJ2CCF [$AdminConfig getid /Node:myNode/
     J2CResourceAdapter:myJ2CRA/J2CConnectionFactory:myJ2CCF/]
17   if {[llength $aJ2CCF] == 0} {
18      # create a J2C connection factory
19      set nameAttr [list name myJ2CCF]
20      set jndiAttr [list jndiName eis/myj2ccf]
21      set authAliasAttr [list authDataAlias myNode/
        defaultSSLSettings]
22      set attrs [list $nameAttr $jndiAttr $authAliasAttr]
23      set aJ2CCF [$AdminConfig create J2CConnectionFactory $aJ2CRA
        $attrs]
24   }
25
26   # configure connection pool
27   set maxConnAttr [list maxConnections 13]
28   set aConnPool [$AdminConfig showAttribute $aJ2CCF connectionPool]
29   if {[llength $aConnPool] == 0} {
30      # create a connection pool using defaults except for maximum
        connections
31      set aConnPool [$AdminConfig create ConnectionPool $aJ2CCF {}]
32   }
33   $AdminConfig modify $aConnPool [list $maxConnAttr]
34
35   $AdminConfig save
```

Manage Security

This section contains tasks to manage security configuration that is effective for the entire security domain.

Global Security

Example 5.73 shows a Jacl script to configure global security with FIPS enabled, detailed in lines 12–27.

Example 5.73 Configuring global security

```
1   set aSec [$AdminConfig getid /Cell:myCell/Security:/]
2   # modify existing security configuration properties
3   set enableAttr [list enable true]
4   set java2SecurityAttr [list enforceJava2Security true]
5   set domainAttr [list useDomainQualifiedUserNames true]
```

Example 5.73   Configuring global security (Continued)

```
 6  set cacheTimeoutAttr [list cacheTimeout 100]
 7  set protocolAttr [list activeProtocol CSI]
 8  set attrs [list $enableAttr $java2SecurityAttr $domainAttr
    $cacheTimeoutAttr $protocolAttr]
 9  $AdminConfig modify $aSec $attrs
10
11  # enable FIPS
12  set properties [lindex [$AdminConfig showAttribute $aSec
    properties] 0]
13  set foundFIPS false
14  if {[llength $properties] != 0} {
15      foreach aProperty $properties {
16          if {[$AdminConfig showAttribute $aProperty name] ==
            "com.ibm.security.userFIPS"} {
17              $AdminConfig modify $aProperty {{value true}}
18              set foundFIPS true
19          }
20      }
21  }
22  if {$foundFIPS == "false"} {
23      set nameAttr [list name com.ibm.security.useFIPS]
24      set valueAttr [list value true]
25      set attrs [list $nameAttr $valueAttr]
26      $AdminConfig create Property $aSec $attrs
27  }
28
29  $AdminConfig save
```

SSL Configuration Repertoires

Example 5.74 shows a Jacl script to configure SSL. Lines 12–25 create a repertoire named myCell/mySSLSettings if one is not configured. Lines 27–35 enable cryptographic token support. Lines 37–55 configure provider, protocol, and cipher suites as custom properties. Line 57 saves the configuration.

Example 5.74   Configuring SSL

```
 1  set aSec [$AdminConfig getid /Cell:myCell/Security:/]
 2  set repertoires [lindex [$AdminConfig showAttribute $aSec
    repertoire] 0]
 3  set foundSSL = false
```

Example 5.74   Configuring SSL (Continued)

```
 4  if {[llength $repertoires] != 0} {
 5     foreach aRepertoire $repertoires {
 6        if {[$AdminConfig showAttribute $aRepertoire alias] ==
           "myCell/mySSLSettings"} {
 7           set foundSSL $aRepertoire
 8        }
 9     }
10  }
11
12  if {$foundSSL == "false"} {
13     # create a repertoire named myCell/mySSLSettings
14     set aliasAttr [list alias myCell/mySSLSettings]
15     set keyFileAttr [list keyFileName \${USER_INSTALL_ROOT}/etc/
        DummyServerKeyFile.jks]
16     set keyPasswordAttr [list keyFilePassword mypassword]
17     set keyFormatAttr [list keyFileFormat JCEK]
18     set trustFileAttr [list trustFileName \${USER_INSTALL_ROOT}/
        etc/DummyServerTrustFile.jks]
19     set trustPasswordAttr [list trustFilePassword mypassword]
20     set trustFormatAttr [list trustFileFormat JCEK]
21     set secLevelAttr [list securityLevel MEDIUM]
22     set settingAttrs [list setting [list $keyFileAttr
        $keyPasswordAttr $keyFormatAttr $trustFileAttr
        $trustPasswordAttr $trustFormatAttr $secLevelAttr]]
23     set attrs [list $aliasAttr $settingAttr]
24     set foundSSL [$AdminConfig create SSLConfig $aSec $attrs
        repertoire]
25  }
26  set ssl [$AdminConfig showAttribute $foundSSL setting]
27  # configure for cryptographic token
28  set enableAttr [list enableCryptoHardwareSupport true]
29  $AdminConfig modify $ssl [list $enableAttr]
30  set crypto [$AdminConfig showAttribute $ssl cryptoHardware]
31  if {[llength $crypto] == 0} {
32     set passwordAttr [list password mypassword]
33     set attrs [list $passwordAttr]
34     $AdminConfig create CryptoHardwareToken $ssl $attrs
35  }
36
37  # configure for custom property
```

Example 5.74   Configuring SSL (Continued)

```
38   set properties [lindex [$AdminConfig showAttribute $ssl
     properties] 0]
39   if {[llength $properties] == 0} {
40      # configure provider property
41      set nameAttr [list name com.ibm.ssl.contextProvider]
42      set valueAttr [list value IBMJSSE]
43      set attrs [list $nameAttr $valueAttr]
44      $AdminConfig create Property $ssl $attrs
45      # configure protocol property
46      set nameAttr [list name com.ibm.ssl.protocol]
47      set valueAttr [list value SSLv3]
48      set attrs [list $nameAttr $valueAttr]
49      $AdminConfig create Property $ssl attrs
50      # configure cipher suites
51      set nameAttr [list name com.ibm.ssl.enabledCipherSuites]
52      set valueAttr [list value
        SSL_DHE_DSS_EXPORT_WITH_DES40_CBC_SHA]
53      set attrs [list $nameAttr $valueAttr]
54      $AdminConfig create Property $ssl $attrs
55   }
56
57   $AdminConfig save
```

Authentication Mechanism—LTPA

Example 5.75 shows a Jacl script to configure an LTPA authentication mechanism. Lines 6–28 use a running security MBean to generate and export LTPA keys. The exported keys are then set in the configuration in lines 30–37. Lines 39–45 enable and configure a single sign on. Line 47 saves the configuration.

Example 5.75   Configuring LTPA

```
1   set aSec [$AdminConfig getid /Cell:myCell/Security:/]
2   set aLTPA [$AdminConfig list LTPA $aSec]
3   if {[llength $aLTPA] != 0} {
4      # modify LTPA to use LTPA keys
5
6      # assuming network deployment environment, for application
       server environment, change process value accordingly.
7      set aRunningSecMBean [$AdminControl queryNames
       type=SecurityAdmin,process=dmgr,*]
```

Example 5.75 Configuring LTPA (Continued)

```
 8    set sharedKey null
 9    set privateKey null
10    set publicKey null
11    if {[llength $aRunningSecMBean] != 0} {
12        puts "Generate LTPA keys"
13        $AdminControl invoke $aRunningSecMBean generateKeys
          mypassword
14        puts "Export LTPA keys"
15        set result [$AdminControl invoke $aRunningSecMBean
          exportLTPAKeys]
16        # look for public, private, and shared keys
17        for {set x 0} {$x < 7} {incr x} {
18            set key [lindex [lindex $result $x] 0]
19            set value [lindex [lindex $result $x] 1]
20            if {[string compare $key com.ibm.websphere.ltpa.3DESKey]
              == 0} {
21                set sharedKey $value
22            } elseif {[string compare $key
              com.ibm.websphere.ltpa.PrivateKey] == 0} {
23                set privateKey $value
24            } elseif {[string compare $key
              com.ibm.websphere.ltpa.PublicKey] == 0} {
25                set publicKey $value
26            }
27        }
28    }
29
30    set passwordAttr [list password mypassword]
31    set sharedAttr [list shared [list [list byteArray $sharedKey]]]
32    set privateAttr [list private [list [list byteArray
      $privateKey]]]
33    set publicAttr [list public [list [list byteArray $publicKey]]]
34    # set timeout in minutes
35    set timeoutAttr [list timeout 100]
36    set attrs [list $passwordAttr $sharedAttr $privateAttr
      $publicAttr $timeoutAttr]
37    $AdminConfig modify $aLTPA $attrs
38
39    # configure single signon
40    set enableAttr [list enable true]
```

Example 5.75   Configuring LTPA (Continued)

```
41      set sslAttr [list requiresSSL false]
42      set domainAttr [list domainName my.com]
43      set signon [$AdminConfig showAttribute $aLTPA singleSignon]
44      set attrs [list $enableAttr $sslAttr $domainAttr]
45      $AdminConfig modify $signon $attrs
46
47      $AdminConfig save
48  }
```

User Registry

Local OS   Example 5.76 shows a Jacl script to configure the user registry for the local operating system. Lines 4–8 specify the user name and password used for WebSphere Application Server security. Lines 11–14 configure a new custom property. Line 16 saves the configuration.

Example 5.76   Configuring local OS user registry

```
 1  set aSec [$AdminConfig getid /Cell:myCell/Security:/]
 2  set userRegistry [$AdminConfig list LocalOSUserRegistry $aSec]
 3  if {[llength $userRegistry] != 0} {
 4      # modify server id and password
 5      set idAttr [list serverId myServerId]
 6      set passwordAttr [list serverPassword myServerPassword]
 7      set attrs [list $idAttr $passwordAttr]
 8      $AdminConfig modify $userRegistry $attrs
 9
10      # Add a property
11      set nameAttr [list name property1]
12      set valueAttr [list value propertyValue1]
13      set attrs [list $nameAttr $valueAttr]
14      $AdminConfig create Property $userRegistry $attrs
15
16      $AdminConfig save
17  }
```

LDAP   Example 5.77 shows a Jacl script to configure LDAP user registry settings. Lines 5–10 modify four general properties of an existing LDAP user registry. Lines 13–20 modify the LDAP server host name. Lines 23–26 modify advanced LDAP user settings to configure certificate map mode. Valid values are EXACT_DN or CERTIFICATE_FILTER. Lines 29–32 configure a custom property. Line 34 saves the configuration.

Example 5.77   Configuring LDAP user registry

```
 1   set aSec [$AdminConfig getid /Cell:myCell/Security:/]
 2   set userRegistry [$AdminConfig list LDAPUserRegistry $aSec]
 3   if {[llength $userRegistry] != 0} {
 4       # modify server id, password, sslConfig and ignore case
         properties
 5       set idAttr [list serverId myServerId]
 6       set passwordAttr [list serverPassword myServerPassword]
 7       set sslConfigAttr [list sslConfig myCell/DefaultSSLSettings]
 8       set ignoreAttr [list ignoreCase true]
 9       set attrs [list $idAttr $passwordAttr $sslConfigAttr
         $ignoreAttr]
10       $AdminConfig modify $userRegistry $attrs
11
12       # modify LDAP server host
13       set endpoints [lindex [$AdminConfig showAttribute $userRegistry
         hosts] 0]
14       if {[llength $endpoints] != 0} {
15           foreach $aEndpoint $endpoints {
16               if {[$AdminConfig showAttribute $aEndpoint port] == 389} {
17                   $AdminConfig modify $aEndpoint {{host myHost}}
18               }
19           }
20       }
21
22       # modify advanced LDAP settings
23       set filter [$AdminConfig showAttribute $userRegistry
         searchFilter]
24       if {[llength $filter] != 0} {
25         $AdminConfig modify $filter {{certificateMapMode EXACT_DN}}
26       }
27
28       # Add a property
29       set nameAttr [list name property1]
30       set valueAttr [list value propertyValue1]
31       set attrs [list $nameAttr $valueAttr]
32       $AdminConfig create Property $userRegistry $attrs
33
```

Example 5.77 Configuring LDAP user registry (Continued)

```
34      $AdminConfig save
35 }
```

Custom Example 5.78 shows a Jacl script to configure a custom user registry. Lines 5–9 configure user name, password, and name of class that implements the com.ibm.websphere.security.UserRegsitry interface. Lines 12–15 create a new custom property. Line 17 saves the configuration.

Example 5.78 Configuring custom user registry

```
 I  set aSec [$AdminConfig getid /Cell:myCell/Security:/]
 2  set userRegistry [$AdminConfig list CustomUserRegistry $aSec]
 3  if {[llength $userRegistry] != 0} {
 4      # configure server id, password, and registry classname
 5      set idAttr [list serverId myServerId]
 6      set passwordAttr [list serverPassword myServerPassword]
 7      set classnameAttr [list customRegistryClassName
         com.ibm.websphere.security.FileRegistrySample]
 8      set attrs [list $idAttr $passwordAttr $classnameAttr]
 9      $AdminConfig modify $userRegistry $attrs
10
11      # Add a property
12      set nameAttr [list name property1]
13      set valueAttr [list value propertyValue1]
14      set attrs [list $nameAttr $valueAttr]
15      $AdminConfig create Property $userRegistry $attrs
16
17      $AdminConfig save
18 }
```

JAAS

Application Logins Example 5.79 shows a Jacl script to configure application logins. Lines 4–6 list all login configurations by their configuration object names. Lines 9–16 look for an existing application login named myAppLogin. Lines 19–26 create an application login named myAppLogin if one is not configured. Lines 29–35 modify existing application login properties. Lines 38–51 look for an application login named myOldAppLogin and deletes it. Line 52 saves the configuration.

Example 5.79   Configuring application login

```
 1   set aSec [$AdminConfig getid /Cell:myCell/Security:/]
 2   set appLogin [$AdminConfig showAttribute $aSec
     applicationLoginConfig]
 3   if {[llength $appLogin] != 0} {
 4       set entries [lindex [$AdminConfig showAttribute $appLogin
         entries] 0]
 5       puts "Login configurations: "
 6       puts $entries
 7
 8       # look for JAAS login module named myAppLogin
 9       set found false
10       foreach aEntry $entries {
11           if {[$AdminConfig showAttribute $aEntry alias] ==
             "myAppLogin"} {
12               puts "Found login configuration named myAppLogin"
13               set found $aEntry
14               break
15           }
16       }
17
18       if {$found == "false"} {
19           # create an application login
20           puts "Create a login configuration named myAppLogin"
21           set aliasAttr [list alias myAppLogin]
22           set strategyAttr [list authenticationStrategy REQUIRED]
23           set moduleClassAttr [list moduleClassName
             com.my.server.common.auth.module.proxy.myProxyImpl]
24           set loginModuleAttr [list loginModules [list [list
             $strategyAttr $moduleClassAttr]]]
25           set attrs [list $aliasAttr $loginModuleAttr]
26           set found [$AdminConfig create JAASConfigurationEntry
             $appLogin $attrs]
27       } else {
28           # modify existing login configuration
29           puts "Modify classname for existing login configuration
             myAppLogin"
30           set loginModules [lindex [$AdminConfig showAttribute $found
             loginModules] 0]
31           foreach aLoginModule $loginModules {
```

Example 5.79 Configuring application login (Continued)

```
32              if {[$AdminConfig showAttribute $aLoginModule
                moduleClassName] ==
                "com.my.server.com.auth.module.proxy.proxyImpl"} {
33                  $AdminConfig modify $aLoginModule {{moduleClassName
                    "com.my.server.com.auth.module.proxy.myProxyImpl"}}
34              }
35          }
36      }
37
38      # look for login configuration named myOldAppLogin
39      set found false
40      foreach aEntry $entries {
41          if {[$AdminConfig showAttribute $aEntry alias] ==
                "myOldAppLogin"} {
42              puts "Found login configuration named myOldAppLogin"
43              set found $aEntry
44              break
45          }
46      }
47      if {$found != "false"} {
48          # remove existing login configuration entry
49          puts "Remove existing login configuration named
                myOldAppLogin"
50          $AdminConfig remove $found
51      }
52      $AdminConfig save
53  }
```

J2C Authentication Data   Example 5.80 shows a Jacl script to configure J2C authentication data. Lines 5–10 create a new J2C authentication data configuration if there is no existing J2C authentication data entry. Lines 12 and 13 display existing authentication data entries by their configuration object names. Lines 15–20 change password property for the existing authentication data entry named myCell/myAuthData. Line 23 saves the configuration.

Example 5.80 Configuring J2C authentication data

```
1  set aSec [$AdminConfig getid /Cell:myCell/Security:/]
2  set authDataEntries [lindex [$AdminConfig showAttribute $aSec
   authDataEntries] 0]
3  if {[llength $authDataEntries] == 0} {
4      # create a auth data named myAuthData
```

Example 5.80   Configuring J2C authentication data (Continued)

```
 5      puts "Create a auth data named myCell/myAuthData"
 6      set aliasAttr [list alias myCell/myAuthData]
 7      set userAttr [list userId myUser]
 8      set passwordAttr [list password myPassword]
 9      set attrs [list $aliasAttr $uesrAttr $passwordAttr]
10      $AdminConfig create JAASAuthData $aSec $attrs
11  } else {
12      puts "JAAS authentication data: "
13      puts $authDataEntries
14
15      foreach aAuthEntry $authDataEntries {
16          if {[$AdminConfig showAttribute $aAuthEntry alias] ==
            "myCell/myAuthData"} {
17              puts "Modify password property for JAAS authentication
                data named myCell/myAuthData"
18              $AdminConfig modify $aAuthEntry {{password myPassword}}
19          }
20      }
21  }
22
23  $AdminConfig save
```

Authentication Protocol

CSIv2 Inbound Authentication   Example 5.81 configures authentication settings for requests received using the OMG Common Secure Interoperability (CSI) authentication protocol.

Example 5.81   Configuring CSIv2 inbound authentication

```
 1  set aSec [$AdminConfig getid /Cell:myCell/Security:/]
 2  set csi [$AdminConfig showAttribute $aSec CSI]
 3  set claim [$AdminConfig showAttribute $csi claims]
 4  if {[regexp CommonSecureInterop $claim] == 1} {
 5      set layers [lindex [$AdminConfig showAttribute $claim layers]
        0]
 6      foreach aLayer $layers {
 7          if {[regexp IdentityAssertionLayer $aLayer] == 1} {
 8              # create trusted server
 9              set serverIdAttr [list serverId myServerId]
10              set attrs [list $serverIdAttr]
```

Example 5.81   Configuring CSIv2 inbound authentication (Continued)

```
11          $AdminConfig create ServerIdentity $aLayer $attrs
12
13          set supportedQOP [$AdminConfig showAttribute $aLayer
            supportedQOP]
14          # modify to enable identity assertion
15          $AdminConfig modify $supportedQOP {{enable true}}
16       }
17       if {[regexp Transportlayer $aLayer] == 1} {
18          set supportedQOP [$AdminConfig showAttribute $aLayer
            supportedQOP]
19          set requiredQOP [$AdminConfig showAttribute $aLayer
            requiredQOP]
20          # set client certificate authentication to required.
21          # To set to supported,
22          # $AdminConfig modify $requiredQOP
            {{establishTrustInClient false}}
23          #$AdminConfig modify $supportedQOP
            {{establishTrustInClient true}}
24          # To set to never, set establishTrustInClient attribute
            to false in both requiredQOP and supportedQOP.
25          $AdminConfig modify $requiredQOP {{establishTrustInClient
            true}}
26          $AdminConfig modify $supportedQOP
            {{establishTrustInClient false}}
27       }
28       if {[regexp MessageLayer $aLayer] == 1} {
29          set supportedQOP [$AdminConfig showAttribute $aLayer
            supportedQOP]
30          set requiredQOP [$AdminConfig showAttribute $aLayer
            requiredQOP]
31          # set basic authentication to required.
32          # To set to supported,
33          # $AdminConfig modify $requiredQOP
            {{establishTrustInClient false}}
34          # $AdminConfig modify $supportedQOP
            {{establishTrustInClient true}}
35          # To set to never, set establishTrustInClient attribute
            to false in both requiredQOP and supportedQOP.
36          $AdminConfig modify $requiredQOP {{establishTrustInClient
            true}}
```

Example 5.81   Configuring CSIv2 inbound authentication (Continued)

```
37              $AdminConfig modify $supportedQOP
                {{establishTrustInClient false}}
38          }
39      }
40
41      # set stateful
42      $AdminConfig modify $claim {{stateful true}}
43
44      $AdminConfig save
45  }
```

CSIv2 Outbound Authentication   Example 5.82 configures authentication settings for
requests sent using the OMG CSI authentication protocol.

Example 5.82   Configuring CSIv2 outbound authentication

```
 I  set aSec [$AdminConfig getid /Cell:myCell/Security:/]
 2  set csi [$AdminConfig showAttribute $aSec CSI]
 3  set perform [$AdminConfig showAttribute $csi performs]
 4  if {[regexp CommonSecureInterop $perform] == 1} {
 5     set layers [lindex [$AdminConfig showAttribute $perform
        layers] 0]
 6     foreach aLayer $layers {
 7        if {[regexp IdentityAssertionLayer $aLayer] == 1} {
 8           set supportedQOP [$AdminConfig showAttribute $aLayer
              supportedQOP]
 9           # modify to enable identity assertion
10           $AdminConfig modify $supportedQOP {{enable true}}
11        }
12        if {[regexp Transportlayer $aLayer] == 1} {
13           set supportedQOP [$AdminConfig showAttribute $aLayer
              supportedQOP]
14           set requiredQOP [$AdminConfig showAttribute $aLayer
              requiredQOP]
15           # set client certificate authentication to required.
16           # To set to supported,
17           # $AdminConfig modify $requiredQOP
              {{establishTrustInClient false}}
18           #$AdminConfig modify $supportedQOP
              {{establishTrustInClient true}}
```

Example 5.82   Configuring CSIv2 outbound authentication (Continued)

```
19          # To set to never, set establishTrustInClient attribute
            to false in both requiredQOP and supportedQOP.
20          $AdminConfig modify $requiredQOP {{establishTrustInClient
            true}}
21          $AdminConfig modify $supportedQOP
            {{establishTrustInClient false}}
22      }
23      if {[regexp MessageLayer $aLayer] == 1} {
24          set supportedQOP [$AdminConfig showAttribute $aLayer
            supportedQOP]
25          set requiredQOP [$AdminConfig showAttribute $aLayer
            requiredQOP]
26          # set basic authentication to required.
27          # To set to supported,
28          # $AdminConfig modify $requiredQOP
            {{establishTrustInClient false}}
29          # $AdminConfig modify $supportedQOP
            {{establishTrustInClient true}}
30          # To set to never, set establishTrustInClient attribute
            to false in both requiredQOP and supportedQOP.
31          $AdminConfig modify $requiredQOP {{establishTrustInClient
            true}}
32          $AdminConfig modify $supportedQOP
            {{establishTrustInClient false}}
33      }
34  }
35
36  # set stateful
37  $AdminConfig modify $perform {{stateful true}}
38
39  $AdminConfig save
40 }
```

CSIv2 Inbound Transport   Example 5.83 configures transport setting for connections accepted using the OMG CSI authentication protocol.

Example 5.83   Configuring CSIv2 inbound transport

```
1  set aSec [$AdminConfig getid /Cell:myCell/Security:/]
2  set csi [$AdminConfig showAttribute $aSec CSI]
3  set claim [$AdminConfig showAttribute $csi claims]
4  if {[regexp CommonSecureInterop $claim] == 1} {
```

Example 5.83   Configuring CSIv2 inbound transport (Continued)

```
 5     set layers [lindex [$AdminConfig showAttribute $claim
       layers] 0]
 6     foreach aLayer $layers {
 7       if {[regexp Transportlayer $aLayer] == 1} {
 8           set supportedQOP [$AdminConfig showAttribute $aLayer
             supportedQOP]
 9           set requiredQOP [$AdminConfig showAttribute $aLayer
             requiredQOP]
10           # configure transport to SSL-required.
11           # To set to SSL-supported,
12           # $AdminConfig modify $requiredQOP {{enableProtection
             false}}
13           # $AdminConfig modify $supportedQOP {{enableProtection
             true}}
14           # To set to TCPIP, set enableProtection attribute to
             false in both requiredQOP and supportedQOP.
15           $AdminConfig modify $requiredQOP {{enableProtection
             true}}
16           $AdminConfig modify $supportedQOP {{enableProtection
             false}}
17
18           # configure SSL settings
19           set serverAuth [$AdminConfig showAttribute $aLayer
             serverAuthentication]
20           $AdminConfig modify $serverAuth {{sslConfig myNode/
             mySSLSettings}}
21
22           $AdminConfig save
23         }
24     }
25  }
```

CSIv2 Outbound Transport   Example 5.84 configures transport setting for connections initiated using OMG CSI authentication protocol.

Example 5.84   Configuring CSIv2 outbound transport

```
 1  set aSec [$AdminConfig getid /Cell:myCell/Security:/]
 2  set csi [$AdminConfig showAttribute $aSec CSI]
 3  set perform [$AdminConfig showAttribute $csi performs]
 4  if {[regexp CommonSecureInterop $perform] == 1} {
```

Example 5.84 Configuring CSIv2 outbound transport (Continued)

```
5    set layers [lindex [$AdminConfig showAttribute $perform
     layers] 0]
6    foreach aLayer $layers {
7      if {[regexp Transportlayer $aLayer] == 1} {
8          set supportedQOP [$AdminConfig showAttribute $aLayer
           supportedQOP]
9          set requiredQOP [$AdminConfig showAttribute $aLayer
           requiredQOP]
10         # configure transport to SSL-required.
11         # To set to SSL-supported,
12         # $AdminConfig modify $requiredQOP {{enableProtection
           false}}
13         # $AdminConfig modify $supportedQOP {{enableProtection
           true}}
14         # To set to TCPIP, set enableProtection attribute to
           false in both requiredQOP and supportedQOP.
15         $AdminConfig modify $requiredQOP {{enableProtection
           true}}
16         $AdminConfig modify $supportedQOP {{enableProtection
           false}}
17
18         # configure SSL settings
19         set serverAuth [$AdminConfig showAttribute $aLayer
           serverAuthentication]
20         $AdminConfig modify $serverAuth {{sslConfig myNode/
           mySSLSettings}}
21
22         $AdminConfig save
23     }
24   }
25 }
```

SAS Inbound Transport Example 5.85 configures transport setting for connections initiated using the IBM Secure Association Service (SAS) authentication protocol.

Example 5.85 Configuring SAS inbound transport

```
1  set aSec [$AdminConfig getid /Cell:myCell/Security:/]
2  set ibm [$AdminConfig showAttribute $aSec IBM]
3  set claim [$AdminConfig showAttribute $ibm claims]
4  if {[regexp SecureAssociationService $claim] == 1} {
```

Example 5.85   Configuring SAS inbound transport (Continued)

```
 5      set layers [lindex [$AdminConfig showAttribute $claim
        layers] 0]
 6      foreach aLayer $layers {
 7        if {[regexp Transportlayer $aLayer] == 1} {
 8            # configure SSL settings
 9            set serverAuth [$AdminConfig showAttribute $aLayer
              serverAuthentication]
10            $AdminConfig modify $serverAuth {{sslConfig myNode/
              mySSLSettings}}
11
12            $AdminConfig save
13        }
14      }
15  }
```

SAS Outbound Transport   Example 5.86 configures transport setting for connections initiated using the IBM SAS authentication protocol.

Example 5.86   Configuring SAS outbound transport

```
 1  set aSec [$AdminConfig getid /Cell:myCell/Security:/]
 2  set ibm [$AdminConfig showAttribute $aSec IBM]
 3  set perform [$AdminConfig showAttribute $ibm performs]
 4  if {[regexp SecureAssociationService $perform] == 1} {
 5      set layers [lindex [$AdminConfig showAttribute $perform
        layers] 0]
 6      foreach aLayer $layers {
 7        if {[regexp Transportlayer $aLayer] == 1} {
 8            # configure SSL settings
 9            set serverAuth [$AdminConfig showAttribute $aLayer
              serverAuthentication]
10            $AdminConfig modify $serverAuth {{sslConfig myNode/
              mySSLSettings}}
11
12            $AdminConfig save
13        }
14      }
15  }
```

Manage Other Environment Elements

This section contains tasks for environment configuration including Web server plug-in, virtual hosts, WebSphere variables, shared libraries, internal replication domains, and naming.

Update Web Server Plug-in

Example 5.87 shows a Jacl script to update the plug-in configuration file. The generated plugin-cfg.xml file is placed in the config directory of your WebSphere install.

Example 5.87 Updating plug-in configuration

```
 I   set pluginGen [$AdminControl completeObjectName
     type=PluginCfgGenerator,*]
 2   $AdminControl invoke $pluginGen generate "c:/WebSphere/
     DeploymentManager c:/WebSphere/DeploymentManager/config mycell
     null null plugin-cfg.xml"
```

Virtual Hosts

Example 5.88 shows a Jacl script to configure a virtual host. Lines 1–6 create a new virtual host named myVH if one does not exist. Lines 10–19 create two host aliases if there is no host alias in the virtual host. Lines 21–26 modify existing host aliases to change port from 9000 to 9010. Lines 29–33 create a new MIME entry for type application/myType. Line 34 saves the configuration.

Example 5.88 Configuring virtual host

```
 I   set aVH [$AdminConfig getid /Node:myNode/VirtualHost:myVH/]
 2   if {[llength $aVH] == 0} {
 3      # create a virtual host
 4      set aNodeParent [$AdminConfig getid /Node:myNode/]
 5      set aVH [$AdminConfig create VirtualHost $aNodeParent
         {{name myVH}}]
 6   }
 7
 8   set aliases [lindex [$AdminConfig showAttributes $aVH aliases] 0]
 9   if {[llength $aliases] == 0} {
10      # create the first host alias
11      set hostAttr [list hostname *]
12      set portAttr [list port 9010]
13      set attrs [list $hostAttr $portAttr]
14      $AdminConfig create HostAlias $aVH $attrs
15      # create the second host alias
16      set portAttr [list port 9012]
```

Example 5.88   Configuring virtual host (Continued)

```
17    set attrs [list $hostAttr $portAttr]
18    # this create command will append the second host alias entry
      into the existing list
19    $AdminConfig create HostAlias $aVH $attrs
20  } else {
21    foreach aAlias $aliases {
22      # modify existing alias to change port
23      if {[$AdminConfig showAttribute $aAlias port] == 9000} {
24        $AdminConfig modify $aAlias {{port 9010}}
25      }
26    }
27  }
28
29  # add a new MIME entry to map new extension mapping
30  set extAttr [list extensions myt]
31  set typeAttr [list type application/myType]
32  set attrs [list $extensions $type]
33  $AdminConfig create MimeEntry $aVH $attrs
34  $AdminConfig save
```

WebSphere Variables

Example 5.89 shows how to manage WebSphere variables in the node scope. Lines 1–6
create a node-level WebSphere variables file if one is not configured. Lines 9–17 look for
a WebSphere variable named MY_HOME. Lines 19–24 create a new variable named
MY_HOME if this variable is not configured. If the variable is configured, lines 27–29
modify the value of the existing WebSphere variable named MY_HOME. Line 32 saves
the configuration.

Example 5.89   Configuring WebSphere variables

```
1  set aNodeVarMap [$AdminConfig getid /Node:myNode/VariableMap:/]
2  if {[llength $aNodeVarMap] == 0} {
3    # create an empty node scope WebSphere variables file
4    set aNodeParent [$AdminConfig getid /Node:myNode/]
5    set aNodeVarMap [$AdminConfig create VariableMap $aNodeParent
       {}]
6  }
7
8  # look for WebSphere variable named MY_HOME
```

Example 5.89 Configuring WebSphere variables (Continued)

```
 9  set entries [lindex [$AdminConfig showAttributes $aNodeVarMap
    entries] 0]
10  set foundEntry false
11  if {[llength $entries] != 0} {
12      foreach aEntry $entries {
13          if {[$AdminConfig showAttribute $aEntry symbolicName] ==
            "MY_HOME"} {
14              set foundEntry $aEntry
15          }
16      }
17  }
18  if {$foundEntry == "false"} {
19      # create a WebSphere variable named MY_HOME
20      set nameAttr [list symbolicName MY_HOME]
21      set valueAttr [list value c:/home]
22      set descAttr [list description "The path to my home directory"]
23      set entryAttr [list $nameAttr $valueAttr $descAttr]
24      $AdminConfig create VariableSubstitutionEntry $aNodeVarMap
        $entryAttr
25  } else {
26      # modify MY_HOME WebSphere variable
27      set valueAttr [list value c:/home]
28      set attrs [list $valueAttr]
29      $AdminConfig modify $foundEntry $attrs
30  }
31
32  $AdminConfig save
```

Shared Libraries

Example 5.90 shows how to configure a shared library that can be used by deployed applications. Lines 1–9 create a shared library named mySharedLibrary in the server scope if one is not configured. You can create a shared library in the cell, node, or server scope. Change lines 1 and 7 to use different scope. Line 1 is to get the configuration object name of mySharedLibrary to determine whether there is an existing library for it or not. Line 7 is to identify the configuration object name of the parent object where you want to create the shared library. Lines 10–14 modify the classpath property of the existing shared library. Line 16 saves the configuration.

Example 5.90 Configuring shared library

```
 I  set aSharedLib [$AdminConfig getid /Node:myNode/Server:myServer/
    Library:mySharedLibrary/]
 2  if {[llength $aSharedLib] == 0} {
 3    # create a shared library named mySharedLibrary
 4    set nameAttr [list name mySharedLibrary]
 5    set classpathAttr [list classPath \${MY_HOME}/mylib/
      mySharedLib.jar]
 6    set attrs [list $nameAttr $classpathAttr]
 7    set aServerParent [$AdminConfig getid /Node:myNode/
      Server:myServer/]
 8    set aSharedLib [$AdminConfig create Library $aServerParent
      $attrs]
 9  } else {
10    # modify existing shared library property
11    set classpathAttr [list classPath \${MY_HOME}/mylib/
      mySharedLib.jar]
12    set attrs [list $classpathAttr]
13    $AdminConfig modify $aSharedLib $attrs]
14  }
15
16  $AdminConfig save
```

Internal Replication Domains

Example 5.91 shows a Jacl script to configure an internal replication domain. Lines 3–9 display the name of existing replicators configured in the cell scope. Lines 13–30 configure a new replicator named myReplicator. Lines 32–36 modify properties of an existing replicator. Lines 40–49 look for an existing replicator entry named myBrokerEntry. If an entry is not found, then lines 51–60 create one. Lines 63–68 configure an application server to define this replicator entry. Lines 71 and 72 modify port property for client. Line 75 saves the configuration.

Example 5.91 Configuring internal replication domain

```
 I  set aCellParent [$AdminConfig getid /Cell:myCell/]
 2  set replicators [$AdminConfig list MultibrokerDomain $aCellParent]
 3  if {[llength $replicators] != 0} {
 4    puts "Existing list of internal replication domains: "
 5    foreach aReplicator $replicators {
 6      set name [$AdminConfig showAttribute $aReplicator name]
 7      puts "  $name"
```

Example 5.91   Configuring internal replication domain (Continued)

```
 8      }
 9  }
10
11  set myReplicator [$AdminConfig getid /Cell:myCell/
    MultibrokerDomain:myReplicator/]
12  if {[llength $myReplicator] == 0} {
13      # create a replicator named myReplicator
14      puts "Create an internal replication domain named myReplicator"
15      set nameAttr [list name myReplicator]
16      set encryptTimeoutAttr [list requestTimeout 5]
17      # valid values for encryption type are DES, TRIPLE_DES, NONE
18      set encryptTypeAttr [list encryptionType NONE]
19      set drsSizeAttr [list size 10]
20      set drsPartitionAttr [list partitionOnEntry false]
21      set drsAttr [list partition [list $drsSizeAttr
        $drsPartitionAttr]]
22      set entrySerializeKindAttr [list entrySerializationKind BYTES]
23      set propertySerializeKindAttr [list propertySerializationKind
        BYTES]
24      set serializationAttr [list serialization [list
        $entrySerializeKindAttr $propertySerializeKindAttr]]
25      set poolConnectionAttr [list poolConnections false]
26      set poolSizeAttr [list size 10]
27      set poolAttr [list pooling [list $poolConnectionAttr
        $poolSizeAttr]]
28      set replicationSettingAttr [list defaultDataReplicationSettings
        [list $encryptTimeoutAttr $encryptTypeAttr $drsAttr
        $serializationAttr $poolAttr]]
29      set attrs [list $nameAttr $replicationSettingAttr]
30      set myReplicator [$AdminConfig create MultibrokerDomain
        $aCellParent $attrs]
31  } else {
32      # modify existing replicator properties
33      set replicatorSetting [$AdminConfig showAttribute $myReplicator
        defaultDataReplicationSettings]
34      $AdminConfig modify $replicatorSetting [list [list
        requestTimeout 10]]
35      set drsPartition [$AdminConfig showAttribute $replicatorSetting
        partition]
36      $AdminConfig modify $drsPartition [list [list size 15]]
37  }
```

Example 5.91   Configuring internal replication domain (Continued)

```
38
39  # check if there is existing replicator entry named myBrokerEntry
40  set replicationEntries [lindex [$AdminConfig showAttribute
    $myReplicator entries] 0]
41  set foundEntry false
42  if {[llength $replicatorEntries] != 0} {
43      foreach aReplicatorEntry $replicatorEntries {
44          if {[$AdminConfig showAttribute $aReplicatorEntry
            brokerName] == "myBrokerEntry"} {
45              set foundEntry $aReplicatorEntry
46              break
47          }
48      }
49  }
50  if {$foundEntry == "false"} {
51      # create a replicator entry named myBrokerEntry
52      set nameAttr [list brokerName myBrokerEntry]
53      set clientHostAttr [list host myBrokerHost]
54      set clientPortAttr [list port 100]
55      set brokerHostAttr [list host myBrokerHost]
56      set brokerPortAttr [list port 101]
57      set clientAttr [list clientEndPoint [list $clientHostAttr
        $clientPortAttr]]
58      set brokerAttr [list brokerEndPoint [list $brokerHostAttr
        $brokerPortAttr]]
59      set attrs [list $nameAttr $clientAttr $brokerAttr]
60      $AdminConfig create MultiBrokerRoutingEntry $myReplicator $attrs
61
62      # configure server myServer to define this replicator entry
63      set domainAttr [list domainName myReplicator]
64      set brokerAttr [list brokerName myBrokerEntry]
65      set enableAttr [list enable true]
66      set attrs [list $domainAttr $brokerAttr $enableAttr]
67      set aServer [$AdminConfig getid /Node:myNode/Server:myServer/]
68      $AdminConfig create SystemMessageServer $aServer $attrs
69  } else {
70      # modify existing replicator entry value
71      set clientEndPoint [$AdminConfig showAttribute $foundEntry
        clientEndPoint]
72      $AdminConfig modify $clientEndPoint [list [list port 100]]
```

Example 5.91   Configuring internal replication domain (Continued)

```
73  }
74
75  $AdminConfig save
```

Naming

Namespace Bindings   Example 5.92 shows how to configure various types of namespace bindings. Line 1 uses cell as the scope. Lines 3–16 configure a string type namespace binding. Lines 19–35 configure an EJB-type namespace binding to a server. Lines 37–52 configure an EJB-type name space binding to a cluster. Lines 54–64 configure a CORBA-type namespace binding. Lines 66–76 configure an indirect-type namespace binding. Line 78 saves the configuration.

Example 5.92   Configuring namespace binding

```
 1  set aCellParent [$AdminConfig getid /Cell:myCell/]
 2  # string type name space binding
 3  set aBinding1 [$AdminConfig getid /Cell:myCell/
    StringNameSpaceBinding:myBinding1/]
 4  if {[llength $aBinding1] == 0} {
 5     # create a string type name space binding
 6     set nameAttr [list name myBinding1]
 7     set nameSpaceAttr [list nameInNameSpace myBindings/myString]
 8     set bindAttr [list stringToBind "String to bind"]
 9     set attrs [list $nameAttr $nameSpaceAttr $bindAttr]
10     set aBinding1 [$AdminConfig create StringNameSpaceBinding
       $aCellParent $attrs]
11  } else {
12     # modify existing name space binding
13     set bindAttr [list stringToBind "new string to bind"]
14     set attrs [list $bindAttr]
15     $AdminConfig modify $aBinding1 $attrs
16  }
17
18  # EJB type name space binding
19  set aBinding2 [$AdminConfig getid /Cell:myCell/
    EjbNameSpaceBinding:myBinding2/]
20  if {[llength $aBinding2] == 0} {
21     # create an EJB type name space binding to a server
22     set nameAttr [list name myBinding2]
23     set nameSpaceAttr [list nameInNameSpace myBindings/myEJB]
```

Example 5.92   Configuring namespace binding (Continued)

```
24      set nodeAttr [list applicationNodeName myNode]
25      set serverNameAttr [list applicationServerName myServer]
26      set locationAttr [list bindingLocation SINGLESERVER]
27      set jndiNameAttr [list ejbJndiName ejb/myEJB]
28      set attrs [list $nameAttr $nameSpaceAttr $nodeAttr
        $serverNameAttr $locationAttr $jndiNameAttr]
29      set aBinding2 [$AdminConfig create EjbNameSpaceBinding
        $aCellParent $attrs]
30    } else {
31      # modify existing EJB type name space binding
32      set jndiNameAttr [list ejbJndiName ejb/myEJB]
33      set attrs [list $jndiName]
34      $AdminConfig modify $aBinding2 $attrs
35    }
36
37    set aBinding3 [$AdminConfig getid /Cell:myCell/
      EjbNameSpaceBinding:myBinding3/]
38    if {[llength $aBinding3] == 0} {
39      # create an EJB type name space binding to a cluster
40      set nameAttr [list name myBinding3]
41      set nameSpaceAttr [list nameInNameSpace myBindings/myEJB]
42      set serverNameAttr [list applicationServerName myCluster]
43      set locationAttr [list bindingLocation SERVERCLUSTER]
44      set jndiNameAttr [list ejbJndiName ejb/myEJB]
45      set attrs [list $nameAttr $nameSpaceAttr $serverNameAttr
        $locationAttr $jndiNameAttr]
46      set aBinding3 [$AdminConfig create EjbNameSpaceBinding
        $aCellParent $attrs]
47    } else {
48      # modify existing EJB type name space binding
49      set jndiNameAttr [list ejbJndiName ejb/myEJB]
50      set attrs [list $jndiName]
51      $AdminConfig modify $aBinding3 $attrs
52    }
53
54    # CORBA type name space binding
55    set aBinding4 [$AdminConfig getid /Cell:myCell/
      CORBAObjectNameSpaceBinding:myBinding4/]
56    if {[llength $aBinding4] == 0} {
57      # create a CORBA type name space binding
```

Example 5.92   Configuring namespace binding (Continued)

```
58      set nameAttr [list name myBinding4]
59      set nameSpaceAttr [list nameInNameSpace myBindings/myCORBA]
60      set urlAttr [list corbanameUrl corbaname:iiop:somehost
        .somecompany.com:2809#stuff/MyCORBAOjbect]
61      set contextAttr [list federatedContext false]
62      set attrs [list $nameAttr $nameSpaceAttr $urlAttr $contextAttr]
63      set aBinding4 [$AdminConfig create CORBAObjectNameSpaceBinding
        $aCellParent $attrs]
64   }
65
66   # indirect type name space binding
67   set aBinding5 [$AdminConfig getid /Cell:myCell/
     IndirectLookupNameSpaceBinding:myBinding5/]
68   if {[llength $aBinding5] == 0} {
69      # create an indirect type name space binding
70      set nameAttr [list name myBinding5]
71      set nameSpaceAttr [list nameInNameSpace myBindings/myIndirect]
72      set urlAttr [list providerURL corbaloc::myCompany.com:9809/
        NameServiceServerRoot]
73      set jndiNameAttr [list jndiName jndi/name/for/EJB]
74      set attrs [list $nameAttr $nameSpaceAttr $urlAttr
        $jndiNameAttr]
75      set aBinding5 [$AdminConfig create
        IndirectLookupNameSpaceBinding $aCellParent $attrs]
76   }
77
78   $AdminConfig save
```

CORBA Naming Service Users   Example 5.93 shows a Jacl script to configure a CORBA naming service user. Lines 3–16 list existing CORBA naming service users for each of the following administrative authorities: Cos Naming Read, Cos Naming Write, Cos Naming Create, and Cos Naming Delete. Lines 17–39 look for an existing user named myCosNamingReadUser with Cos Naming Read authority. If this user is not found, then line 44 creates a new user. It is assumed that the user name myCosNamingReadUser exists in the active user registry. Lines 48–57 delete all the myCosNamingReadUser users regardless of the granted authority level. Line 59 saves the configuration.

Example 5.93   Configuring CORBA naming service user

```
1   set roleAssignExts [$AdminConfig list RoleAssignmentExt]
2   # list all CORBA naming service users
```

Example 5.93   Configuring CORBA naming service user (Continued)

```
3   foreach aRoleAssignExt $roleAssignExts {
4     set secRoleId [$AdminConfig showAttribute $aRoleAssignExt role]
5     # get the role name
6     set secRoleName [$AdminConfig showAttribute $secRoleId
      roleName]
7     if {$secRoleName == "CosNamingCreate" || $secRoleName ==
      "CosNamingDelete" || $secRoleName == "CosNamingRead" ||
      $secRoleName == "CosNamingWrite"} {
8         puts "Users with $secRoleName authority: "
9         set users [lindex [$AdminConfig showAttribute
          $aRoleAasignExt users] 0]
10        if {[llength $users] != 0} {
11            foreach aUser $users {
12                puts [$AdminConfig showAttribute $aUser name]
13            }
14        }
15    }
16  }
17  set username myCosNamingReadUser
18  # valid roles are CosNamingRead, CosNamingWrite, CosNamingCreate,
    CosNamginDelete
19  set rolePick CosNamingRead
20  # check whether user myCosNamingReadUser with Cos Naming Read
    authority already exists
21  set found false
22  set foundRoleAssignExt ""
23  foreach aRoleAssignExt $roleAssignExts {
24    set secRoleId [$AdminConfig showAttribute $aRoleAssignExt role]

25    # get the role name
26    set secRoleName [$AdminConfig showAttribute $secRoleId
      roleName]
27    if {$secRoleName == $rolePick} {
28        set foundRoleAssignExt $aRoleAssignExt
29        set users [lindex [$AdminConfig showAttribute
          $aRoleAssignExt users] 0]
30        foreach aUser $users {
31            # check if user already exists
32            if {[$AdminConfig showAttribute $aUser name] ==
              $username} {
33                set found true
```

Example 5.93   Configuring CORBA naming service user (Continued)

```
34              break
35          }
36      }
37      break
38   }
39 }
40
41 if {$found == "false"} {
42     # assuming myCosNamingReadUser is included in the active user
       registry
43     puts "Create a new user $username with $rolePick authority"
44     $AdminConfig create UserExt $foundRoleAssignExt [list [list
       name $username]]
45 }
46
47 # Found all the myCosNamingReadUser users and delete them
48 set deleteUser myCosNamingReadUser
49 foreach aRoleAssignExt $roleAssignExts {
50     set users [lindex [$AdminConfig showAttribute $aRoleAssignExt
       users] 0]
51     foreach aUser $users {
52         if {[$AdminConfig showAttribute $aUser name] ==
           $deleteUser} {
53             puts "Removing $aUser"
54             $AdminConfig remove $aUser
55         }
56     }
57 }
58
59 $AdminConfig save
```

CORBA Naming Service Groups   Example 5.94 shows a Jacl script to configure CORBA naming service groups. Lines 3–16 list existing CORBA naming service groups for each of the following administrative authorities: Cos Naming Read, Cos Naming Write, Cos Naming Create, and Cos Naming Delete. Lines 17–39 look for an existing group named myCosNamingDeleteGroup with Cos Naming Delete authority. If there is no such group, then line 44 creates a new group. It is assumed that the group name myCosNamingDeleteGroup exists in the active user registry. Lines 48–57 delete all the myCosNamingDeleteGroup groups regardless of the granted authority. Line 59 saves the configuration.

Example 5.94   Configuring CORBA naming service group

```
 1  set roleAssignExts [$AdminConfig list RoleAssignmentExt]
 2  # list all CORBA naming service groups
 3  foreach aRoleAssignExt $roleAssignExts {
 4     set secRoleId [$AdminConfig showAttribute $aRoleAssignExt role]
 5     # get the role name
 6     set secRoleName [$AdminConfig showAttribute $secRoleId
        roleName]
 7     if {$secRoleName == "CosNamingCreate" || $secRoleName ==
        "CosNamingDelete" || $secRoleName == "CosNamingRead" ||
        $secRoleName == "CosNamingWrite"} {
 8        puts "Groups with $secRoleName authority: "
 9        set groups [lindex [$AdminConfig showAttribute
           $aRoleAasignExt groups] 0]
10        if {[llength $groups] != 0} {
11           foreach aGroup $groups {
12              puts [$AdminConfig showAttribute $aGroup name]
13           }
14        }
15     }
16  }
17  set groupname myCosNamingDeleteGroup
18  # valid roles are CosNamingRead, CosNamingWrite, CosNamingCreate,
    CosNamginDelete
19  set rolePick CosNamingDelete
20  # check whether group myCosNamingDeleteGroup with Cos Naming
    Delete authority already exists
21  set found false
22  set foundRoleAssignExt ""
23  foreach aRoleAssignExt $roleAssignExts {
24     set secRoleId [$AdminConfig showAttribute $aRoleAssignExt role]
25     # get the role name
26     set secRoleName [$AdminConfig showAttribute $secRoleId
        roleName]
27     if {$secRoleName == $rolePick} {
28        set foundRoleAssignExt $aRoleAssignExt
29        set groups [lindex [$AdminConfig showAttribute
           $aRoleAssignExt groups] 0]
30        foreach aGroup $groups {
31           # check if group already exists
32           if {[$AdminConfig showAttribute $aGroup name] ==
              $groupname} {
```

Example 5.94   Configuring CORBA naming service group (Continued)

```
33                    set found true
34                    break
35                }
36            }
37        break
38        }
39  }
40
41  if {$found == "false"} {
42      # assuming myCosNamingDeleteGroup is included in the active
        user registry
43      puts "Create a new group $groupname with $rolePick authority"
44      $AdminConfig create GroupExt $foundRoleAssignExt [list [list
        name $groupname]]
45  }
46
47  # Found all the myCosNamingDeleteGroup group name and delete them
48  set deleteGroup myCosNamingDeleteGroup
49  foreach aRoleAssignExt $roleAssignExts {
50      set groups [lindex [$AdminConfig showAttribute $aRoleAssignExt
        groups] 0]
51      foreach aGroup $groups {
52          if {[$AdminConfig showAttribute $aGroup name] ==
            $deleteGroup} {
53              puts "Removing $aGroup"
54              $AdminConfig remove $aGroup
55          }
56      }
57  }
58
59  $AdminConfig save
```

Manage System Administration

This section contains tasks to manage cells, deployment manager, nodes, and node agents.

Cell

Example 5.95 configures a cell. Line 1 queries for the cell configuration object. Line 3 modifies a property in the cell configuration object. Lines 6–11 create a custom property. Line 13 saves the configuration.

Example 5.95 Configuring cell

```
 1  set aCell [$AdminConfig getid /Cell:myCell/]
 2  # modify cellDiscoveryProtocol to use UDP
 3  $AdminConfig modify $aCell {{cellDiscoveryProtocol UDP}}
 4
 5  # create a custom property
 6  set nameAttr [list name property1]
 7  set valueAttr [list value property1Value]
 8  set requireAttr [list required false]
 9  set typeAttr [list type java.lang.String]
10  set attrs [list $nameAttr $valueAttr $requireAttr $typeAttr]
11  $AdminConfig create TypedProperty $aCell $attrs
12
13  $AdminConfig save
```

Deployment Manager

This section contains tasks to perform configuration and run-time operation on deployment manager.

Configuration   The configuration tasks for deployment manager include ORB service, administrative services, diagnostic trace service, logging and tracing, custom services, process definition, end points, and HTTP transports. All of these tasks except for logging and tracing are provided in section Manage Application Servers. For logging and tracing tasks, refer to section Logs and Traces for scripting examples.

Run Time   Example 5.96 stops the deployment manager. If the current scripting client is connected to the deployment manager that you are stopping, you will no longer be able to use this instance of the scripting client. For a task to view run-time read-only information, refer to Example 5.24. You can modify the task to obtain the run-time object name of a deployment manager.

Example 5.96 Stopping deployment manager

```
set dmgr [$AdminControl queryNames type=Server,name=dmgr,*]
$AdminControl invoke $dmgr stop
```

Nodes

This section contains tasks to perform configuration and run-time operation on nodes.

Get a List of Nodes   Run the following command to list all the nodes in the configuration:

```
$AdminConfig list Node
```

Remove a Node from the Cell   Example 5.97 shows a Jacl script to remove a node from the configuration.

Example 5.97   Removing a node

```
set aNode [$AdminConfig getid /Node:myNode/]
$AdminConfig remove $aNode
$AdminConfig save
```

Synchronize a Node   Example 5.98 shows a Jacl script to synchronize a node's repository with the cell repository.

Example 5.98   Synchronizing a node

```
set aRunningNodeSync [$AdminControl queryNames
type=NodeSync,node=myNode,process=nodeagent,*]
$AdminControl invoke $aRunningNodeSync sync
```

Full Synchronize   Example 5.99 shows a Jacl script to perform a full synchronization of a node's repository. To perform a full synchronization of the repository in the deployment manager, replace nodeagent with dmgr as the process name and mynode with the node name of your deployment manager as the node name in the queryNames commands.

Example 5.99   Full synchronization of a node

```
set aRunningConfigRepo [$AdminControl queryNames
type=ConfigRepository,node=myNode,process=nodeagent,*]
$AdminControl invoke $aRunningConfigRepo refresh RepositoryEpoch
set aRunningNodeSync [$AdminControl queryNames
type=NodeSync,node=myNode,process=nodeagent,*]
$AdminControl invoke $aRunningNodeSync sync
```

Stop a Node   Example 5.100 shows a Jacl script to stop a node.

Example 5.100   Stopping a node

```
set aRunningNode [$AdminControl queryNames
type=Server,node=myNode,processType=NodeAgent,*]
$AdminControl invoke $aRunningNode stop
```

Modify Configuration of a Node   This section provides task scripts to configure general and custom properties of a node configuration object. Example 5.101 shows a Jacl script to configure the discovery protocol property.

Example 5.101   Configuring general property of a node

```
set aNode [$AdminConfig getid /Node:myNode/]
# valid values for discovery protocol are UDP, TCP, and MULTICAST
$AdminConfig modify $aNode [list [list discoveryProtocol TCP]]
$AdminConfig save
```

Example 5.102 shows a Jacl script to configure custom properties of a node. Lines 6–11 list all existing properties. Lines 14–20 check if there is an existing property named property1. Lines 23–30 create a new property named property1 if property1 is not configured. Line 32 saves the configuration.

Example 5.102   Configuring custom properties of a node

```
 I   set aNode [$AdminConfig getid /Node:myNode/]
 2
 3   set props [lindex [$AdminConfig showAttribute $aNode
     properties] 0]
 4
 5   # list all properties
 6   if {[llength $props] != 0} {
 7      puts "Existing properties:"
 8      foreach aProp $props {
 9          puts [$AdminConfig showall $aProp]
10      }
11   }
12
13   # look for property named property1
14   set found false
15   foreach aProp $props {
16      if {[$AdminConfig showAttribute $aProp name] == "property1"} {
17          set found $aProp
18          break
19      }
20   }
21
22   # if property1 is not found, create one
23   if {$found == "false"} {
24      puts "Create a new property"
25      set nameAttr [list name property1]
26      set valueAttr [list value property1Value]
27      set attrs [list $nameAttr $valueAttr]
```

Example 5.102 Configuring custom properties of a node (Continued)

```
28      set prop [$AdminConfig create Property $aNode $attrs]
29      puts [$AdminConfig showall $prop]
30  }
31
32  $AdminConfig save
```

Node Agents

This section contains tasks to perform configuration and run-time operation on node agents.

Get a List of Node Agents   Run the following command to get a list of node agents:

```
$AdminConfig list NodeAgent
```

Stop a Node Agent   Example 5.103 shows a Jacl script to stop a node agent.

Example 5.103 Stopping a node agent

```
set aRunningNodeAgent [$AdminControl queryNames
type=NodeAgent,node=myNode,*]
$AdminControl invoke $aRunningNodeAgent stopNode
```

Restart a Node Agent   Example 5.104 shows a Jacl script to restart a node agent.

Example 5.104 Restarting a node agent

```
set aRunningNodeAgent [$AdminControl queryNames
type=NodeAgent,node=myNode,*]
$AdminControl invoke $aRunningNodeAgent restart {true true}
```

Restart All Servers on a Node Agent   Example 5.105 shows a Jacl script to restart all servers on a node. Line 1 gets hold of all the running server MBeans. Lines 2–5 stop each running server. Lines 7–10 start the servers again.

Example 5.105 Restarting all servers on a node

```
1   set runningServers [$AdminControl queryNames
    type=Server,node=myNode,type=ManagedProcess,*]
2   foreach aRunningServer $runningServers {
3       set name [$AdminControl getAttribute $aRunningServer name]
4       $AdminControl stopServer $name myNode
5   }
6
7   foreach aRunningServer $runningServers {
```

Example 5.105   Restarting all servers on a node (Continued)

```
 8      set name [$AdminControl getAttribute $aRunningServer name]
 9      $AdminControl startServer $name myNode
10  }
```

Modify Configuration of a Node Agent   This section provides task scripts to configure file transfer service and file synchronization service properties. For other node agent properties, follow similar scripts provided in the section Manage Application Servers.

Example 5.106 shows a Jacl script to configure the file transfer service properties. Line 4 obtains the file transfer service configuration object from the node agent for the node myNode. Lines 7–13 modify two general properties. Lines 16–21 create a custom property. Line 23 saves the configuration.

Example 5.106   Configuring file transfer service properties

```
 1   set aNodeServer [$AdminConfig getid /Node:myNode/Server
     :nodeagent/]
 2   # get configuration object for NodeAgent
 3   set aNodeAgent [$AdminConfig list NodeAgent $aNodeServer]
 4   set aFileTransferService [$AdminConfig showAttribute $aNodeAgent
     fileTransferService]
 5
 6   # modify general properties
 7   set retriesCountAttr [list retriesCount 2]
 8   # wait time is specified in number seconds
 9   set retriesWaitAttr [list retryWaitTime 5]
10   set attrs [list $retriesCountAttr $retriesWaitAttr]
11   puts "Modify general properties for file transfer service"
12   $AdminConfig modify $aFileTransferService $attrs
13   puts [$AdminConfig show $aFileTransferService]
14
15   # add a new custom property
16   puts "Create a new property"
17   set nameAttr [list name property1]
18   set valueAttr [list value property1Value]
19   set attrs [list $nameAttr $valueAttr]
20   set prop [$AdminConfig create Property $aFileTransferService
     $attrs]
21   puts [$AdminConfig showall $prop]
22
23   $AdminConfig save
```

Example 5.107 shows a Jacl script to configure file synchronization service properties. Line 4 obtains the file synchronization service configuration object from the node agent for the node myNode. Lines 7–13 modify two general properties. Lines 16–21 create a custom property. Line 23 saves the configuration.

Example 5.107 *Configuring file synchronization service properties*

```
 1  set aNodeServer [$AdminConfig getid /Node:myNode/Server
    :nodeagent/]
 2  # get configuration object for NodeAgent
 3  set aNodeAgent [$AdminConfig list NodeAgent $aNodeServer]
 4  set aFileSyncService [$AdminConfig showAttribute $aNodeAgent
    fileSynchronizationService]
 5
 6  # modify general properties
 7  set synchOnStartupAttr [list synchOnServerStartup true]
 8  # synchronization interval is in number of minutes
 9  set synchIntervalAttr [list synchInterval 2]
10  set attrs [list $synchOnStartupAttr $synchIntervalAttr]
11  puts "Modify general properties of a file synchronization service"
12  $AdminConfig modify $aFileSyncService $attrs
13  puts [$AdminConfig show $aFileSyncService]
14
15  # add a new custom property
16  puts "Create a new property"
17  set nameAttr [list name property1]
18  set valueAttr [list value property1Value]
19  set attrs [list $nameAttr $valueAttr]
20  set prop [$AdminConfig create Property $aFileSyncService $attrs]
21  puts [$AdminConfig showall $prop]
22
23  $AdminConfig save
```

Troubleshooting

This section contains tasks to configure log, trace, and performance monitoring settings to aid in debugging problems.

Logs and Traces

Diagnostic Trace   Example 5.108 shows a Jacl script to configure tracing information of a server. Lines 1–7 modify the configuration property. Lines 9–13 modify the run-time property. Line 4 shows the syntax of setting up multiple component paths to trace. Line 12 shows the syntax of setting up a single component path to trace. The change in the run-time property in line 12 is not persistent.

Example 5.108   Configuring diagnostic trace

```
 I  # modify configuration trace spec property of diagnostic trace
    service for a server
 2  set aServer [$AdminConfig getid /Server:myServer/]
 3  set aTraceService [$AdminConfig list TraceService $aServer]
 4  set specAttr [list startupTraceSpecification
    com.ibm.ws.management.*=all=enabled:com.ibm.websphere.management.
    *=all=enabled]
 5  set attrs [list $specAttr]
 6  $AdminConfig modify $aTraceService $attrs
 7  $AdminConfig save
 8
 9  # modify runtime trace spec property for running object myServer
10  set aRunningTraceService [$AdminControl queryNames
    type=TraceService,process=myServer,*]
II  if {[llength $aRunningTraceService] != 0} {
12      $AdminControl setAttribute $aRunningTraceService
        traceSpecification com.ibm.ws.management.*=all=enabled
13  }
```

Client Trace   Run the following AdminControl command to enable client trace without restarting the scripting client:

```
$AdminControl trace
   com.ibm.ws.management.*=all=enabled:com.ibm.websphere.management
   .*=all=enabled
```

JVM Logs   Example 5.109 shows how to modify configuration settings of JVM System.out and System.err logs for an application server.

Example 5.109   Configuring JVM logs

```
 I  # modify configuration settings of JVM System.out and System.err
    logs for a server
 2  set aServer [$AdminConfig getid /Node:myNode/Server:myServer/]
 3  set outputStream [$AdminConfig showAttribute $aServer
    outputStreamRedirect]
 4  # change the log file name
 5  set fileNameAttr [list fileName \${SERVER_LOG_ROOT}/out.log]
```

Example 5.109   Configuring JVM logs (Continued)

```
 6  # change the rotation file size to 2 MB
 7  set rolloverSizeAttr [list rolloverSize 2]
 8  # change rotation policy based on time
 9  set rolloverTypeAttr [list rolloverType TIME]
10  set rolloverPeriodAttr [list rolloverPeriod 12]
11  set baseHourAttr [list baseHour 24]
12  # suppress formatting
13  set formatAttr [list formatWrites false]
14  set attrs [list $fileNameAttr $rolloverSizeAttr $rolloverTypeAttr
    $rolloverPeriodAttr $baseHourAttr $formatAttr]
15  $AdminConfig modify $outputStream $attrs
16
17  set errorStream [$AdminConfig showAttribute $aServer
    errorStreamRedirect]
18  # change the log file name
19  set fileNameAttr [list fileName \${SERVER_LOG_ROOT}/err.log]
20  # change number of history log files
21  set backupAttr [list maxNumberOfBackupFiles 2]
22  set attrs [list $fileNameAttr $backupAttr]
23  $AdminConfig modify $errorStream $attrs
24
25  $AdminConfig save
```

Process Logs   Example 5.110 shows a Jacl script to configure the file settings to which stdout and stderr streams write.

Example 5.110   Configuring process logs

```
 1  # modify configuration setting for files that stdout and stderr
    streams write
 2  set aServer [$AdminConfig getid /Node:myNode/Server:myServer/]
 3  set outputRedirect [$AdminConfig list OutputRedirect $aServer]
 4  set errAttr [list stderrFilename \ ${SERVER_LOG_ROOT}/
    nativeStderr.log]
 5  set outAttr [list stdoutFilename \$ {SERVER_LOG_ROOT}/
    nativeStdout.log]
 6  set attrs [list $errAttr $outAttr]
 7  $AdminConfig modify $outputRedirect $attrs
 8  $AdminConfig save
```

IBM Service Logs   Example 5.111 shows a Jacl script to configure the settings for the IBM service log, which is also known as the activity log.

Example 5.111   Configuring activity log

```
 1   set aServer [$AdminConfig getid /Node:myNode/Server:myServer/]
 2   set loggingService [$AdminConfig list RASLoggingService $aServer]
 3   # change to disable correlation ID
 4   set correlationAttr [list enableCorrelationId false]
 5   # change message filtering to log service, warning, error
 6   set filterAttr [list messageFilterLevel SERVICE]
 7   # change the service log size to 4 MB
 8   set sizeAttr [list size 4]
 9   set attrs [list $correlationAttr $filterAttr]
10   $AdminConfig modify $loggingService $attrs
11   set serviceLog [$AdminConfig showAttribute $loggingService
     serviceLog]
12   set attrs [list $sizeAttr]
13   $AdminConfig modify $serviceLog $attrs
14   $AdminConfig save
```

Configuration Problems

Example 5.112 shows a Jacl script to configure document validation and perform a configuration validation. Valid validation levels are none, low, medium, high, and highest. Validation results are logged in the default wsadmin.valout file located in the logs directory of your WebSphere install directory. The validation report location property is configurable in the wsadmin.properties file. Each configuration problem logged in the report contains the severity of the problem, the problem configuration type and object name, and a descriptive error message. The following is an example of a configuration problem error message:

```
WASX7195I: Severity 1; line 0; target
"Websphere:_Websphere_Config_Data_Type=EndPoint,_Websphere_Config
_Data_Id=cells/BAMBIENetwork/nodes/
BAMBIE:serverindex.xml#EndPoint_1070689358017";
CHKW2517E: The port assignment, host , port 7873, of end point
DRS_CLIENT_ADDRESS in server entry clusterMember1, is the same
as another port assignment.
```

Example 5.112   Configuring document validation

```
$AdminConfig setValidationLevel MEDIUM
$AdminConfig setCrossDocumentValidationEnabled true
$AdminConifg validate
```

PMI Request Metrics

Example 5.113 shows a Jacl script to configure PMI request metrics. Line 1 gets hold of a PMI request metric configuration object. Lines 2–7 modify its general properties. Lines 10–19 list the existing set of filters and the filter values associated with each filter. Line 21 saves the configuration.

Example 5.113   Configuring PMI request metrics

```
 I  set aPMI [$AdminConfig list PMIRequestMetrics]
 2  # change to enable PMI request metrics
 3  set enableAttr [list enable true]
 4  # change to have full detail trace
 5  set traceAttr [list traceLevel DEBUG]
 6  set attrs [list $enableAttr $traceAttr]
 7  $AdminConfig modify $aPMI $attrs
 8
 9  # list existing filters
10  set filters [lindex [$AdminConfig showAttribute $aPMI filters] 0]
11  foreach aFilter $filters {
12      puts "Filter type: [$AdminConfig showAttribute $aFilter type]"
13      puts "   enabled: [$AdminConfig showAttribute $aFilter enable]"
14      set filterValues [lindex [$AdminConfig showAttribute $aFilter
        filterValues] 0]
15      foreach aFilterValue $filterValues {
16          puts "   filter value: [$AdminConfig showAttribute
            $aFilterValue value]"
17          puts "      enable: [$AdminConfig showAttribute
            $aFilterValue enable]"
18      }
19  }
20
21  $AdminConfig save
```

ONLINE INTERACTIVE HELP

The scripting client provides general and dynamic help on using the tool and its commands. You can use the online help for the running objects to help you in writing your scripts with the AdminControl commands. There are `help` commands provided in each scripting object to obtain general help and specific help on each command. Using the AdminConfig object as an example, the following help command

In Jacl:

```
$AdminConfig help
```

In Jython:

```
print AdminConfig.help()
```

returns the static help information on all the commands available in the AdminConfig object. To get help on a specific command, you can provide the command name as an argument to the `help` command, for example, running

In Jacl:

```
$AdminConfig help create
```

In Jython:

```
print AdminConfig.help('create')
```

results in the following help information for the `create` command:

```
WASX7054I: Method: create

    Arguments: type, parent, attributes

    Description: Create a configuration object of the type named by
    "type", the parent named by "parent", using the attributes
    supplied by "attributes."

    Method: create

    Arguments: type, parent, attributes, parent attribute name,

    Description: Create a configuration object of the type named by
    "type", the parent named by "parent", using the attributes
    supplied by "attributes" and the attribute name in the parent
    given by "parent attribute name"
```

The same set of `help` commands is available in AdminControl and AdminApp objects. For AdminApp object, help is also available for the installation options. To get help on a specific option, you can provide the option name as an argument to the `help` command, for example, running

In Jacl:

```
$AdminApp help update.ignore.old
```

In Jython:

```
print AdminApp.help('update.ignore.old')
```

results in the following online help information:

```
WASX7367I: "update.ignore.old" option; this option specifies
    that when an application is updated, the bindings from the
    the old version are ignored during the reinstall operation.
    This option only has meaning if the "update" option is
    specified; otherwise it is ignored.
```

There is also a separate Help scripting object that provides general help, online information about the running MBeans, and help on messages. Running the help command on this Help object provides the following output:

```
WASX7028I: The Help object has two purposes:

     First, provide general help information for the the objects
supplied by wsadmin for scripting: Help, AdminApp, AdminConfig, and
AdminControl.

     Second, provide a means to obtain interface information about
MBeans running in the system.  For this purpose, a variety of
commands are available to get information about the operations,
attributes, and other interface information about particular
MBeans.

     The following commands are supported by Help; more detailed
information about each of these commands is available by using the
"help" command of Help and supplying the name of the command as an
argument.

attributes      given an MBean, returns help for attributes
operations      given an MBean, returns help for operations
constructors    given an MBean, returns help for constructors
description     given an MBean, returns help for description
notifications   given an MBean, returns help for notifications
classname       given an MBean, returns help for classname
all             given an MBean, returns help for all the above
help            returns this help text
AdminControl    returns general help text for the AdminControl object
AdminConfig     returns general help text for the AdminConfig object
AdminApp        returns general help text for the AdminApp object
wsadmin         returns general help text for the wsadmin script
                    launcher
message         given a message id, returns explanation and user action
                    message
```

As shown in the general help output, the commands to get online help information on the running MBeans are **all**, **attributes**, **classname**, **constructors**, **description**, **notification**, and **operations**. You can obtain individual command help for each of these commands by running   .

In Jacl:

```
$Help help commandName
```

In Jython:

```
print Help.help(commandName)
```

For example,

In Jacl:

```
$Help help operations
```

In Jython:

```
print Help.help('operations')
```

All seven commands require a running MBean object name as their argument. For the `operations` command, a second argument can be provided to obtain more detailed help on a specific operation. For example,

In Jacl:

```
set runningAppManager [$AdminControl queryNames
    type=ApplicationManager,process=server1,*]
$Help attributes $runningAppManager
$Help operations $runningAppManager
$Help operations $runnginAppManager stopApplication
```

In Jython:

```
runningAppManager =
AdminControl.queryNames('type=ApplicationManager,process=
    server1,*')
print Help.attributes(runningAppManager)
print Help.operations(runningAppManager)
print Help.operations(runnginAppManager, 'stopApplication')
```

Another useful command in the Help scripting object is the `message` command. The `message` command is provided as an aid to understand the probable cause and solution to the problem described in a warning or error message. For example, you receive a WASX7115E error when running the AdminApp `install` command to install an application. Running the following `message` command on this message identifier,

In Jacl:

```
$Help message WASX7115E
```

In Jython:

```
print Help.message('WASX7115E')
```

results in the following output:

```
Explanation: wsadmin failed to read an ear file when preparing
    to copy it to a temporary location for AdminApp processing.
User action: Examine the wsadmin.traceout log file to
    determine the problem; there may be file permission
    problems.
```

The user action specifies the recommended action to correct the problem. It is important to understand that in some cases the user action might not be able to provide corrective actions to cover all the possible causes of an error. It is an aid to provide you with information to troubleshoot a problem.

PROBLEM DETERMINATION USING WSADMIN

Wsadmin Trace Log

If you receive an error when running a script or a command with wsadmin, the top-level error message is displayed at the command prompt. Additional diagnostic error information is reported in the default wsadmin.traceout file located in the logs directory of your WebSphere install. If you have changed the wsadmin trace log file location, then the diagnostic information is logged in the specified log file. The additional information logged includes the stack trace where the error is thrown and the nested error message and its stack traces if any. If the error is instantiated from WebSphere, the error message includes a message identifier such as WASX7115E. You can use the message command in the Help object to find out more about this error. Refer to section Online Interactive Help for a message command example.

Run-Time Log

The wsadmin trace log provides the stack trace for any reported error. It also contains other trace and logging information for the client codes. If the reported error is originated from the WebSphere server run time, more detailed information regarding this error is provided in server log files. There are two types of logs for each server process. They are JVM logs and process logs. The default files for JVM logs are logs/*serverName*/SystemOut.log and logs/*serverName*/SystemErr.log in your WebSphere install. The default files for process logs are logs/*serverName*/native_stdout.log and logs/*serverName*/native_stderr.log in your

WebSphere install. These file name properties are configurable. Consult the appropriate logs if you have changed these log file properties. For example, if you are using wsadmin to connect to the deployment manager process, the logs files are logs/dmgr/SystemOut.log, logs/dmgr/SystemErr.log, logs/dmgr/native_stdout.log, and logs/dmgr/native_stderr.log in your deployment manager machine. If you are using your deployment manager machine to connect to a managed server, the server log files are located in the node machine where this managed server resides. If your managed server is server1, then the log files are logs/ server1/SystemOut.log, logs/server1/SystemErr.log, logs/server1/native_stdout.log, and logs/server1/native_stderr.log.

Configuration Validation

If a reported error is on configuration, you can perform a configuration validation to learn more about the problems that exist in the current configuration. Refer to section Configuration Problems on how to perform a configuration validation and view the validation report.

COMMON ADMIN SCENARIOS USING WSADMIN

Two end-to-end scenarios are provided to show a potentially useful sequence of common actions using the scripting client wsadmin.

Scenario 1—Install and Start an Application on a New Server

Example 5.114 shows a Jacl script to provide an end-to-end scenario for creating a new server and installing an application on the new server. Lines 1–5 set up four values to be used for the rest of the script. The values are node name, server name, application name, and application file name. Lines 7–21 perform error checking on the provided server and node names. Lines 23–26 create a new server. Lines 29–36 perform error checking on the provided application name. You can provide an empty string as the application name if you want to use the display name of the application file or the application file name as the default application name. Lines 39–43 perform error checking on the application file name. Lines 46–52 install a new application on the newly created server. Notice that in lines 49–52 the appname option is not included if the application name is an empty string. Line 55 saves the configuration. Lines 58–70 check for the existence of a NodeSync MBean and perform node synchronization if the MBean is present and the property to perform node synchronization when starting a server is disabled. Line 74 starts the server and its installed application.

Example 5.114   Scenario 1: Install and start an application on a new server

```
 1   # Initialize global variables to be used in creating server and
     installing application. Change these values to customerize for
     your environment.
 2   set nodeName myNode
```

Example 5.114 Scenario 1: Install and start an application on a new server (Continued)

```
 3  set serverName myServer
 4  set appName myApp
 5  set earFile /myEar/myApp.ear
 6
 7  # check if server of the same name already exists
 8  puts "Check if a server with the name $serverName already exists"
 9  set serverObject [$AdminConfig getid /Node:$nodeName/
    Server:$serverName/]
10  if {[llength $serverObject] != 0} {
11      puts "Error: server $serverName already exists on node
        $nodeName. Rerun the script with a different server and/or
        node name."
12      exit
13  }
14
15  # check if this is an existing node name
16  puts "Check if there is an existing node $nodeName"
17  set nodeObject [$AdminConfig getid /Node:$nodeName/]
18  if {[llength $nodeObject] == 0} {
19      puts "Error: node $nodeName does not exist in the current cell"
20      exit
21  }
22
23  # use default template to create the new server
24  puts "Creating a new server $serverName"
25  set attrs [list [list name $serverName]]
26  set myServerObject [$AdminConfig create Server $nodeObject $attrs]
27
28  # check if application with the same name already exists
29  if {[llength $appName] != 0} {
30      puts "Check if application with the same name $appName already
        exists"
31      set existingApps [$AdminApp list]
32      if {[regexp $appName $existingApps] == 1} {
33          puts "Error: application with the same name $appName already
            exists"
34          exit
35      }
36  }
37
```

Example 5.114   Scenario 1: Install and start an application on a new server (Continued)

```
38  # check if application file is set
39  puts "Check if application file is specified"
40  if {[llength $earFile] == 0} {
41     puts "Error: application file name is not specified"
42     exit
43  }
44
45  # install a new application
46  puts "Installing a new application $appName"
47  set options [list -node $nodeName]
48  lappend options -server $serverName
49  if {[llength $appName] != 0} {
50     lappend options -appname $appName
51  }
52  $AdminApp install $earFile $options
53
54  puts "Saving the configuration"
55  $AdminConfig save
56
57  # if it is a network deployment environment, perform a node sync
    as necessary
58  puts "Check for network deployment environment"
59  set nodeSync [$AdminControl queryNames
    type=NodeSync,node=$nodeName,*]
60  if {[llength $nodeSync] == 0} {
61     puts "NodeSync MBean is not available, assuming it is not
       network deployment environment"
62  } else {
63     # perform a node sync to update the configuration if the
       serverStartupSyncEnabled is set to false
64     set enabled [$AdminControl getAttribute $nodeSync
       serverStartupSyncEnabled]
65     if {$enabled == "false"} {
66        puts "Performing a node sync on $nodeName"
67        $AdminControl invoke $nodeSync sync
68        puts "Done with node sync"
69     }
70  }
71
```

Example 5.114 Scenario 1: Install and start an application on a new server (Continued)

```
72  # start the new server which in turn will start the new
    application installed on this server
73  puts "Starting the new server $serverName"
74  $AdminControl startServer $serverName $nodeName
75
76  puts "Done"
```

Scenario 2—Install and Start an Application on a New Cluster

Example 5.115 shows a Jacl script to provide an end-to-end scenario for creating a new cluster and installing an application on the new cluster. Lines 1–9 set up various values to be used for the rest of the script. The values are cell name, list of node names, list of server names for each node, list of weights matching the list of servers, cluster name, application name, and application file name. Lines 11–45 perform error checking on the provided cell, node, cluster, and server member names. Lines 47–53 create a new cluster and lines 55–71 create its cluster members. Lines 73–81 perform error checking on the provided application name. You can provide an empty string as the application name if you want to use the display name of the application file or the application file name as the default application name. Lines 83–88 perform error checking on the application file name. Lines 90–96 install a new application on the newly created cluster. Notice that in lines 93–95 the appname option is not included if the application name is an empty string. Line 99 saves the configuration. Lines 101–117 check for the existence of NodeSync MBean for each node that includes a newly created cluster member. Node synchronization is performed if the Node-Sync MBean is present and the property to perform node synchronization when starting a server is disabled. Line 120 looks for the ClusterMgr MBean. Line 125 invokes the retrieve-Clusters method in the ClusterMgr MBean to load the newly created cluster. Once the newly created cluster is loaded, it creates a new MBean for it. Line 127 locates this MBean and then calls its start method to start the new cluster in line 129. Lines 130–139 wait in a loop until the cluster either starts successfully or stops because of an unexpected problem.

Example 5.115 Scenario 2: Install and start an application on a new cluster

```
1  # Initialize global variables to be used in creating cluster and
   installing application
2  set cellName myCell
3  set nodeList {myNode myNode2}
4  # serverList and weightList have to be provided in a nested
   list format, i.e. one nested list per node specified in nodeList.
   Even if there is only one cluster in a node, it has to be
   provided as a list.
```

Example 5.115   Scenario 2: Install and start an application on a new cluster (Continued)

```
 5   set serverList {{myClusterServer1 myClusterServer2}
     {myClusterServer3}}
 6   set weightList {{10 10} {20}}
 7   set clusterName myCluster
 8   set appName myClusterApp
 9   set earFile /myEar/myClusterApp.ear
10
11   # check if this is an existing cell
12   set cellObject [$AdminConfig getid /Cell:$cellName/]
13   if ([llength $cellObject] == 0) {
14      puts "Error: cell $cellName does not exist in the
        configuration"
15      exit
16   }
17
18   # check if cluster of the same name already exists
19   puts "Check if a cluster with the name $clusterName already
     exists"
20   set clusterObject [$AdminConfig getid /Cell:$cellName/
     ServerCluster:$clusterName/]
21   if {[llength $clusterObject] != 0} {
22      puts "Error: cluster $clusterName already exists on cell
        $cellName. Rerun the script with a different cell and/or
        cluster name."
23      exit
24   }
25   set nodeIndex 0
26   # check if specified nodes and server names exist
27   foreach node $nodeList {
28      # check if node exists
29      puts "Check if node $node exists"
30      set nodeObject [$AdminConfig getid /Cell:$cellName/Node
        :$node/]
31      if {[llength $nodeObject] == 0} {
32         puts "Error: node $node does not exist in the cell
           $cellName"
33         exit
34      }
35      set sList [lindex $serverList $nodeIndex]
36      foreach server $sList {
```

Example 5.115   Scenario 2: Install and start an application on a new cluster (Continued)

```
37        puts "Check if server $server exists on node $node"
38        set serverObject [$AdminConfig getid /Cell:$cellName/
          Node:$node/Server:$server/]
39        if {[llength $serverObject] != 0} {
40            puts "Error: server $server already exists on node
              $node"
41            exit
42        }
43     }
44     incr nodeIndex
45  }
46
47  # create a new cluster
48  puts "Creating a new cluster $clusterName"
49  set nameAttr [list name $clusterName]
50  set descAttr [list description "My cluster"]
51  set stateMAttr  [list stateManagement [list [list initialState
    STOP]]]
52  set attrs [list $nameAttr $descAttr $stateMAttr]
53  set clusterObject [$AdminConfig create ServerCluster $cellObject
    $attrs]
54
55  # create new cluster member
56  set nodeIndex 0
57  foreach node $nodeList {
58     set nodeObject [$AdminConfig getid /Cell:$cellName/Node
       :$node/]
59     set servers [lindex $serverList $nodeIndex]
60     set weights [lindex $weightList $nodeIndex]
61     set serverIndex 0
62     foreach server $servers {
63        set nameAttr [list memberName $server]
64        set weightAttr [lindex $weights $serverIndex]
65        puts "Creating new cluster member $server"
66        set attrs [list $nameAttr $weightAttr]
67        $AdminConfig createClusterMember $clusterObject
          $nodeObject $attrs
68        incr serverIndex
69     }
70     incr nodeIndex
```

Example 5.115   Scenario 2: Install and start an application on a new cluster (Continued)

```
71  }
72
73  # check if application with the same name already exists
74  if {[llength $appName] != 0} {
75      puts "Check if application with the same name $appName
        already exists"
76      set existingApps [$AdminApp list]
77      if {[regexp $appName $existingApps] == 1} {
78          puts "Error: application with the same name $appName
            already exists"
79          exit
80      }
81  }
82
83  # check if application file is set
84  puts "Check if application file is specified"
85  if {[llength $earFile] == 0} {
86      puts "Error: application file name is not specified"
87      exit
88  }
89
90  # install a new application
91  puts "Installing new application $appName onto cluster
    $clusterName"
92  set options [list —cluster $clusterName]
93  if {[llength $appName] != 0} {
94      lappend options —appname $appName
95  }
96  $AdminApp install $earFile $options
97
98  puts "Saving the configuration"
99  $AdminConfig save
100
101 # if it is a network deployment environment, perform node sync
    as necessary
102 puts "Check for network deployment environment"
103 foreach node $nodeList {
104     set nodeSync [$AdminControl queryNames type=NodeSync,
        node=$node,*]
105     if {[llength $nodeSync] == 0} {
```

Example 5.115   Scenario 2: Install and start an application on a new cluster (Continued)

```
106         puts "NodeSync MBean is not available, assuming it is
            not network deployment environment"
107         break
108     } else {
109         # perform a node sync to update the configuration if
            the serverStartupSyncEnabled is set to false
110         set enabled [$AdminControl getAttribute $nodeSync
            serverStartupSyncEnabled]
111         if {$enabled == "false"} {
112             puts "Performing a node sync on node $node"
113             $AdminControl invoke $nodeSync sync
114             puts "Done with node sync on node $node"
115         }
116     }
117 }
118
119 # look for ClusterMgr MBean to refresh the list of clusters
120 set runningClusterMgr [$AdminControl completeObjectName
    type=ClusterMgr,cell=$cellName,*]
121 if {[llength $runningClusterMgr] == 0} {
122     puts "Not able to find ClusterMgr MBean. You have to start
        the cluster $clusterName manually"
123 } else {
124     puts "Refresh the list of clusters to load the new cluster
        $clusterName"
125     $AdminControl invoke $runningClusterMgr retrieveClusters
126     # locate the cluster MBean for the new cluster
127     set runningCluster [$AdminControl completeObjectName
        type=Cluster,name=$clusterName,*]
128     puts "Starting the new cluster $clusterName"
129     $AdminControl invoke $runningCluster start
130     set state [$AdminControl getAttribute $runningCluster state]
131     puts —nonewline "Waiting for cluster to start .."
132     while {$state != "websphere.cluster.running" && $state !=
        "websphere.cluster.stopped"}
133         # sleep for 100 milliseconds
134         after 100
135         set state [$AdminControl getAttribute $runningCluster
            state]
136         puts —nonewline ".."
137     }
```

Example 5.115   Scenario 2: Install and start an application on a new cluster (Continued)

```
138     puts "\nCluster state is $state"
139  }
140
141  puts "Done"
```

Administration Programming Interfaces

WebSphere Application Server 5.0 supports a Java programming interface for developing administrative programs. In fact, all of the administrative tools supplied with the product are written according to the API, which is based on the industry standard JMX specification.

To completely describe this interface would require an entire book by itself, so in this chapter we aim to give you a quick introduction to JMX and then cover the major components of the administrative interface: operational management, configuration management, and application management. We will supply example code that shows how to accomplish common administrative tasks.

JMX

Introduction to JMX

Before you start to develop your own administration client program, it is important that you familiarize yourself with JMX.

JMX is the Java standard for managing an application's resources. The management architecture defined by JMX is divided into three levels (see Figure 6.1).

- The bottom level is management instrumentation. Each manageable resource is described by an interface that specifies the attributes it has, the operations it supports, and the notifications it sends. This resource is a managed bean (MBean).
- The middle level is the management agent. Each managed process contains a JMX agent that includes an MBean server, which provides a registry and access

point for MBeans. Management clients must use the MBean server to access the
registered MBeans.

- The top level of the architecture is identified, but undefined in the current level of
  the JMX specification. It is the distributed services level, and its role is to facilitate
  remote access to JMX agents. This task is accomplished through connectors, which
  provide a protocol-independent, location-transparent, client-side interface to the
  MBean server (e.g., an RMI connector), or protocol adapters, which provide
  protocol-specific, server-side access to the MBean server (e.g., an HTTP adapter).

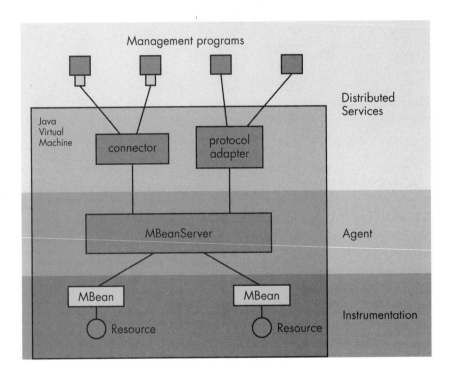

Figure 6.1
The JMX architecture.

JMX in WebSphere

JMX is at the core of Application Server's administration capabilities. The application server
contains a JMX agent. All of the system components are instrumented as MBeans. Application Server's JMX agent supports two types of connectors, RMI/IIOP and SOAP/HTTP(S),
which provide remote access to the server's resources. All of the administration tools
included with Application Server use these JMX facilities to accomplish their functions.

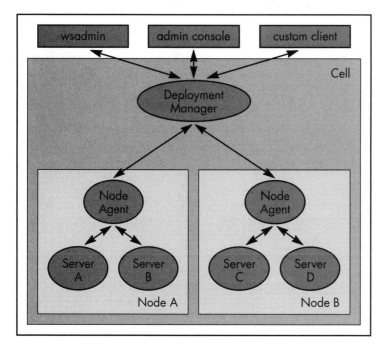

Figure 6.2
WebSphere Network Deployment topology.

In a Base Application Server installation, servers exist and are administered individually. An administrative client connects directly to the application server in this environment. In a Network Deployment installation, (see Figure 6.2) a hierarchical topology groups application servers within nodes, and groups nodes within a cell. Administrative servers exist at the node level (node agents) and at the cell level (the Deployment Manager), and act as aggregation points for the administrative services in the subordinate servers. MBeans in all servers on a node are visible through that node agent, and MBeans in all nodes are visible through the Deployment Manager. Therefore, by connecting to the Deployment Manager, you can invoke operations, get and set attributes, and receive notifications for any MBean in the cell. Application Server provides an AdminService class that reflects the standard JMX MBeanServer interface, and wraps the MBeanServer so that it takes part in implementing this distributed management functionality.

OPERATIONAL MANAGEMENT

The AdminClient Interface

Because you're writing a client program, you need a connection to the desired server and you need a means to invoke methods on remote MBeans. The AdminClient interface provides these capabilities. When an AdminClient object is created, it provides a proxy to the remote AdminService object through one of the supported JMX connectors. As a proxy to the remote AdminService, the AdminClient also reflects the MBeanServer interface. However, the AdminClient does not include methods of the MBeanServer that are not applicable on the client side of the connection.

Use the following code to create an AdminClient object that is connected to a server:

```
Properties clientProps = new Properties();
clientProps.setProperty(AdminClient.CONNECTOR_TYPE,
                        AdminClient.CONNECTOR_TYPE_SOAP);
clientProps.setProperty(AdminClient.CONNECTOR_HOST,
                        "localhost");
clientProps.setProperty(AdminClient.CONNECTOR_PORT, "8880");

AdminClient adminClient = null;
try {
    adminClient = AdminClientFactory.createAdminClient(clientProps);
}
catch (ConnectorException e) {
    System.out.println("Exception creating admin client: " + e);
}
```

First, set up a Properties object with the properties required to get to your desired server. In this case, you will use the SOAP connector to reach the server; for the connector type, use the value AdminClient.CONNECTOR_TYPE_SOAP. For simplicity, you will run the client program on the same machine as the server; use localhost for the host name. To access a remote host instead of a local host, simply use a network-resolvable name for that host. The final property that you need to set is the port number on which the server's SOAP connector is listening. In a single server installation, the default port number for the application server's SOAP connector is 8880. In a Network Deployment installation, the default port number for the Deployment Manager's SOAP connector is 8879. You can find a server's SOAP connector port number definition in the SOAP_CONNECTOR_ADDRESS end point in the serverindex.xml configuration document for the node in which your server is defined.

After the connection properties are set, you can use the AdminClientFactory class and the Properties object to create an AdminClient object that is connected to your chosen server. Depending on factors such as your desired protocol and security environment, you might need to set other properties. For more detailed information about the AdminClient interface and additional creation examples, refer to the AdminClient javadoc.

Accessing MBeans

Once you obtain an `AdminClient` instance, you can use it to access managed resources in the application and administration servers. Each managed resource registers an MBean with the MBeanServer in its process. In JMX, management programs do not directly access MBeans. Instead, they must direct requests to the MBeanServer and reference MBeans by name. An MBean name takes the form of an ObjectName, which consists of a domain name followed by an unordered list of one or more key properties. The syntax looks like this:

```
[domainName]:property=value[,property=value]*
```

The domain name provides a partitioning of the ObjectName namespace within the JMX agent. It is optional; if it is not present, then the MBean server will use a default domain name. For WebSphere Application Server, the domain name is conveniently WebSphere.

A key property is a name–value pair. An ObjectName's list of key properties can consist of any number of key properties, but at least one needs to exist. The ordering of key properties in the list does not matter. Table 6.1 shows the most important key property names that WebSphere Application Server administration uses.

Table 6.1   Important ObjectName Key Property Names

Property name	Description
type	The resource type that the MBean represents.
name	The name identifier for the individual instance of the MBean.
cell	The name of the cell in which the MBean is executing.
node	The name of the node in which the MBean is executing.
process	The name of the process in which the MBean is executing.

Some MBeans in Application Server use additional key properties. However, Table 6.1 contains the most important, minimally required key properties. An MBean without these key properties can be registered with the MBeanServer in an Application Server process, but such an MBean cannot participate in the distributed enhancements that Application Server adds (e.g., request routing, distributed event notification, etc.).

If you know the complete set of key properties for an ObjectName, then you can use it to
find the MBean it identifies. However, it is usually more practical and convenient to find
MBeans without having to know all of their key properties. You can do this by using a wildcard character, * , for any key properties that you do not need to match. Table 6.2 provides
some examples of ObjectNames with wildcard key properties that match single or multiple
MBeans.

Table 6.2   Example of ObjectNames with Wildcard Key Properties

ObjectName Pattern	Description
:type=Server,	All MBeans of type Server
:node=Node1,type=Server,	All MBeans of type Server on Node1
:type=JVM,process=server1,node=Node1,	The JVM MBean in the server named server1 node Node1
:process=server1,	All MBeans in all servers named server1
:process=server1,node=Node1,	All MBeans in the server named server1 on Node1

The following example shows how to find the MBean for the server named server1 on the
node named MyNode:

```
String serverName = "server1";
String nodeName = "MyNode";
ObjectName queryName = new ObjectName
    ("WebSphere:*,type=Server,process=" + serverName + ",node=" +
    nodeName);
ObjectName server = null;
Set s = adminClient.queryNames(queryName, null);
if (!s.isEmpty())
    server = (ObjectName)s.iterator().next();
else
    System.out.println("Server MBean was not found");
```

Begin by building an ObjectName with a query string that specifies the key properties of
type, process, and node. By using a wildcard for the remaining key properties, this pattern
will match the ObjectNames for all MBeans of type Server in process server1 on node
MyNode. Because server names are unique per node, this is sufficient to identify the MBean
that you want. Next, give this ObjectName to the queryNames method of AdminClient,
which will perform the remote call to the AdminService to obtain the set of MBean Object-
Names that match the query. (The null second parameter to this method is a query expression (QueryExp) object that you can use as an additional query over the MBeans that match

the ObjectName pattern in the first parameter.) Finally, use the set's iterator to get the first (and, in this case, only) element, which is the server's MBean ObjectName.

Now that you have access to an MBean what can you do?

Using MBeans

What a specific MBean lets you do depends on the management interface that it exposes. It might declare attributes that you can get or set. It might declare operations that you can invoke. It might declare notifications for which you can register listeners. For the MBeans provided by Application Server, you can find information about the interfaces they support in the MBean javadoc. This javadoc is also installed with Application Server in the \web subdirectory under the product installation root directory.

Getting and Setting Attributes

The following example shows how to get an attribute, in this case the process ID (PID) of the server MBean from the preceding example.

```
try
{
    String pid = (String)adminClient.getAttribute(server, "pid");
}
catch (Exception e)
{
    System.out.println("Exception invoking getAttribute: " + e);
}
```

The call to getAttribute takes an MBean ObjectName and an attribute name as parameters and returns an Object. In this case the attribute type as defined by the server MBean is a String, so that is how we cast the return value.

The server MBean's attributes are all read-only so there are none that we can set via a call to setAttribute. For an example of setting an attribute let's use the messageFilterLevel attribute of the server's RasLoggingService MBean, which specifies what filtering is applied to the server's logs.

```
try
{
    Attribute attr = new Attribute("messageFilterLevel", "SERVICE");
    adminClient.setAttribute(rasLoggingService, attr);
}
catch (Exception e)
{
    System.out.println("Exception invoking setAttribute: " + e);
}
```

Here we create a new Attribute object with the name of the attribute we wish to set and an Object specifying the attribute value, in this case the String "SERVICE," and use it in the call to setAttribute along with the ObjectName of the target MBean.

Invoking Operations

The following example invokes one of the operations available on a NodeAgent MBean. It starts the application server named MyServer:

```
String opName = "launchProcess";
String signature[] = { "java.lang.String" };
Object params[] = { "MyServer" };
try
{
    adminClient.invoke(nodeAgent, opName, params, signature);
}
catch (Exception e)
{
    System.out.println("Exception invoking launchProcess: " + e);
}
```

The AdminClient.invoke method is a generic means of invoking any operation on any MBean. The parameters are:

- The ObjectName of the target MBean
- The name of the operation
- An Object array that contains the operation parameters
- A String array that contains the operation signature

In this case, the launchProcess operation has a single parameter: a string that identifies the server to start.

The invoke method returns an Object instance that the calling code could then cast to the correct return type for the invoked operation. The launchProcess operation is declared void so you can ignore the return value in this example.

Using Event Notifications

Registering for Event Notification

Besides managing resources, JMX also supports monitoring of administrative events. Certain events produce notifications, for example, when a server starts. Management applications might declare their interest in these events by registering as a notification listener. WebSphere Application Server provides a full implementation of the JMX notification model, and provides additional functions so that you can receive notifications in a distributed environment. The following is an example of how an object can register itself for event notifications emitted from your node agent MBean:

```
adminClient.addNotificationListener(nodeAgent, this, null, null);
```

In this example, the first parameter is the ObjectName for the node agent MBean. The second parameter identifies the listener object, which must implement the NotificationListener interface. In this case, the calling object is the listener. The third parameter is a filter (javax.management.NotificationFilter) that you can use to indicate which notifications you want to receive. When you leave this value as null, you will receive all notifications from this MBean. The final parameter is a hand back object that you can have JMX return to you when it emits a notification.

If your MBean is located on another server in the cell, you can still receive its notifications even though your administrative client program might be connected to the Deployment Manager server. This is because all notifications flow to the upstream server. For example, a notification from an application server will first flow to the local node agent and from there to the Deployment Manager.

Another enhanced feature that Application Server provides is the ability to register as a notification listener of multiple MBeans with one call. This is done via the addNotification-ListenerExtended method of AdminClient, an extension of the standard JMX addNotificationListener method. This extension method even lets you register for MBeans that are not currently active. This is important in situations where you would like to monitor events from resources that can be stopped and restarted during the lifetime of your administrative client program.

Handling Event Notifications

Objects receive JMX event notifications via the handleNotification method, which is defined by the NotificationListener interface and which any event receiver must implement. The following example is an implementation of handleNotification that reports the notifications that it receives.

```
public void handleNotification(Notification n, Object handback)
{
    System.out.println("*******************************************");
    System.out.println("* Notification received at "
        + new Date().toString());
    System.out.println("* type = " + n.getType());
    System.out.println("* message = " + n.getMessage());
    System.out.println("* source = " + n.getSource());
    System.out.println("* seqNum = "
```

```
        + Long.toString(n.getSequenceNumber()));
    System.out.println("* timeStamp = " + new Date(n.getTimeStamp()));
    System.out.println("* userData = " + n.getUserData());
    System.out.println("*****************************************");
}
```

CONFIGURATION MANAGEMENT

As discussed in earlier chapters, there is a distinction in WebSphere between operational administration and configuration administration. You can use the MBeans in any running server to control the operation of the system. As we have just seen, you can get and set attributes and invoke operations to control the behavior of the system. However, such operational changes do not affect the persistent configuration of the system. The WebSphere administration API provides a configuration service as the means for managing the system configuration.

This service allows you to query or modify your WebSphere Application Server configuration. For instance, you can use the configuration service to find all the servers in the cell, modify some server configuration parameters, or configure a new data source. In fact, the configuration service can provide the same configuration functions that are available using the admin console and the AdminConfig object in the wsadmin scripting interface.

Configuration Objects

As we saw in Chapter 2, WebSphere Application Server configuration is composed of a set of XML documents stored in the config directory under the root directory of the installation. A configuration object is an XML element inside a configuration document that defines configurations of run-time components in WebSphere Application Server. The following are two examples of configuration objects in a server's configuration from the server.xml document. The first is the trace service configuration:

```
<services XMI:type="traceservice:TraceService" XMI:id="TraceService_1"
    enable="true"
    startupTraceSpecification="*=all=disabled"
    traceOutputType="SPECIFIED_FILE" traceFormat="BASIC"
    memoryBufferSize="8">
    <traceLog XMI:id="TraceLog_1" fileName="${SERVER_LOG_ROOT}/
        trace.log" rolloverSize="20" maxNumberOfBackupFiles="1"/>
</services>
```

Here is the process configuration:

```
<processDefinition XMI:type="processexec:JavaProcessDef"
    XMI:id="JavaProcessDef_1" executableName="${Java_HOME}/bin/Java"
    workingDirectory="${USER_INSTALL_ROOT}"
```

```
executableTargetKind="Java_CLASS"
executableTarget="com.ibm.ws.runtime.WsServer">
<execution XMI:id="ProcessExecution_1" processPriority="20"
    runAsUser="" runAsGroup=""/>
<ioRedirect XMI:id="OutputRedirect_1"
    stdoutFilename="${SERVER_LOG_ROOT}/native_stdout.log"
    stderrFilename="${SERVER_LOG_ROOT}/native_stderr.log"/>
<monitoringPolicy XMI:id="MonitoringPolicy_1"
    maximumStartupAttempts="3" pingInterval="60" pingTimeout="300"
    autoRestart="true" nodeRestartState="STOPPED"/>
<jvmEntries XMI:id="JavaVirtualMachine_1"
    verboseModeClass="false" verboseModeGarbageCollection="false"
    verboseModeJNI="false" initialHeapSize="0" maximumHeapSize="256"
    runHProf="false" hprofArguments="" debugMode="false"
    debugArgs="-DJava.compiler=NONE -Xdebug -Xnoagent
      -Xrunjdwp:transport=dt_socket,server=y,
      suspend=n,address=7777" genericJvmArguments="">
  <classpath></classpath> <bootClasspath></bootClasspath>
</jvmEntries>
</processDefinition>
```

As you can see, configuration objects can be nested, meaning one object can contain other configuration objects.

The Configuration Service Interfaces

The primary interface of the configuration service is ConfigService. Through this interface you can locate configuration objects, edit them, create them, and delete them. To begin using the ConfigService in an administrative client program you will first need to get a reference to it.

Similar to the way we used an AdminClient as a remote proxy to the AdminService running in a server, we need to have a remote proxy for the configuration service in the server (Figure 6.3).

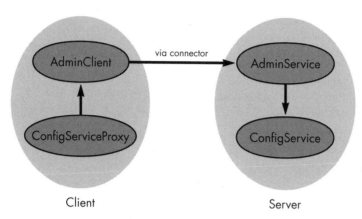

Figure 6.3
Using ConfigServiceProxy from remote client.

The following code snippet shows how to get a reference to the ConfigService in a remote client process via a ConfigServiceProxy object, and using the AdminClient object we obtained in the previous section.

```
// create a config service proxy object.
ConfigService configService = new ConfigServiceProxy(adminClient);
```

An important concept to introduce before proceeding with more details about using the configuration service is how configuration updates are grouped. Imagine that one client is in the middle of making a series of configuration changes to a server while another client tries to start the server. As the server is starting, the configuration changes are partially complete. Because of this the server has inconsistent configuration data and encounters an error during initialization. To avoid a scenario like this, all changes made through the ConfigService are grouped together within a session and held in a private workspace until an explicit save is performed. The configuration service provides a Session object (com.ibm.websphere.management.Session) for this purpose and creating a session is usually the next thing a client should do after getting a reference to the ConfigService:

```
// create a session
Session session = new Session();
```

This session object will be used in subsequent calls to the ConfigService as you query and modify the configuration.

As a client completes a set of related configuration changes it will want to save them from the session's workspace into the repository. The ConfigService provides a save method to accomplish this:

```
// save the accumulated changes.
configService.save(session, false);
```

It is not necessary to save after every configuration modification. The rule of thumb is to save the configuration when you are ready to publish the configuration updates you made within the session to the repository, enabling the rest of the system to use the updated configuration.

Because all the configuration changes made in a session are not pushed into the config directory until you save the session, you also will not see any unsaved configuration changes made in other concurrent sessions. When users concurrently update the same configuration document through different sessions, the conflict is detected by the save method. The boolean value in the save call above is the overwriteOnConflict flag, where a false value means that the call would fail if another user has concurrently modified the same configuration document, and true means the call would overwrite the other concurrent modification. Overwriting other config updates is not recommended as a normal course of business because it could result in an inconsistent configuration. It is intended for careful use in interactive clients where the user knows by the nature of the change or by coordination with other administrators that it is safe to overwrite the changes. To help a user make this decision, you can query the list of conflict documents with the `getConflictDocuments` method of the ConfigService.

The session will need to be cleaned up when the client's work is finished. The ConfigService provides a discard method to release all the resources used by the session when you are done. Failing to do so can waste resources and potentially cause a memory leak if the client is long running.

```
configService.discard(session);
```

In addition to releasing all the resources owned by the session, this method also discards all the changes made since the previous save. Therefore, it can also be used to throw away any unsaved changes if you choose not to complete the session, for example, in case of a failure.

Identifying Configuration Objects

The ConfigService uses an ObjectName to uniquely identify configuration objects in the same way that JMX uses an ObjectName to uniquely identify an MBean registered in the MBeanServer. However, instead of the key properties we used with MBeans, the ConfigService uses the key properties in Table 6.3, where the property names are constants defined in the com.ibm.websphere.management.configservice.SystemAttributes class.

Table 6.3   ConfigService Key Properties

Property Name	Description
_WEBSPHERE_CONFIG_DATA_ID	An opaque handle that uniquely identifies this config object
_WEBSPHERE_CONFIG_DATA_TYPE	The type of this config object, (e.g., DataSource, Server, ServerCluster, etc.)
_WEBSPHERE_CONFIG_DATA_DISPLAY_NAME	The name of this config object (e.g., the name of a Server)

The configuration service provides a ConfigServiceHelper class that offers various helper methods to manipulate ObjectNames, such as constructing an ObjectName or retrieving information from an ObjectName. For example, this class provides a `getObjectLocation` method to derive the location information from the ObjectName.

Locating Configuration Objects

Before you can affect the configuration of an object you must first get a reference to it. The ConfigService provides two methods named `queryConfigObjects` and `resolve` to obtain the IDs of configuration objects. Much like the `queryNames` method we saw on the Admin-Service interface, the `queryConfigObjects` method of the ConfigService allows you to find the configuration objects that match some query pattern. Here is how you could find the names of all the existing servers:

```
ObjectName scope = null;
ObjectName pattern = ConfigServiceHelper.createObjectName
    (null, "Server");
ObjectName[] servers = configService.queryConfigObjects
    (session, scope, pattern, null);
```

The `queryConfigObjects` method provides a scoped search functionality based on the config object type, name, or both. Values for the scope can be a Cell, Node, Server, Application, or Cluster config object. If null is specified for the query scope, the method will search the entire configuration, which can be expensive. However, the search algorithm is optimized to handle common scenarios, such as listing all the servers or nodes or J2EE applications in a cell. The final parameter in the queryConfigObejcts call, like the `AdminService.queryNames` method, is a JMX query expression (QueryExp) that can be used as a secondary filter of the matching results.

The `resolve` method is another easy and efficient way to query for configuration objects. Here is an example of finding the server named server1 on the node named MyNode.

```
ObjectName server;
ObjectName[] servers = configService.resolve(session,
"Node=MyNode:Server=server1");
if (servers.length > 0)
    server = servers[0];
```

The resolve method takes the session object and a containment path string as parameters and, like queryConfigObjects, it also returns an array of ObjectNames. In this case, we know that server names are unique within a node, so if server1 exists on MyNode it will be the only element in the array.

The format of the containment path argument is type=name:type=name:... For example, "Node=MyNode:Server=server1:Application=myAppServer." The type is the configuration data type and is required. The name is the configuration data name and is optional. If the name is not specified, all instances of the type are matched. The name field can be double quoted to preserve spaces in the name. If the name field is not quoted, any space around the name will be trimmed.

Using Configuration Objects

Now that you know how to find existing configuration objects you can proceed to work with their configurations.

Modifying Configuration Objects

You can use the getAttribute and setAttribute methods to query and modify various attribute values on a configuration object. As an example, the following code snippet gets the TraceService for server1 and sets its startupTraceSpecification attribute with the new value "*=all=enabled" using the setAttribute method, and then verifies the change using the getAttribute method.

```
// query to get the trace service component in the server.
ObjectName pattern = ConfigServiceHelper.createObjectName
    (null, "TraceService");
ObjectName traceService = configService.queryConfigObjects
    (session, server, pattern, null)[0];

// set the server's trace specification to new value.
String newTrace = "*=all=enabled";
AttributeList attrList = new AttributeList();
attrList.add(new Attribute("startupTraceSpecification", newTrace));
configService.setAttributes(session, traceService, attrList);
```

```
// verify the new setting.
newTrace = (String) configService.getAttribute(session, traceService,
  "startupTraceSpecification");
System.out.println("new trace is" + newTrace);
```

Using Attribute Lists

The javax.management.AttributeList class from the JMX specification is used to represent the configuration information of config objects. An AttributeList is a collection of attribute objects that are name and value pairs. Because AttributeList is a generic data structure, ConfigServiceHelper offers several helper methods to construct and traverse an AttributeList.

Any attribute list returned from config service contains two system attributes defined by config service:

- SystemAttributes._WEBSPHERE_CONFIG_DATA_ID
- SystemAttributes._WEBSPHERE_CONFIG_DATA_TYPE.

The following sections discuss how AttributeList represents configuration information for various types of attributes.

Simple Attributes   If the attribute type is one of the simple Java types, such as String, Integer, Boolean, and so on, the value of the attribute is directly used in the attribute list. For example, the AttributeList that represents the TraceService config object (shown here) contains an attribute named enable with a Boolean value of true, and a startupTraceSpecification attribute with a string value of "*=all=disabled."

```
<services XMI:type="traceservice:TraceService" XMI:id="TraceService_1"
    enable="true" startupTraceSpecification="*=all=disabled"
    traceOutputType="SPECIFIED_FILE" traceFormat="BASIC"
    memoryBufferSize="8">
    <traceLog XMI:id="TraceLog_1" fileName="${SERVER_LOG_ROOT}/trace.log"
        rolloverSize="20" maxNumberOfBackupFiles="1"/>
</services>
```

Complex Attributes   If the attribute type is complex, the attribute value is represented as an AttributeList, (i.e., a nested attribute list). The TraceService config object shown previously has a complex type attribute named traceLog, the value of which is a nested AttributeList with the attributes filename, rolloverSize, and maxNumberOfBackupFiles.

Collection Attributes   If the attribute type is a collection, the attribute value in AttributeList is java.util.List. For instance, the DataSource config object in the *resources.xml* file (shown here) has a collection type attribute ResourceProperties, thus its attribute value is a list object and each element inside is also an AttributeList that represents a ResourceProperty config object.

```
<factories XMI:type="resources.jdbc:DataSource" XMI:id="DataSource_1"
    name="Default Datasource" jndiName="DefaultDatasource"
    description="Datasource for the WebSphere Default Application"
    category="default" authMechanismPreference="BASIC_PASSWORD"
    statementCacheSize="0" datasourceHelperClassname=
    "com.ibm.websphere.rsadapter.CloudscapeDataStoreHelper"
    relationalResourceAdapter="builtin_rra">
    <propertySet XMI:id="DB2a-J2EEResourcePropertySet_1a">
        <resourceProperties XMI:id="res_prop_template_DB2j_5_1"
            name="databaseName" type="java.lang.String"
            value="${WAS_INSTALL_ROOT}/bin/DefaultDB"
            description="Location of Cloudscape default Database."/>
        <resourceProperties XMI:id="res_prop_template_DB2j_5_2"
            name="remoteDataSourceProtocol" type="java.lang.String"
            value=""/>
        <resourceProperties XMI:id="res_prop_template_DB2j_5_3"
            name="shutdownDatabase" type="java.lang.String" value=""/>
        <resourceProperties XMI:id="res_prop_template_DB2j_5_4"
            name="dataSourceName" type="java.lang.String" value=""/>
    </propertySet>
    <connectionPool XMI:id="ConnectionPool_1"
        connectionTimeout="1000" maxConnections="30"
        minConnections="1" reapTime="180" unusedTimeout="1800"
        purgePolicy="FailingConnectionOnly"/>
</factories>
```

Although you can use the `setAttributes` method to modify the value of collection type attributes, the drawback is that it replaces the whole collection rather than allowing you to modify individual elements in the list. The `addElement` and `removeElement` methods are provided to make finer modifications for collection type attributes.

The `createConfigData` method can also be used to add a complex type element into a collection. It creates a config object with the specified attribute list and adds it at the end. The advantage of addElement here is that you can specify the position of the created object, whereas the advantage of using `createConfigData` is that it returns the ID of the created config object, which you can use to process the config object further.

The following code snippet illustrates how to add a J2EEResourceProperty object into the propertySet for a DataSource config object.

```
// get the J2EEResourcePropertySet object
AttributeList value = configService.getAttributes(session,
    newDataSource, new String[]{"propertySet"}, false);
ObjectName propertySet = (ObjectName)
    ConfigServiceHelper.getAttributeValue(value,  "propertySet");


// create a J2EEResourceProperty object and add into the list of
resourceProperties.attrList.clear();
ConfigServiceHelper.setAttributeValue(attrList, "name",
    "DatabaseName");
ConfigServiceHelper.setAttributeValue(attrList, "type",
    "Java.lang.String");
ConfigServiceHelper.setAttributeValue(attrList, "value", "myDatabase");
ObjectName prop = configService.createConfigData(session, propertySet,
"resourceProperties", "J2EEResourceProperty", attrList);
```

This code generates the following XML fragment in the DataSource config object:

```
<propertySet XMI:id="J2EEResourcePropertySet_1">
   <resourceProperties XMI:id="res_prop_1" name="DatabaseName"
   type="Java.lang.String" value="myDatabase" />
</propertySet>
```

Reference Attributes   Reference attributes do not contain a value directly. Instead, they refer to other config objects defined elsewhere, such as the relationalResourceAdapter attribute on the DataSource config object shown in the previous section. The ID of the referred config object is used as the value for any reference attributes; in this case, the value of the relationalResourceAdapter attribute is the ID of the referred J2CResourceAdapter config object.

Creating Configuration Objects

Creating a Server   Let's start with an example of creating a server. In the following code, a new server is created using the `createConfigData` method of the ConfigService. Typically, you only need to specify the name attribute. ConfigService will set up log directories and properly resolve port conflicts. After creating the server, you can make further attribute modifications using the `setAttributes` method.

```
// query to get the config object ID for the node
// where we want to create the new server.
ObjectName node = configService.resolve(session, "Node=" +
    nodeName)[0];

// create a new application server.
AttributeList attrList = new AttributeList();
ConfigServiceHelper.setAttributeValue(attrList, "name", serverName);
ObjectName newServer = configService.createConfigData(session, node,
    "Server", "Server", attrList);
```

The createConfigData method requires you to specify the parent and the attribute name of the created config object. As described earlier, config objects can be nested and modeled as attributes on the parent. However, because WebSphere Application Server configuration data is stored in a group of configuration documents, the parent and the new config object might reside in different documents. In this case, a newly created config object cannot be modeled as an attribute on a parent. For example, a Node config object logically contains multiple Server config objects but the Node config object is stored in a node.xml file, and Server config objects are stored in server.xml files; thus a Server is not an attribute of a Node. The ConfigService uses the term *relationship* to describe the logical containment among config objects that reside in different configuration documents.

Each relationship has a name and value:

- The name of a relationship describes the type of logical containment among config objects.
- The value of a relationship is a collection of related config objects, which can be empty.

When the parent and the new config object are in different configuration documents, the relationship name should be used rather than the attribute name for the createConfigData method. In the sample code, the first Server is the relationship name between the node and the newly created server. Figure 6.4 shows the names of relationships for a Node config object.

The parent relationship associates a config object with its containing config object, which in this case is a cell config object. Other relationships associate a config object with whatever types of config objects it logically contains. Typically, the relationship name describes the type of contained config objects; the "server" relationship describes the servers on the node, and so on. The following code sample shows how to get the cell config object that contains the specified node, and how to get the servers on that node. The set of relationships a config object has is determined by its type. You can use the getRelationship and getRelationships methods to obtain relationship values.

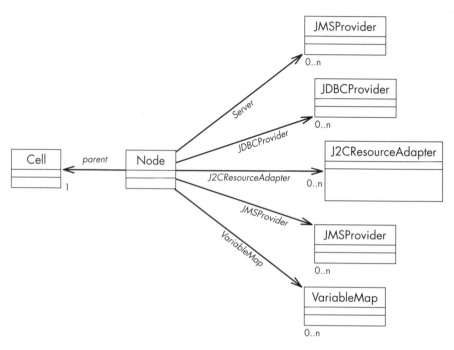

Figure 6.4
Node relationships.

```
// get the Cell config object.
ObjectName cell = configService.getRelationship(session, node,
    "parent")[0];
// list servers on the node
ObjectName[] servers = configService.getRelationship(session, node,
    "Server");
```

Creating a JDBCProvider and DataSource   Configuring a JDBC provider is quite different from one database vendor (and one implementation) to another, so the ConfigService provides the createConfigDataByTemplate method to enable you to specify a template for the created object. This method creates a blank config object, copies the configuration data from the selected template to the created config object, and then applies the specified attribute values on top of it. You can specify a system-defined template (several are available for common database vendors and implementations) or specify an existing config object to use as a template instead.

System-defined templates are stored in the templates directory, under the config directory, and are used only during config object creation time. The ConfigService provides the queryTemplates method to query all the system-defined templates. The following sample code

queries all the JDBCProvider templates defined in the system, and uses the Cloudscape
JDBC Provider 5.0 template to create a new JDBC provider.

```
String jdbcProviderTemplateName = "Cloudscape JDBC Provider 5.0";
ObjectName[] templates = configService.queryTemplates(session,
    "JDBCProvider");
ObjectName match = null;
for (int i = 0; i < templates.length; i++) {
    System.out.println("JDBCProvider template " + templates[i]);
    if (jdbcProviderTemplateName.
       equals(ConfigServiceHelper.getDisplayName(templates[i])))  {
       match = templates[i];
       break;
    }
}
System.out.println("found JDBCProvider template " + match);


// create an instance of embedded JDBC provider using template.
attrList.clear();
ConfigServiceHelper.setAttributeValue(attrList, "name",
   jdbcProviderName);
ObjectName jdbcProvider = configService.createConfigDataByTemplate(
   session, newServer, "JDBCProvider", attrList, match);
```

After the JDBC provider is created you can use the createConfigData method to create a
DataSource as follows:

```
// create a JDBC data source for the application.
ConfigServiceHelper.setAttributeValue(attrList, "name",
   dataSourceName);
ConfigServiceHelper.setAttributeValue(attrList, "jndiName", "foo");
ObjectName newDataSource = configService.createConfigData(session,
   jdbcProvider,  "DataSource", "DataSource", attrList);
```

Deleting Configuration Objects

Deleting configuration objects is much easier than creating them. Simply call the delete-
ConfigData method to delete any config object. Note that deleting a parent config object
removes all the child config objects as well. For instance, if you delete a JDBC provider, the
DataSources defined underneath it are deleted implicitly.

APPLICATION MANAGEMENT

Application Preparation

J2EE applications and modules include an XML-based deployment descriptor that specifies various J2EE artifacts (e.g., EJB definitions, security role definitions, ejb-refs, resource-refs, etc.) pertaining to the application or the modules. These artifacts define various unresolved references that are used by the application logic. The J2EE specification requires that these artifacts be mapped to J2EE platform-specific (in this case, WebSphere-specific) information during deployment of J2EE applications on such platforms.

The Application Assembly Tool, installed as a part of the WebSphere Application Server product, as well as the application management support provided by WebSphere systems management, facilitates collection of such WebSphere-specific information that is used to resolve references defined in various deployment descriptors in a J2EE application. This information is stored in the application EAR file and is colocated with the deployment descriptors. Figure 6.5 shows the structure of an EAR file that is populated with WebSphere-specific deployment information.

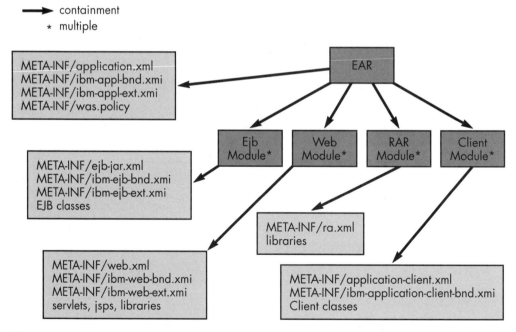

Figure 6.5
EAR file containing WebSphere-specific deployment information.

The WebSphere application management architecture provides a set of classes that allows deployers to collect WebSphere-specific deployment information (hereafter called binding information) and store it in the application EAR file. Such an EAR file can then be installed into a WebSphere configuration, using application management interfaces described later in the "Installing Applications" section. The rest of this section explains, using a programming example, how an EAR file can be populated with binding information.

The following are the major steps in the application preparation process:

- Create AppDeploymentController instance.
- Obtain AppDeploymentTask instances.
- Manipulate task data as necessary.
- Save task data back into EAR file and obtain install options.

Create AppDeploymentController

The AppDeploymentController takes an EAR file as an argument and creates a sequence of steps, represented by AppDeploymentTask objects (hereafter called tasks). The tasks are typically presented to the deployer to collect binding information, or are manipulated programmatically. The following code excerpt shows how to create an AppDeploymentController instance:

```
// create preferences to pass in the locale information
Hashtable prefs = new Hashtable();
prefs.put(AppConstants.APPDEPL_LOCALE, Locale.getDefault());

// create a controller instance for EAR file
// specified by a fully qualified path in earName
AppDeploymentController flowController =
  AppDeploymentController.readArchive (earName, prefs);
```

Obtain AppDeploymentTask Instances

After creating AppDeploymentController, you can iterate over the task objects that it creates. Each task collects a specific kind of binding information for various modules in the application or for the application itself. A task has the attributes (and corresponding getters/setters as applicable) as shown in Table 6.4.

Table 6.4   Task Attributes

Attribute	Description
name	A unique task name.
taskData	A two-dimensional array (table) of strings. The first row of the table contains the column headings for the task (e.g., name of the module, module URI, JNDI name, etc). The rest of the rows represent application-specific information.
requiredColumns	An array of boolean indicating if a task column must have a non-null value.
mutableColumns	An array of boolean indicating if the task data in a specific column index can be changed by the deployer.
isTaskDisabled	A boolean indicating if the task should be considered for manipulation.

Table 6.5 lists various task names that are typically created by AppDeploymentController for a J2EE 1.3 (and J2EE 1.2) application. You might notice more tasks if the application contains WebSphere Enterprise extensions.

Table 6.5   Typical Task Names

AppDeploymentTask Name	Description	Task Column Names

MapRolesToUsers	Allows you to specify users or groups for a security role. Each row of task data represents a single security role. Multiple users or groups for a role are separated by |. Possible values for special role columns, such as `role.everyone`, `role.all.auth.user` are `App-Constants.YES_KEY` or `AppConstants.NO_KEY`.	`role,`
		`role.everyone,`
		`role.all.auth.user,`
		`role.user,`
		`role.group`

MapRunAsRolesToUsers	Allows you to specify credentials for a run-as role. Each row of task data represents a single run-as role.	`role, userName,` `password`
BindJndiForEJBNonMessageBinding	Allows you to specify JNDI names for EJBs. This JNDI name is used to look up EJB Homes from client programs. A row of task data specifies a single EJB for which JNDI name can be supplied.	`EJBModule, EJB,` `uri, JNDI`
BindJndiForEJBMessageBinding	Allows you to specify a listener port name for message-driven beans (MDBs). Each row of task data represents a single MDB.	`EJBModule, EJB,` `uri, listenerPort`

Table 6.5   Typical Task Names (Continued)

AppDeploymentTask Name	Description	Task Column Names
MapEJBRefToEJB	Allows you to specify JNDI names of EJBs that are bound to ejb-refs. Each row of task data represents a single ejb-ref defined in an EJB or in a Web module.	`module, EJB, uri, referenceBinding, class, JNDI`
MapResRefToEJB	Allows you to specify JNDI names of resources defined in WebSphere configuration that are bound to resource-refs. Each row of task data represents a single resource-ref defined in an EJB or in a Web module.	`AppVersion, ModuleVersion, module, EJB, uri, referenceBinding, resRef.type, oracleRef, JNDI`
MapResEnvRefToRes	Allows you to specify JNDI names of resources defined in WebSphere configuration that are bound to resource-env-refs. Each row of task data represents a single resource-env-ref defined in an EJB or in a Web module.	`module, EJB, uri, referenceBinding, resEnvRef.type, JNDI`
DataSourceFor10EJBModules	Allows you to specify JNDI name of the default data source used for an EJB module that contains EJB1.x beans. Each row of task data represents a single EJB module.	`AppVersion, EJBModule, uri, JNDI, userName, password`
DataSourceFor20EJBModules	Allows you to specify JNDI name of the default connection factory used for an EJB module that contains EJB2.x beans. Each row of task data represents a single EJB module.	`AppVersion, EJBModule, uri, JNDI`
DataSourceFor10CMPBeans	Allows you to specify JNDI name of the data source to be used for an EJB1.x bean with container managed persistence. A row of task data represents a single EJB.	`AppVersion, EJBVersion, EJBModule, EJB, uri, JNDI, userName, password`
DataSourceFor20CMPBeans	Allows you to specify JNDI name of the connection factory to be used for an EJB2.x bean with container managed persistence. A row of task data represents a single EJB.	`AppVersion, EJBVersion, EJBModule, EJB, uri, JNDI`

Table 6.5   Typical Task Names (Continued)

AppDeploymentTask Name	Description	Task Column Names
MapWebModToVH	Allows you to specify virtual hosts for Web modules. Each row of task data represents a Web module in the application for which virtual host information is to be collected.	`webModule, uri, virtualHost`
EnsureMethodProtectionFor10EJB	Allows you to specify if all unprotected methods of an EJB1.x module should be made inaccessible. Each task row represents a single EJB1.x module. Possible values for `method.denyAllAccessPermission` column are `AppConstants.YES_KEY` or `AppConstants.NO_KEY`.	`EJBModule, uri, method.denyAllAccessPermission`
EnsureMethodProtectionFor20EJB	Allows you to specify protection level for unprotected methods of EJB2.x beans in EJB modules. Each row of task data specifies method protection per EJB module. Possible values of `method.protectionType` column are `AppConstants.APPDEPL_METHOD_PROTECTION_UNCHECK` or `AppConstants.APPDEPL_METHOD_PROTECTION_EXCLUDE`.	`EJBModule, uri, method.protectionType`
AppDeploymentOptions	Allows you to specify various deployment-specific options. This task has only two rows. The first row specifies the option name and the second row has the corresponding option value. Possible values for columns such as `preCompileJSPs, deployejb, distributeApp, useMetaDataFromBinary, createMBeansForResources` are `AppConstants.YES_KEY` or `AppConstants.NO_KEY`.	`preCompileJSPs, installed.ear.destination, distributeApp useMetaDataFromBinary, deployejb, appname, createMBeansForResources, reloadInterval, reloadEnabled`

Table 6.5 Typical Task Names (Continued)

AppDeploymentTask Name	Description	Task Column Names
EJBDeployOptions	Allows you to specify various options that can be passed when you want to deploy EJB modules during application installation. This task has only two rows. The first row specifies the option name and the second row has the corresponding option value.	`deployejb.classpath,` `deployejb.rmic,` `deployejb.dbtype,` `deployejb.dbschema`
MapModulesToServers	Allows you to specify the target servers or clusters for modules in an application. Each row of task data represents one module in the application. The server target is specified as `WebSphere:cell=cellName, node=nodeName, server=serveName` and cluster target is specified as `WebSphere:cell=cellName, cluster=clusterName`. Multiple targets can be specified for a given module by delimiting them with "+".	`module, uri, server`

The URI column in various tasks uniquely identifies a module in the application using the format `<moduleURI,ddURI>` as its value, where `moduleURI` is the module file name defined in the application's deployment descriptor, and `ddURI` is the URI of the deployment descriptor within the module (for standard deployment descriptor) or the URI of the alternate deployment descriptor for the module, as defined in the application's deployment descriptor. For example, if an application has a Web module in MyWeb.war and the module uses a standard deployment descriptor, then the value of the URI column in various tasks for this module is MyWeb.war,WEB-INF/web.xml. Thus the URI column value always guarantees a unique identification of a module.

The following code excerpt shows how to obtain tasks from AppDeploymentController:

```
AppDeploymentTask task = flowController.getFirstTask();
while (task != null)
{
    // manipulate task data as necessary
    task = flowController.getNextTask();
}
```

Manipulate Task Data

Using task name, task column names, and the J2EE artifact for which binding information is to be supplied, the task data can be modified if the corresponding column is marked as mutable. The following sample code shows how binding information can be supplied for a specific task. In this example, we are specifying users for a security role: Consider that the application has a security role named Role1, and that you need to assign users User1 and User2 to that role:

```
if (task.getName().equals ("MapRolesToUsers")
    && !task. isTaskDisabled()
{
    // find out column index for role and user column
    // refer to the table above to find the column names
    int roleColumn = -1;
    int userColumn = -1;
    String[] colNames = task.getColumnNames();
    for (int i=0; i < colNames.length; i++)
    {
        if (colNames[i].equals ("role"))
            roleColumn = i;
        else if (colNames[i].equals ("role.user"))
            userColumn = i;
    }
    // iterate over task data starting at row 1 as row0 is
    // column names
    String[][]data = task.getTaskData();
    for (int i=1; i < data.length; i++)
    {
        if (data[i][roleColumn].equals ("Role1"))
        {
        data[i][userColumn]="User1|User2";
        break;
        }
    }
    // now that the task data is changed, save it back
    task.setTaskData (data);
}
```

Similar logic can be used to specify all other types of binding information, such as JNDI names for EJBs, virtual host names for Web modules, and so on, in various tasks. (The task information and the preceding sample code do not allow you to collect binding information for application client modules. You need to use the Client Configuration tool shipped with WebSphere Application Server to configure application clients.)

Save EAR File and Obtain Install Options

After all the necessary binding information has been supplied in various tasks, the task data should be saved back into the EAR file so that the populated EAR file can be installed into the WebSphere configuration. In addition to the binding information that is stored in the EAR file, there are several other deployment options that are collected by tasks, such as AppDeploymentOptions, EJBDeployOptions, and MapModulesToServers. These options are not saved in the EAR file but should be passed when the application is installed into the WebSphere configuration. After the task data is manipulated as necessary and the EAR file is saved, these options can be obtained from AppDeploymentController as a hash table. Alternately, these options can be passed directly during application installation, as explained later, and in the javadoc for installApplication API of com.ibm.websphere.management.application.AppManagement interface.

The following code shows how to save the task data into the EAR file and get generated installation options:

```
// the following line of code saves the task data
// in the EAR file specified as earName in step 1
flowController.saveAndClose();

// get the installation options
Hashtable options =
     flowController.getAppDeploymentSavedResults();
```

Managing Applications

The application management support in WebSphere Application Server provides functions such as installing and uninstalling applications, editing of binding information for installed applications, updating the entire application, exporting the application, and so on. This functionality is provided through the com.ibm.websphere.management.application.AppManagement interface, which is exposed as a JMX-based AppManagement MBean in WebSphere Application Server, and can be accessed by code running on the server or in a stand-alone administrative client program. When using WebSphere Application Server Network Deployment, the AppManagement MBean is only present in the Deployment Manager that facilitates centralized configuration and administration.

AppManagementProxy

The com.ibm.websphere.management.application.AppManagementProxy class provides uniform access to application management functionality, regardless of whether it is accessed from the server process, administrative client process, or a stand-alone Java program in the absence of WebSphere Application Server. The following code excerpts demonstrate how to obtain an AppManagementProxy instance in a variety of cases:

To access AppManagement function from the code that is running in WebSphere Application Server (e.g., as a custom service), use:

```
AppManagement appMgmt =
    AppManagementProxy. getJMXProxyForServer();
```

You can then use the AppManagement interface to perform operations such as installation of applications.

To access application management functionality from outside WebSphere Application Server via a JMX-based AppManagement MBean, you need to first create an AdminClient to establish a connection to the WebSphere server, as described earlier.

```
// create AppManagement proxy object
AppManagement appMgmt =
    AppManagementProxy. getJMXProxyForClient (adminClient);
```

Figure 6.6 shows the request flow when using the AppManagementProxy object to communicate with an AppManagement MBean.

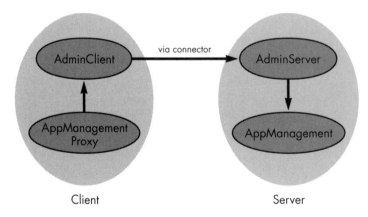

Figure 6.6
Using AppManagementProxy from remote client.

After obtaining an AppManagementProxy, you can perform various management functions such as installation, uninstallation, editing, and so on. However, before exploring the details of various application management functions, it is necessary to understand how the session concept from ConfigService works with application management functions.

Session Sharing

ConfigService allows you to create a session, which is a temporary staging area where all the configuration modifications can be saved. Saving the session saves all the updates from the session into the WebSphere configuration repository. The application management logic supports session sharing with ConfigService. Thus, it is possible to make all the application specific changes in the same session as the one created by config service. Saving such a session saves all the updates, including the ones that are application-specific. All the methods on the AppManagement interface take the last parameter as (String *workspaceID*). Here is a sample API:

```
public void installApplication (String localEarPath,
    String appName, Hashtable properties,
    String workspaceID) throws AdminException;
```

(The exceptions are the setApplicationInfo and setModuleInfo APIs, which do take (String *workspaceID*) as a parameter, but not as the last parameter.)

Passing a null value for this parameter indicates that there is no session sharing, and thus configuration changes made as a result of this operation are always saved in the configuration repository if the operation succeeds. The following steps demonstrate session sharing with config service:

1. Obtain ConfigService as described earlier.
2. Create a session as described earlier.
3. Pass in the session information to AppManagement:
```
AppManagement appMgmt = ...
appMgmt.installApplication
    (earPath, appName, properties, session.toString());
```
4. Save the session after all necessary changes are made:
```
configService.save(session, false);
```

Installing Applications

An EAR file that is populated with WebSphere-specific binding information can be installed into a WebSphere configuration using the installApplication API on the AppManagement interface.

The javadoc for installApplication API on com.ibm.websphere.management.application .AppManagement interface explains various options that can be passed during application installation, and also shows a code sample. These options can also be collected during the application preparation phase.

When the session in which the application deployment takes place is saved, the application EAR file, as well as the application metadata (which includes deployment descriptor and WebSphere-specific bindings and deployment descriptor extensions), are stored in the configuration repository. Additionally, a *deployment.xml* file is also created for each deployed application. It contains information about various deployment attributes and module-to-target (server and/or cluster) mappings. These files are stored in the configuration in the directory structure shown in Table 6.6.

Table 6.6   Directory Structure for EAR File and Application Metadata

EAR file	`$WAS_HOME/config/cells/cellName/applications/appName.ear/appName.ear`
Metadata	`$WAS_HOME/config/cells/cellName/applications/appName.ear/deployments/` `appName/<<all metadata files>> $WAS_HOME/config/cells/cellName/` `applications/appName.ear/deployments/appName/deployment.xml`

After the deployment-specific files are created in the WebSphere configuration repository (and in the case of WebSphere Application Server Network Deployment configuration, as the master repository configuration is synchronized with each node that the application modules are expected to run on), the application EAR file is extracted in the install destination location of the target node (see Figure 6.7). This location is specified during application installation using the option AppConstants.APPDEPL_INSTALL_DIR. The WebSphere Application Server run time reads the application business logic (e.g., EJB classes, servlets, JSPs) from the install destination location, while serving application client requests. However, the application metadata (e.g., deployment descriptor, WebSphere-specific bindings) is read by the server run time only during application startup. The metadata is read either from the configuration repository or from the install destination, depending on the APPDEPL _USE_BINARY_CONFIG option specified during application installation. This option is saved in deployment.xml as the useMetadataFromBinaries attribute. The default behavior is to read the metadata from the configuration repository.

The default install destination is ${APP_INSTALL_ROOT}/cellName/appName.ear, which is typically $WAS_HOME/installedApps/cellName/appName.ear. If an application is deployed on heterogeneous nodes, then the install destination (AppConstants.APPDEPL _INSTALL_DIR option specified during installation) should be defined as a variable with platform-specific values for individual nodes.

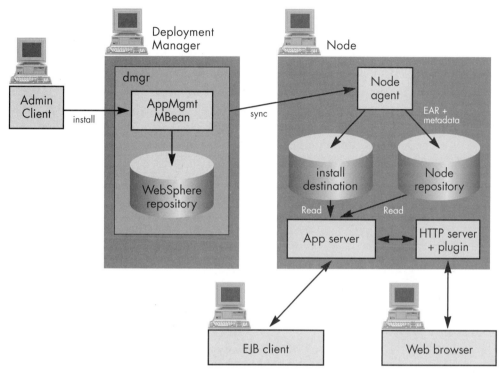

Figure 6.7
Application deployment in Network Deployment configuration.

Uninstalling Applications

An uninstall operation removes the application from the WebSphere configuration, thus removing it from all the servers and clusters that it runs on. Use the uninstallApplication API to uninstall applications.

To remove an application from a specific server or a cluster, or all the servers on a specific node, you can edit the application information, as explained in the next section.

After the application is uninstalled from the WebSphere configuration repository (and in the case of WebSphere Application Server Network Deployment configuration, as the master repository configuration is synchronized with each node on which the application modules are deployed), the EAR file extracted into the install destination of the target node during application installation is deleted. The application is stopped, if running, before the extracted EAR file is deleted from the target node.

Editing Applications

Most of the application binding information and application options that are specified during installation can be modified postinstall by editing an existing application. Certain options, such as EJB deployment, JSP precompilation, and so on, are only available at installation time. The edit operation involves the following steps:

1. Get information about an installed application.

Use the getApplicationInfo method on the AppManagement interface to get a list of AppDeploymentTask instances.

```
// Get information for an application with name appName
// Pass Locale information as the preference
Hashtable prefs = new Hashtable();
prefs.put(AppConstants.APPDEPL_LOCALE, Locale.getDefault());
Vector allTasks =
     appMgmt.getApplicationInfo (appName, prefs, null);
```

2. Manipulate task data as necessary.

The vector returned in the first step contains various AppDeploymentTask instances that are same as the ones explained in Table 6.5. These tasks can be manipulated as explained previously.

3. Save changes back into the installed application.

Use the setApplicationInfo method on the AppManagement interface to save the changes back to the configuration repository or to the session.

```
// Set information for an application with name appName
// Pass Locale information as the preference
Hashtable prefs = new Hashtable();
prefs.put(AppConstants.APPDEPL_LOCALE, Locale.getDefault());
appMgmt.setApplicationInfo (appName, prefs, null, allTasks);
```

After the edited application is saved in the WebSphere configuration repository (and in the case of WebSphere Application Server Network Deployment configuration, as the master repository configuration is synchronized with each node on which the application modules are deployed), the following actions are taken on each target node:

- If the application is running on the target node, then it is stopped and restarted for the new binding information and deployment options to take effect.
- If the application is completely removed from the target node by editing the MapModulesToServers task, then the EAR file extracted in the install destination of the target node as a result of application installation is deleted. Conversely, if the application is newly deployed on the application servers of the target node, then the EAR file is extracted in the install destination.

Redeploying (Updating) Configurations

It is quite common for application developers to continue to develop and fix applications in their development environment even after the application is deployed on a production system. To replace a deployed J2EE application with its new revision, the AppManagement interface provides a redeployApplication API. This function uninstalls the deployed application and installs the new revision with the same application name.

If the application is updated in the WebSphere configuration repository while it is running, then the running application is first stopped, the old EAR file is deleted from the install destination, the new EAR file is extracted in the install destination, and the application is restarted.

Starting and Stopping Applications

WebSphere Application Server provides an ApplicationManager MBean in each application server that allows you to start or stop applications on that server. Since WebSphere Application Server Version 5.0.1, the AppManagement interface also provides startApplication and stopApplication APIs. These functions start and stop applications on all the targets (servers and clusters) on which the application is deployed.

Using the ConfigService for Deployment Options

There are additional attributes related to a deployed application that are not exposed during or after application installation using AppDeploymentTask objects. These attributes are saved in the *deployment.xml* file that is created in the configuration repository for each deployed application. These attributes include the following:

- startingWeight: Specifies the order in which applications are started when the server starts up; applications are started in the ascending order of their starting weight.
- classloaderMode: Specifies the order in which classes are searched by the application classloader; default is PARENT_FIRST, which means classes are looked for in the following places in order: process, application, module. The other option is PARENT_LAST.

Refer to the configuration javadoc for the classes in the appdeployment package to learn about all of the application deployment attributes.

BUILDING AND RUNNING AN ADMINISTRATIVE CLIENT PROGRAM

When you are ready to build an administrative client program, you simply need to run javac and set the classpath to pick up the necessary JMX and WebSphere Application Server JAR files. The JAR files typically consist of *jmxc.jar*, *admin.jar*, and *wsexception.jar*. If Application Server is installed in C:\DeploymentManager, then the `javac` command would look as follows:

```
javac -classpath c:\DeploymentManager\lib\admin.jar;
   c:\DeploymentManager\lib\wsexception.jar;
   c:\DeploymentManager\lib\jmxc.jar AdminClientExample.java
```

Run your administrative client program by setting up the run-time environment so that the program can find all of the necessary requirements. Many of the batch or script files in the bin directory under the Application Server installation root perform a similar function. The following code snippet is an example of a Microsoft Windows batch file that runs an administrative client program named AdminClientExample; it is packaged in a JAR file of the same name. It uses the setupCmdLine.bat script that is installed in the Application Server bin directory to set up the necessary environment for the process:

```
@echo off
call "%~dp0setupCmdLine.bat"
"%JAVA_HOME%\bin\java" -classpath "%WAS_CLASSPATH%;
   %WAS_HOME%\lib\admin.jar;%WAS_HOME%\lib\wasjmx.jar;
   c:\test\AdminClientExample.jar" AdminClientExample %*
```

SAMPLE TASKS

The Web site that accompanies this book includes several Java programs that illustrate the administrative topics presented in this chapter. Here is a description of each program:

- Example1.java—Create a new application server.
- Example2.java—Install a new application.
- Example3.java—Target an installed application to a server.
- Example4.java—Start an application server.
- Example5.java—Stop an application server.
- Example6.java—Start an application.
- Example7.java—Stop an application.
- Example8.java—Update an existing application.

WHERE TO FIND ADDITIONAL INFORMATION

We only touched on the bare essentials of JMX in this chapter and there is much more that you might want to learn about. There are many good sources of information on JMX, from articles on Java developer Web sites to entire books. The place to start, though, would be the official Sun site at *http://java.sun.com/products/JavaManagement*.

There are three sets of documentation pertaining to WebSphere administration that are important to know about:

- WebSphere administration API—This is the javadoc for the classes that comprise the administration API and it is included in the ovrall Application Server API section of the javadocs in the WebSphere Information Center. To find it you need to use the left navigation pane, expand Qiuck Reference and then expand Javadoc and select Application Server API. There you will find the detailed documentation on AdminClient, ConfigService, AppManagement, and many other classes.
- WebSphere MBean documentation—This is the documentation for the MBeans provided by WebSphere presented in javadoc format. You can find this in the Info Center just below the Application Server API just mentioned. It is also installed with the Appliation Server in the `web/mbeanDocs` directory.
- WebSphere configuration documentation—This documentation describes the configuration objects and will be useful for configuration management programming. You will also find this in the javadoc section of the Info Center under the heading of "Server configuation API" and it is also installed with the Application Server in the `web/configDocs` directory.

Administrative Integration on z/OS

T he administrative features of WebSphere Version 5 are common to all WebSphere platforms, including IBM z/OS operating system platform for z/Series Enterprise Servers. In addition to these common features, there are additional administrative features present in the WebSphere Version 5 product specifically designed to enhance product operation on the z/OS platform. The purpose of this appendix is to introduce you to these additional features.

PROCESS MODEL INTEGRATION

The process model for WebSphere on z/OS is a multiprocess federation, consisting of one control process and one or more servant processes. The control process executes only authorized WebSphere systems. Its purpose is to host communication end points, provide authentication point of control, and serve as the registration point for recoverable resources. The servant processes contain the WebSphere system components that support the J2EE programming model and host J2EE applications. Figure A.1 illustrates this process model.

The control process hosts only authorized WebSphere system functions. Communications, security, and transaction control are deeply integrated with z/OS operating system services such as high-speed SRB mode TCP/IP sockets, System Access Facility (SAF), Resource Recovery Services (RRS), z/OS Workload Manager (WLM), and Automatic Restart Manager (ARM). The z/OS operating system upholds high standards of system integrity. Process separation of application code from system code adheres to these standards.

Each servant process provides all APIs in the J2EE programming model as well as WebSphere extensions. All servant processes are clones of one another. Servants can be dynamically added and removed on demand in response to system workload by the z/OS WLM

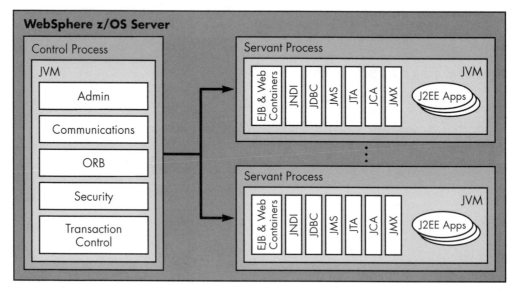

Figure A.1
z/OS Application Server process model.

working in conjunction with the server's control process. The servant process is where your J2EE application runs. In the event of a terminating error, z/OS automatically starts a replacement servant process. This resiliency increases the robustness of the server.

Each z/OS process has a job name that is eight characters or less. There is an additional field in the server's definition through which the job name is specified. The job name is known as *short name* in the server configuration. Figure A.2 shows the placement of the short name field in the server's configuration.

Application Servers >
server1

An application server is a server which provides services required to run enterprise applications. ⓘ

Configuration		

General Properties		
Name	server1	ⓘ The display name for the server.
Initial State	Started ▾	ⓘ The execution state requested when the server is first started.
Application classloader policy	Multiple ▾	ⓘ Specifies whether there is a single classloader for all applications ("Single") or a classloader per application ("Multiple").
Application class loading mode	Parent first ▾	ⓘ Specifies the class loading mode when the application classloader policy is "Single"
short Name	BBOS001	ⓘ An optional short name for this server (8 chars or less)
Unique Id	BA749CE714131C23000000DC000000010939041C	ⓘ Specifies unique identifier for this server.

Apply | OK | Reset | Cancel

Figure A.2
Server short name property.

The WebSphere z/OS server registers with z/OS WLM to enable dynamic management of the servant processes. This registration requires a unique eight-character WLM Application Environment name. This name is specified in the WebSphere cluster definition, again, as a short name. Figure A.3 shows the placement of this field.

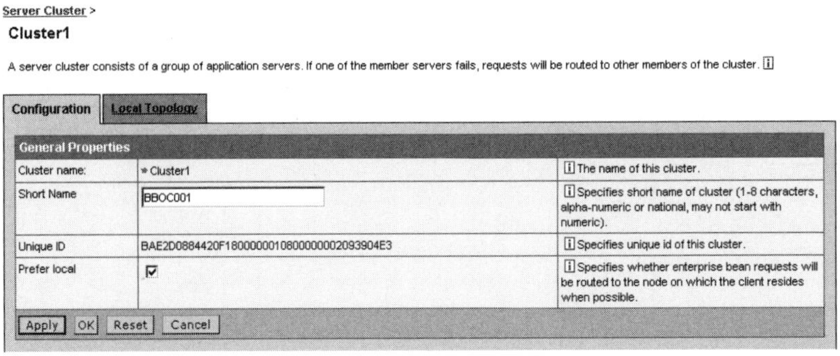

Server Cluster >
Cluster1

A server cluster consists of a group of application servers. If one of the member servers fails, requests will be routed to other members of the cluster. [i]

Configuration	Local Topology		
General Properties			
Cluster name:	* Cluster1		[i] The name of this cluster.
Short Name	BBOC001		[i] Specifies short name of cluster (1-8 characters, alpha-numeric or national, may not start with numeric).
Unique ID	BAE2D0884420F1800000010800000002093904E3		[i] Specifies unique id of this cluster.
Prefer local	☑		[i] Specifies whether enterprise bean requests will be routed to the node on which the client resides when possible.

Apply | OK | Reset | Cancel

Figure A.3
Cluster short name property.

The number of servants is controlled through a policy setting that is passed by the control process when it registers with z/OS WLM. Each server has a *server instance* configuration to specify this policy. The default configuration runs with only a single servant process. The server can be placed in scalable mode by enabling multiple servants and specifying a minimum and maximum number of servants. This policy can be defined through the configuration page shown in Figure A.4.

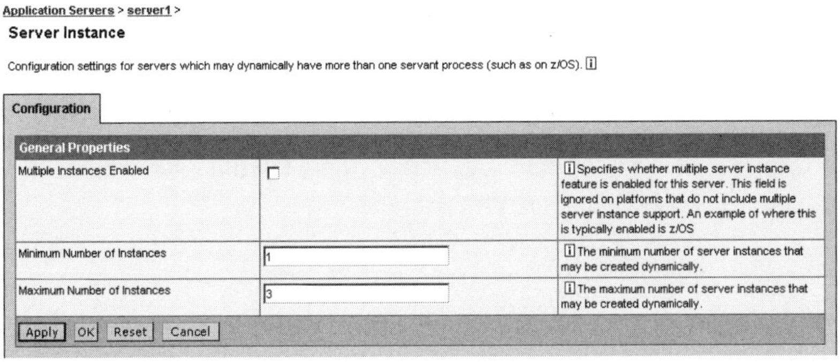

Application Servers > server1 >
Server Instance

Configuration settings for servers which may dynamically have more than one servant process (such as on z/OS). [i]

Configuration		
General Properties		
Multiple Instances Enabled	☐	[i] Specifies whether multiple server instance feature is enabled for this server. This field is ignored on platforms that do not include multiple server instance support. An example of where this is typically enabled is z/OS
Minimum Number of Instances	1	[i] The minimum number of server instances that may be created dynamically.
Maximum Number of Instances	3	[i] The maximum number of server instances that may be created dynamically.

Apply | OK | Reset | Cancel

Figure A.4
z/OS server instance configuration.

The settings for each process type, control or servant, are separately configurable. When you select the server's process definition configuration in the Administrative Console, you are presented with a collection view through which either the control or servant configuration can be selected, as shown in Figure A.5.

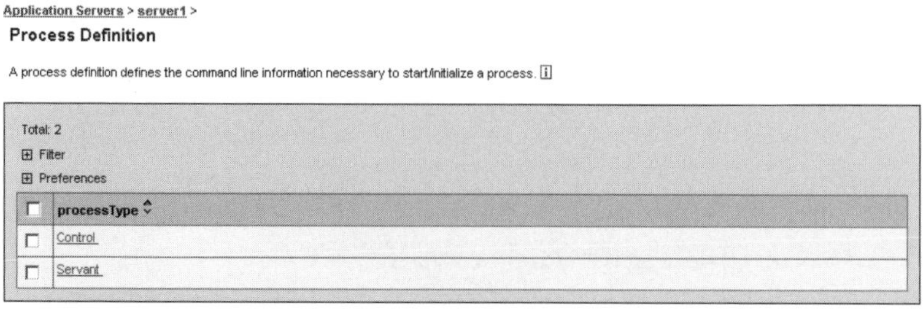

Figure A.5
z/OS process definition collection page.

OPERATIONS MODEL INTEGRATION

The WebSphere z/OS server supports the UNIX operational commands, such as `start-Server.sh` and `stopServer.sh`. However, z/OS operations commonly are performed through the z/OS Operations Interfaces, which include the z/OS Operator Console, System Command Interface (MGRE), and Write-to-Operator (WTO).

System `START` and `STOP` commands are used to control the server life cycle. Starting and stopping a WebSphere z/OS server through the z/OS Operations Interfaces is done with these commands. These command strings are stored in the server's process definitions for use by other operational facilities.

The control process definition includes the start command string for starting the control process. This command string is comprised of a *Start Command* and *Start Command Args*. The two are concatenated to produce the full `START` command. The full `START` command is used internally by the `startServer.sh` UNIX command so that the server is started using the same mechanism whether it is launched directly through the z/OS Operator Console, through Automation using MGRE, or through the UNIX command interface. Figure A.6 shows the configuration for the z/OS System `START` command.

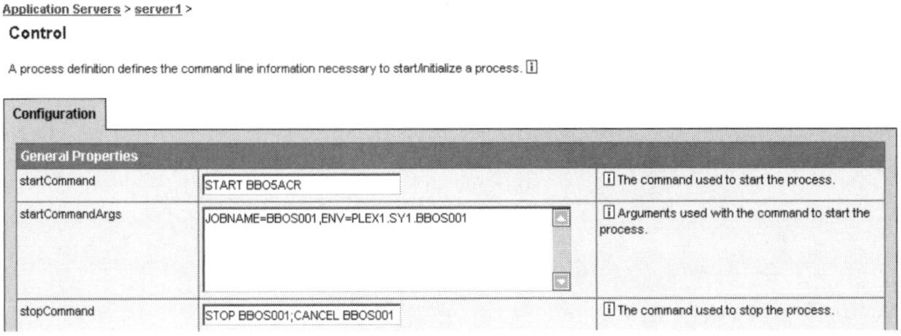

Application Servers > server1 >
Control

A process definition defines the command line information necessary to start/initialize a process. ⓘ

Configuration		
General Properties		
startCommand	START BBO5ACR	ⓘ The command used to start the process.
startCommandArgs	JOBNAME=BBOS001,ENV=PLEX1.SY1.BBOS001	ⓘ Arguments used with the command to start the process.
stopCommand	STOP BBOS001;CANCEL BBOS001	ⓘ The command used to stop the process.

Figure A.6
z/OS Application Server Start command.

The syntax for the START command follows:

```
START <JCL proc name>
        ,JOBNAME=<server short name>
        ,ENV=<cell short name>.<node short name>.<server short name>
```

Where:

- <JCL proc name> specifies the name of the Job Control Language procedure from the System PROCLIB data set concatenation used to start this server.
- JOBNAME=<server short name> specifies the z/OS job name of this server.
- ENV=<cell short name>.<node short name>.<server short name> is a file system convention that specifies a shortcut to the location of the server's configuration files. This shortcut is implemented as a UNIX file system (HFS) symbolic link. For example:

    ```
    /WebSphere/V5R0M0/PLEX1.SY1.BBOS001
    ```

    is a symbolic link to

    ```
    /WebSphere/V5R0M0/AppServer/config/cells/PLEX1Network
            /nodes/System1/servers/server1
    ```

The cell and node short names are found in the cell and node configuration. These values are specified during initial product configuration through the WebSphere z/OS Customization Dialog. These values are viewable through the Administrative Console in the cell and node configuration pages (see Figures A.7 and A.8).

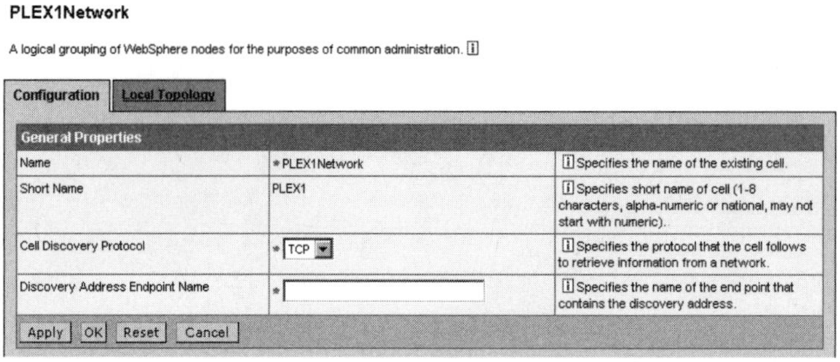

PLEX1Network

A logical grouping of WebSphere nodes for the purposes of common administration. ⓘ

Configuration	Local Topology

General Properties		
Name	* PLEX1Network	ⓘ Specifies the name of the existing cell.
Short Name	PLEX1	ⓘ Specifies short name of cell (1-8 characters, alpha-numeric or national, may not start with numeric).
Cell Discovery Protocol	* TCP ▾	ⓘ Specifies the protocol that the cell follows to retrieve information from a network.
Discovery Address Endpoint Name	*	ⓘ Specifies the name of the end point that contains the discovery address.

Apply OK Reset Cancel

Figure A.7
z/OS Cell short name.

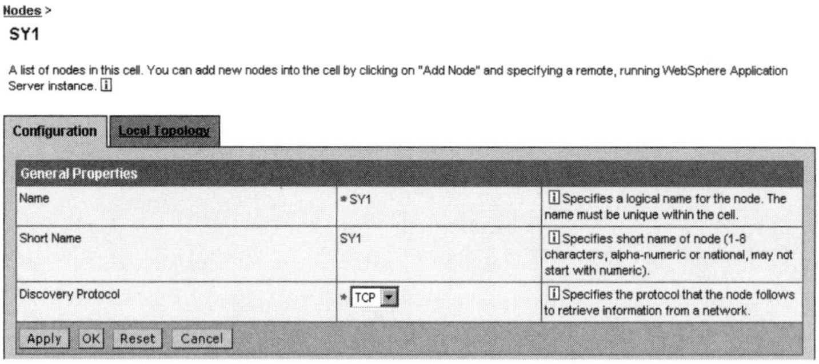

Nodes >
SY1

A list of nodes in this cell. You can add new nodes into the cell by clicking on "Add Node" and specifying a remote, running WebSphere Application Server instance. ⓘ

Configuration	Local Topology

General Properties		
Name	* SY1	ⓘ Specifies a logical name for the node. The name must be unique within the cell.
Short Name	SY1	ⓘ Specifies short name of node (1-8 characters, alpha-numeric or national, may not start with numeric).
Discovery Protocol	* TCP ▾	ⓘ Specifies the protocol that the node follows to retrieve information from a network.

Apply OK Reset Cancel

Figure A.8
z/OS Node short name.

The servant process is started under control of z/OS WLM. When the server control process registers with z/OS WLM, the JCL procedure name and START command parameters to start the servant process are passed to WLM on the registration call. When WLM decides to start a servant process, it issues the START command through MGRE. Figure A.9 shows the configuration for a servant process' START command:

Application Servers > server1 >
Servant

A process definition defines the command line information necessary to start/initialize a process. ⓘ

Configuration

General Properties		
startCommand	BBO5ASR	ⓘ The command used to start the process.
startCommandArgs	JOBNAME=&MVMSSNM.S,ENV='PLEX1.SY1.&MVMSSNM.'	ⓘ Arguments used with the command to start the process.

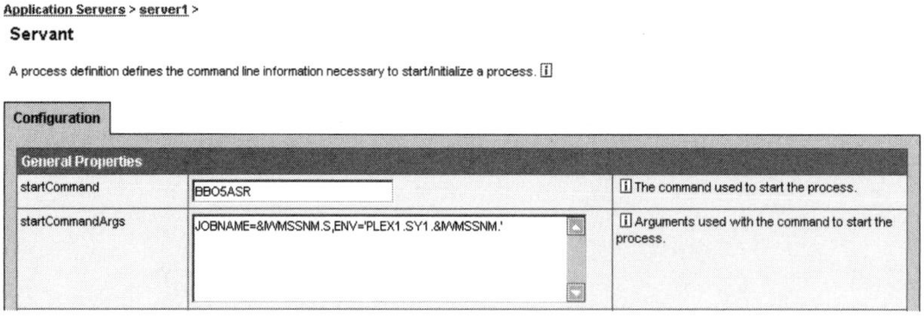

Figure A.9
z/OS servant process START command.

A z/OS server is typically started using the control process START command issued through the z/OS Operator Console. Figure A.10 shows the result of issuing this command:

```
START BBO5ACR,JOBNAME=BBOS001,ENV=PLEX1.SY1.BBOS001:
```

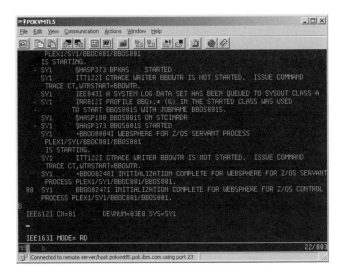

Figure A.10
z/OS Operator Console issuing START command.

The system messages (WTOs) report on the progress of the server's initialization. Separate messages are issued for both control and servant processes. The use of WTO messages enables z/OS automation products (e.g., IBM Tivoli NetView) to monitor and manage WebSphere z/OS servers.

Integration with z/OS system facilities includes exposing the WebSphere server jobs through conventional operations interfaces, such as System Display and Service Facility (SDSF). Figure A.11 shows the control and one servant process for server1.

Figure A.11
z/OS system display and service facility.

The ProcStep column in the preceding display clearly indicates whether the process type is control (BBOCTL) or servant (BBOSR). The JCL for these two procedures is shown here:

Control Process JCL (BBO5ACR)

```
//BBO5ACR  PROC ENV=,PARMS=' ',Z=BBO5ACRZ
//  SET ROOT='/WebSphere/V5R0M0'
//BBOCTL  EXEC PGM=BBOCTL,REGION=0M,
// PARM='TRAP(ON,NOSPIE),ENVAR("_EDC_UMASK_DFLT=007") / &PARMS.'
//BBOENV DD PATH='&ROOT/&ENV/was.env'
//  INCLUDE MEMBER=&Z
```

Servant Process JCL

```
//BBO5ASR  PROC ENV=,PARMS=' ',Z=BBO5ASRZ
//  SET ROOT='/WebSphere/V5R0M0'
//BBOSR  EXEC PGM=BBOCTL,REGION=0M,
// PARM='TRAP(ON,NOSPIE),ENVAR("_EDC_UMASK_DFLT=007") / &PARMS.'
//BBOENV DD PATH='&ROOT/&ENV/was.env'
//  INCLUDE MEMBER=&Z
```

The WebSphere z/OS server is similarly stopped using the z/OS System STOP command. Like the START command, the STOP command is configured in the control process definition and is used by the UNIX stopServer.sh line command. WLM uses an internal mechanism to stop servant processes, so there is no STOP command configuration in the servant process definition. Using the z/OS Operator Console, the following command would be used to stop server1:

STOP BBOS00I

Like the START command, the STOP command issues WTO that enable z/OS automation. Figure A.12 shows these messages.

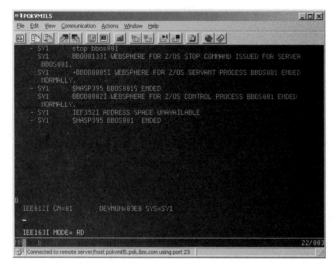

Figure A.12
z/OS server STOP messages.

WORKLOAD MANAGEMENT MODEL INTEGRATION

In addition to using z/OS WLM to make on-demand provisioning decisions for a server's servant processes, WLM is further exploited in a z/OS Sysplex configuration. A z/OS Sysplex is a hardware cluster running two or more z/OS instances. The systems in a z/OS Sysplex are interconnected using high-speed bus-level transports and share a specialized hardware memory device called the coupling facility. The coupling facility supports multiple Sysplex-wide functions, including the following:

- DB2, CICS, and IMS data sharing.
- Sysplex-wide lock manager (GRS).
- Sysplex-wide logging (System Logger).
- Sysplex-wide workload management (z/OS WLM).
- Sysplex-wide peer recovery (ARM).

- Sysplex member services (XCF).
- Sysplex-wide TCP IP communications (Sysplex Distributor).

A common workload management and distribution configuration for z/OS Sysplex leverages the distributed dynamic virtual IP address (DVIPA) capability of Sysplex Distributor. A DVIPA is a logical, multistack IP address. It is typically spread across multiple z/OS instances. Each instance of the DVIPA listens on the same port number. This enables dynamically managed workload balancing through WLM and supports failover.

The WebSphere z/OS server supports use of DVIPAs for both Web and EJB traffic. Sessionless Web traffic can be managed by routing the work from the network devices directly to the z/OS Sysplex's DVIPA configuration. Sessional Web traffic can be routed first to a Web server and then using the WebSphere HTTP plug-in, to either a DVIPA (for new sessions) or a specific z/OS TCP IP stack (for existing sessions).

EJB traffic is managed by establishing connections through the WebSphere z/OS Location Service daemon. The location service supports CORBA locate requests, connecting a EJB requestor with a server that hosts the requested EJB. The location service is cluster-aware and exploits z/OS WLM to make routing decisions among cluster members. The location service daemon is replicated in a z/OS sysplex and uses a DVIPA to support connection balancing and failover. Figure A.13 depicts the configuration for WebSphere z/OS TCP IP configuration.

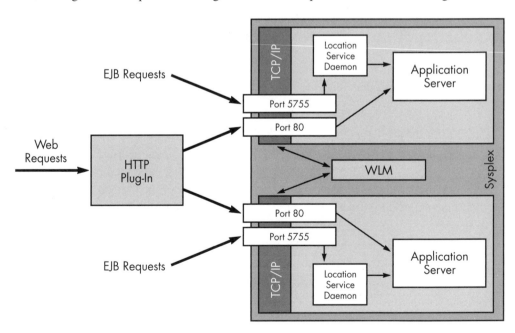

Figure A.13
z/OS TCP/IP configuration.

The configuration for the z/OS Location Service Daemon is accessible through the Administrative Console. A link to this configuration page is accessible through the System Administration tree list, found at the left side of the Administrative Console and enables configuration of the daemon's job name, host, ports, and SSL configuration (see Figure A.14).

Location Service Daemon

This panel specifies configuration settings for the location service daemon for this cell. Changes made to these settings apply to the entire cell and to the location service daemon instance on each node in the cell. [i]

Configuration		
General Properties		
Job Name	* BBODMNC	[i] Specifies z/OS JOBNAME of location service daemon.
Host Name	* BOSSXXXX.PLEX1.L2.IBM.COM	[i] Specifies host name to be used when contacting location service daemon.
Port	* 5755	[i] Specifies port location service daemon listens on for un-encrypted communication.
SSL Port	* 5756	[i] Specifies port location service daemon listens on for encrypted communication.
SSL Settings	* PLEX1Manager/DefaultIIOPSSL ▼	[i] Specifies a list of pre-defined SSL settings to choose from for connections. These are configured at the SSL repertoire panel.
Apply OK Reset Cancel		

Figure A.14
z/OS Location Service daemon configuration.

SECURITY MODEL INTEGRATION

The z/OS security domain differs from the Distributed security domain by several distinguishing features:

1. Additional global security features

2. Two types of SSL repertoires

3. JSSE (JDK SSL)

4. System SSL (z/OS-native SSL)

5. Optional use of SAF repository as an alternative to key ring file

6. ICSF authentication mechanism (based on z/Series HW cryptographic processor)

7. SAF local OS registry settings

8. zSAS configuration in place of SAS Inbound/Outbound configuration

Global Security

The z/OS security domain has the following additional configuration options: default remote and local identifies for unauthenticated client requests, and options for application and connector thread identity enablement.

These additional configuration options are configurable through the configuration page shown in Figure A.15, which is accessible through the Global Security page's additional Properties list.

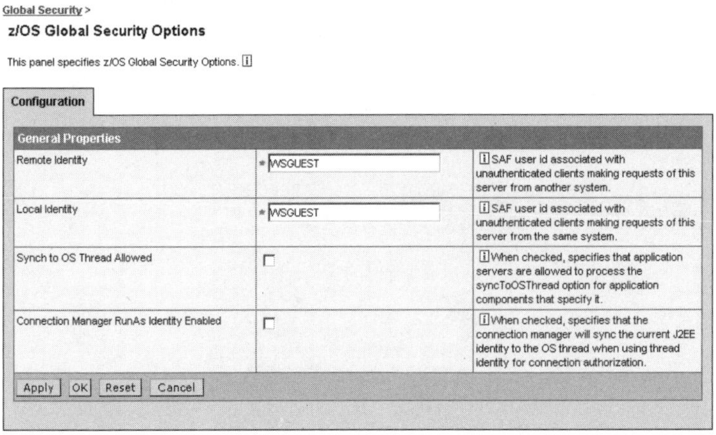

Global Security >
z/OS Global Security Options

This panel specifies z/OS Global Security Options. ⓘ

Configuration		
General Properties		
Remote Identity	＊ WSGUEST	ⓘ SAF user id associated with unauthenticated clients making requests of this server from another system.
Local Identity	＊ WSGUEST	ⓘ SAF user id associated with unauthenticated clients making requests of this server from the same system.
Synch to OS Thread Allowed	☐	ⓘ When checked, specifies that application servers are allowed to process the syncToOSThread option for application components that specify it.
Connection Manager RunAs Identity Enabled	☐	ⓘ When checked, specifies that the connection manager will sync the current J2EE identity to the OS thread when using thread identity for connection authorization.

Apply | OK | Reset | Cancel

Figure A.15
z/OS security configuration options.

SSL

The z/OS system supports two different SSL types: JSSE and System SSL (SSSL):

1. JSSE (Java Secure Socket Extension) is the SSL type supported on JDK TCP IP sockets.
2. SSSL is the SSL type supported natively on z/OS TCP IP sockets.

JSSE and SSSL support different cipher suites, and SSSL has fewer configuration options. The SSL Repertoire Configuration page allows for the choice of creating either JSSE or SSSL repertoires, and has an additional type column to allow easy identification of repertoires by type (see Figure A.16).

SSL Configuration Repertoires

Specifies the list of defined Secure Socket Layer configurations. ⓘ

Total: 10	
⊞ Filter	
⊞ Preferences	

New SSSL Repertoire   New JSSE Repertoire   Delete

☐	Alias ⇕	Type ⇕
☐	PLEX1Manager/DefaultHTTPS	SSSL
☐	PLEX1Manager/DefaultIIOPSSL	SSSL
☐	PLEX1Manager/DefaultSOAPSSLSettings	JSSE
☐	PLEX1Manager/DefaultSSLSettings	JSSE
☐	PLEX1Manager/RACFJSSESettings	JSSE
☐	SY1/DefaultHTTPS	SSSL
☐	SY1/DefaultIIOPSSL	SSSL
☐	SY1/DefaultSOAPSSLSettings	JSSE
☐	SY1/DefaultSSLSettings	JSSE
☐	SY1/RACFJSSESettings	JSSE

Figure A.16
z/OS SSL repertoire collection.

The SSSL repertoire uses only the SAF registry for storing certificates. It does not have a separate trust file. Therefore fewer options are present on the configuration page for an SSSL repertoire (see Figure A.17).

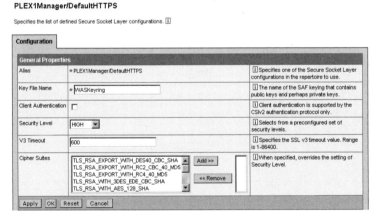

SSL Configuration Repertoires >
PLEX1Manager/DefaultHTTPS

Specifies the list of defined Secure Socket Layer configurations. ⓘ

Figure A.17
z/OS SSL repertoire configuration.

JSSE and SSSL repertoires support different cipher suites.

JSSE Ciphers

- SSL_DHE_DSS_EXPORT_WITH_DES40_CBC_SHA
- SSL_DHE_DSS_WITH_3DES_EDE_CBC_SHA
- SSL_DHE_DSS_WITH_DES_CBC_SHA
- SSL_DHE_RSA_EXPORT_WITH_DES40_CBC_SHA
- SSL_DHE_RSA_WITH_3DES_EDE_CBC_SHA
- SSL_DHE_RSA_WITH_DES_CBC_SHA
- SSL_DH_anon_EXPORT_WITH_DES40_CBC_SHA
- SSL_DH_anon_EXPORT_WITH_RC4_40_MD5
- SSL_DH_anon_WITH_3DES_EDE_CBC_SHA
- SSL_DH_anon_WITH_DES_CBC_SHA
- SSL_DH_anon_WITH_RC4_128_MD5
- SSL_RSA_EXPORT_WITH_DES40_CBC_SHA
- SSL_RSA_EXPORT_WITH_RC2_CBC_40_MD5
- SSL_RSA_EXPORT_WITH_RC4_40_MD5
- SSL_RSA_WITH_3DES_EDE_CBC_SHA
- SSL_RSA_WITH_DES_CBC_SHA
- SSL_RSA_WITH_NULL_MD5 SSL_RSA_WITH_NULL_SHA
- SSL_RSA_WITH_RC4_128_MD5
- SSL_RSA_WITH_RC4_128_SHA

SSSL Ciphers

- TLS_RSA_EXPORT_WITH_DES40_CBC_SHA
- TLS_RSA_EXPORT_WITH_RC2_CBC_40_MD5
- TLS_RSA_EXPORT_WITH_RC4_40_MD5
- TLS_RSA_WITH_3DES_EDE_CBC_SHA
- TLS_RSA_WITH_AES_128_SHA
- TLS_RSA_WITH_AES_256_SHA
- TLS_RSA_WITH_DES_CBC_SHA
- TLS_RSA_WITH_IDEA_CBC_SHA
- TLS_RSA_WITH_NULL_MD5
- TLS_RSA_WITH_NULL_SHA
- TLS_RSA_WITH_RC4_128_MD5
- TLS_RSA_WITH_RC4_128_SHA

A WAS z/OS server utilizes both JDK and native sockets. It uses JDK sockets for the SOAP HTTP connector. It uses native sockets for HTTP and RMI sockets. This means that the SOAP HTTP connector uses a JSSE repertoire, and the HTTP transports and ORB ports use SSSL repertoires. To enhance usability, those pages on the console that expose an SSL repertoire selection use type-specific selection lists so that the correct SSL type can be selected. This means:

- The following configuration elements expose only SSSL repertoire types in their SSLSettings drop-down lists:
  - CSI Inbound Transport
  - CSI Outbound Transport
  - zSAS Transport
- The SOAP connector sslConfig property exposes only JSSE repertoire types in its drop-down list as shown in Figure A.18.

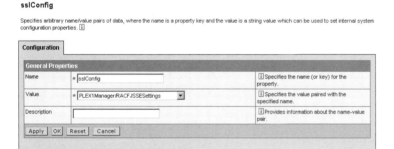

Figure A.18
z/OS SOAP connector SSL configuration.

SAF Key Ring

SSSL repertoires use only the SAF registry as a key ring store. JSSE repertoires can use either file system or the SAF registry for a key ring store. The benefit of the SAF repository as a key ring store is that it is shared by all z/WAS nodes in the same z/OS Sysplex (see Figure A.19).

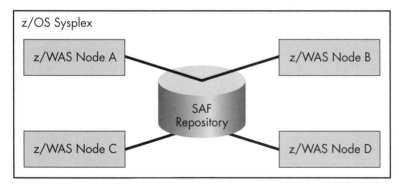

Figure A.19
z/OS SAF repository.

This is a benefit because all certificates are shared. Therefore certificates need not be imported into multiple registries to enable SSL connections between those nodes that are in the same security domain. However, this quality of service is available only to WebSphere nodes in the same z/OS Sysplex.

The SAF repository is the only key ring store option for SSSL repertoires. JSSE repertoires have a choice of either file system or SAF. If file system is chosen, the configuration considerations are identical to those of a WebSphere Distributed node. If SAF is chosen, the configuration considerations are the same as SSSL. The JSSE key ring (and trust ring) decision is made using a simple URL pattern:

```
[file:][<file-spec>] | [safkeyring:][<key ring name>]
```

Where:

```
<file-spec> is a fully qualified file system name.
<key ring name> is a valid SAF key ring name.
```

ICSF

The Integrated Cryptographic Security Facility (ICSF) is an alternate authentication mechanism available to WebSphere z/OS application servers. It exploits the z/Series Cryptographic Coprocessor Facility as the basis of its function. It is available only to WebSphere nodes in the same z/OS Sysplex.

A separate configuration page, shown in Figure A.20, is accessible through the admin console navigation bar:

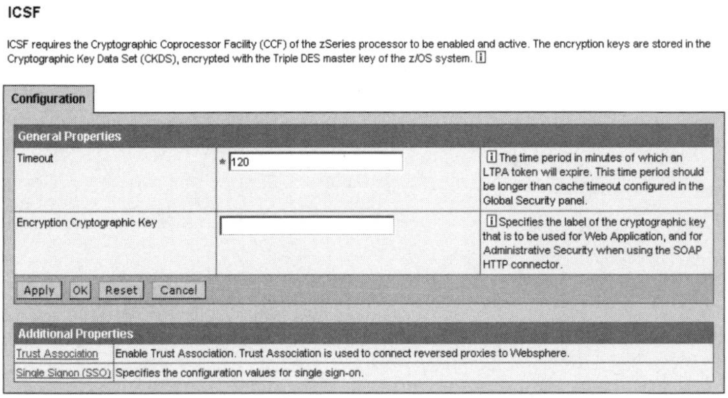

Figure A.20
z/OS ICSF configuration.

Local OS

SAF is the local OS for WebSphere z/OS. Unlike the local OS found on other platforms, the z/OS local OS is inherently common and shared among all WebSphere z/OS nodes in the same Sysplex. The configurable elements of the SAF local OS are different than the local OS of distributed platforms as follows:

- **No user ID or password is configured.** This is because WebSphere z/OS servers authenticate and are assigned identity through SAF-managed policy that is configured outside of WebSphere. This mechanism is the SAF Started Procedures Class.
- **User ID case policy.** SAF user IDs are traditionally uppercase. Based on local policy, the WebSphere z/OS customer can choose uppercase (default) or mixed case.

The local OS configuration page for z/OS is shown in Figure A.21.

Local OS User Registry

The user registry for the local operating system of the application server. When security is enabled and any of these properties are changed, please go to the GlobalSecurity panel and click Apply or OK to validate the changes. [i]

Configuration		
General Properties		
Local OS Type	SAS	[i] Use the "Custom Properties" link to configure the SAS.
Ignore Case	☐	[i] When set to true, a case insensitive authorization check will be performed.
Apply OK Reset Cancel		
Additional Properties		
Custom Properties	A set of arbitrary user registry configuration properties whose names are specific to a given type of pluggable registry.	

Figure A.21
z/OS local OS configuration.

zSAS

The SAS authentication protocol on the WebSphere z/OS platform is logically the same as SAS on distributed platforms. However, its configurable elements differ significantly from its distributed sibling. Because its configuration characteristics are so dissimilar, it was even given a different identity: *zSAS*.

The zSAS authentication protocol has only one configuration policy for both inbound and outbound requests. In contrast, SAS offers both. Additionally, zSAS has several additional options not found in SAS:

- Basic authentication
- Client certificate
- Kerberos
- User ID password
- User ID passticket

- Identity assertion inbound
- Identity assertion outbound
- Allow unauthenticated clients

The configuration page for zSAS is shown in Figure A.22.

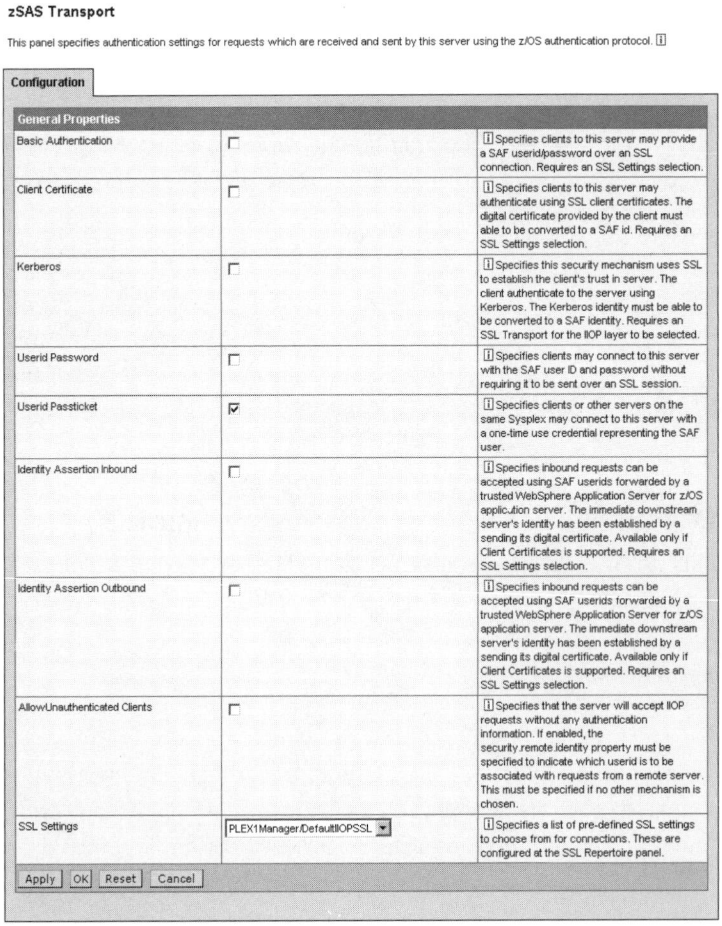

zSAS Transport

This panel specifies authentication settings for requests which are received and sent by this server using the z/OS authentication protocol. ⓘ

Configuration		
General Properties		
Basic Authentication	☐	ⓘ Specifies clients to this server may provide a SAF userid/password over an SSL connection. Requires an SSL Settings selection.
Client Certificate	☐	ⓘ Specifies clients to this server may authenticate using SSL client certificates. The digital certificate provided by the client must able to be converted to a SAF id. Requires an SSL Settings selection.
Kerberos	☐	ⓘ Specifies this security mechanism uses SSL to establish the client's trust in server. The client authenticate to the server using Kerberos. The Kerberos identity must be able to be converted to a SAF identity. Requires an SSL Transport for the IIOP layer to be selected.
Userid Password	☐	ⓘ Specifies clients may connect to this server with the SAF user ID and password without requiring it to be sent over an SSL session.
Userid Passticket	☑	ⓘ Specifies clients or other servers on the same Sysplex may connect to this server with a one-time use credential representing the SAF user.
Identity Assertion Inbound	☐	ⓘ Specifies inbound requests can be accepted using SAF userids forwarded by a trusted WebSphere Application Server for z/OS application server. The immediate downstream server's identity has been established by a sending its digital certificate. Available only if Client Certificates is supported. Requires an SSL Settings selection.
Identity Assertion Outbound	☐	ⓘ Specifies inbound requests can be accepted using SAF userids forwarded by a trusted WebSphere Application Server for z/OS application server. The immediate downstream server's identity has been established by a sending its digital certificate. Available only if Client Certificates is supported. Requires an SSL Settings selection.
AllowUnauthenticated Clients	☐	ⓘ Specifies that the server will accept IIOP requests without any authentication information. If enabled, the security.remote.identity property must be specified to indicate which userid is to be associated with requests from a remote server. This must be specified if no other mechanism is chosen.
SSL Settings	PLEX1Manager/DefaultIIOPSSL ▼	ⓘ Specifies a list of pre-defined SSL settings to choose from for connections. These are configured at the SSL Repertoire panel.

Apply OK Reset Cancel

Figure A.22
z/OS zSAS configuration.

WebSphere Version 5 Run-Time MBeans

This Appendix identifies each JMX MBean included with the WebSphere Application Server Version 5 product. Full documentation of all attributes, operations, and notifications for each MBean is available in an html table that is installed with each copy of the WebSphere product. Instructions for accessing the MBean documentation shipped with WebSphere are included at the end of this appendix.

OVERALL LIST OF JMX MBEAN TYPES IN WEBSPHERE VERSION 5

The following list documents all of the WebSphere Application Server Version 5 run-time MBeans supplied with the product.

AdminOperations—miscellaneous administrative functions, available in any WebSphere JVM.

Application—represents a running J2EE application, available in any WebSphere JVM where the application is executing.

ApplicationManager—control logic for starting and stopping applications, available in any Application Server JVM.

AppManagement—administrative logic for deploying and updating J2EE applications, available only in administrative JVMs.

CellSync—configuration synchronization logic that executes against the master cell repository, available only in the Deployment Manager JVM.

Cluster—represents a WebSphere cluster of application servers, available only in the Deployment Manager JVM.

ClusterMgr—administrative logic for locating, starting, and stopping Cluster MBeans, available only in the Deployment Manager JVM.

ConfigRepository—interface to the configuration repository for performing document level operations, available only in administrative JVMs.

ConfigService—interface for performing individual object configuration, available only in administrative JVMs.

ConnectionFactory—represents the connection factory portion of any J2EE resource, available in any WebSphere JVM within the scope of this resource configuration.

ControlAdminService—interface to the Control JVM for the z/OS platform, available only on z/OS.

DataSource—represents a WebSphere V5 JDBC DataSource, available in any WebSphere JVM within the scope of this resource configuration.

DataSourceCfgHelper—MBean for testing JDBC DataSources, available WebSphere administration server JVMs.

DeployedObject—parent MBean for J2EE applications and their component parts, available in any WebSphere JVM where the application is executing.

DeploymentManager—represents the control interface to the Deployment Manager server, available only in the Deployment Manager JVM.

Discovery—administrative logic for discovering other WebSphere servers, available in all WebSphere JVMs.

DynaCache—represents the caching functions of the server, available in any Application Server JVM.

EJB—represents any Enterprise Java Bean portion of a J2EE application, available in any WebSphere JVM where the application is executing.

EJBContainer—represents the Container environment for the EJB portion of a J2EE application, available in any JVM that includes such a container in its component set.

EJBModule—represents the EJB portion of a J2EE application, available in any WebSphere JVM where the application is executing.

EmbeddedJMSAdministration—provides function for the embedded and integral JMS provider.

EntityBean—represents any EntityBean portion of a J2EE application, available in any WebSphere JVM where the application is executing.

J2CConnectionFactory—represents a connection factory for a J2C resource adapter, available in any JVM within the configuration scope of that resource.

J2CResourceAdapter—represents the provider library for a J2C resource adapter, available in any JVM within the configuration scope of that resource.

J2EEResourceFactory—parent MBean for all resource factories, available in any JVM within the configuration scope of that resource.

J2EEResourceProvider—parent MBean for all resource provider libraries, available in any JVM within the configuration scope of that resource.

JDBCProvider—represents the provider library for a JDBC driver, available in any JVM within the configuration scope of that resource.

JMSAdministration—basic administration function for JMS providers.

JMSBasicFunction—used to perform application like function for JMS, such as sending or receiving messages.

JMSDestination—represents a JMS destination resource factory, available in any JVM within the configuration scope of that resource.

JMSProvider—represents the provider library for a JMS resource provider, available in any JVM within the configuration scope of that resource.

JMSServer—represents the message broker and queue manager functions for the JMS runtime component, available in any JVM that includes such a component in its component set.

JMXConnector—represents individual connectors between WebSphere administrative processes, available in all WebSphere JVMs.

JSP—represents a JavaServer Page portion of a J2EE application, available in any WebSphere JVM where the application is executing.

JVM—the control logic for the JVM in the managed process, available in every WebSphere JVM.

ListenerPort—control logic for the incoming port used by the WebSphere MessageListenerService, available in any JVM that includes such a component in its component set.

MailProvider—represents the provider library for a JavaMail resource provider, available in any JVM within the configuration scope of that resource.

MessageDrivenBean—represents any J2EE 1.3 MessageDrivenBean portion of a J2EE application, available in any WebSphere JVM where the application is executing.

Module—parent MBean for J2EE application component parts, available in any WebSphere JVM where the application is executing.

NameServer—represents the name server control functions, available in all WebSphere JVMs.

NodeAgent—represents the control interface to the Node Agent server, available only in the Node Agent JVM.

NodeSync—configuration synchronization logic that executes against the remote node repository, available only in the Node Agent JVM.

NotificationService—control logic for the service that propagates JMX notifications, available in every WebSphere JVM.

ORB—represents the CORBA Object Request Broker component, available in all WebSphere JVMs.

Perf—the performance metrics management interface, available in every WebSphere JVM.

PluginCfgGenerator—logic to control the generation of the configuration file to be used by the Web Server plug-in, available in administrative JVMs.

PmiRmJmxService—control logic for PMI Request Metric service, available in every WebSphere JVM.

RasLoggingService—control logic for the logging functions within the JVM, available in every WebSphere JVM.

ResourceAdapter—represents the provider library for a JCA resource adapter, available in any JVM within the configuration scope of that resource.

ResourceAdapterModule—represents the embedded JCA resource portion of a J2EE application, available in any WebSphere JVM where the application is executing.

SecurityAdmin—represents the management interface for the Security system, available in every WebSphere JVM.

Server—represents the process control elements for any WebSphere logical server JVM.

Servlet—represents the Servlet portion of a J2EE application, available in any WebSphere JVM where the application is executing.

SessionBean—represents the Session Bean EJB portion of a J2EE application, available in any WebSphere JVM where the application is executing.

SessionManager—control logic for application session state management, available in any Application Server JVM.

StatefulSessionBean—represents the Stateful Session Bean portion of a J2EE application, available in any WebSphere JVM where the application is executing.

StatelessSessionBean—represents the Stateless Session Bean portion of a J2EE application, available in any WebSphere JVM where the application is executing.

SystemMetrics—interface to retrieve platform specific system statistics, only available in the Node Agent JVM.

ThreadPool—represents individual thread pool sets within the JVM, available in all WebSphere JVMs.

TraceService—the service for controlling trace behavior in a process, available in all WebSphere JVMs.

Transaction—represents individual transactions, available in all WebSphere JVMs.

TransactionService—the service for managing individual Transactions, available in all WebSphere JVMs.

URLProvider—represents the resource provider library for URL resources.

WAS40DataSource—represents a legacy WebSphere 4 JDBC DataSource, as opposed to a WebSphere 5 DataSource configuration.

WebContainer—represents the Container environment for Web Applications, available in any JVM that includes such a container in its component set.

WebModule—represents the WebApp portion of a J2EE application, available in any WebSphere JVM where the application is executing.

WLMAppServer—interface for retrieving Workload Management statistics from a Server, available in any JVM participating in workload balancing.

WMQQueueDefiner—control logic to query and update a WebSphere MQ Queue, available in administrative JVMs.

WSGW—management interface for WebServices Gateway component, available in any JVM executing the WebServices Gateway feature.

INDIVIDUAL MBEAN DOCUMENTATION

Each WebSphere runtime MBean may have attributes, operations, and notifications that it exposes for administrative logic to control. The complete documentation for each MBean supplied with WebSphere is installed and available with the product in a directory under the main install directory.

Under the main install directory for the product, there is a directory named web. And under that directory is another directory named mbeanDocs. In the mbeanDocs directory are several html files, one for each MBean supplied with WebSphere. There is also an *index.html* file that ties all of the individual MBean files together in a top-level navigation tree. If you open the *index.html* file in your browser, you will see an top-level page similar to Figure B.1.

Clicking on any one of the MBeans from the navigation list in the left-hand frame of the index page will take you to the page that contains the detailed documentation for that particular MBean, as shown in Figure B.2.

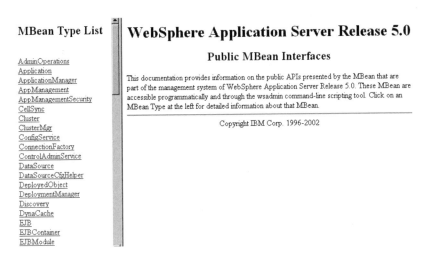

Figure B.1
WebSphere JMX MBean index.

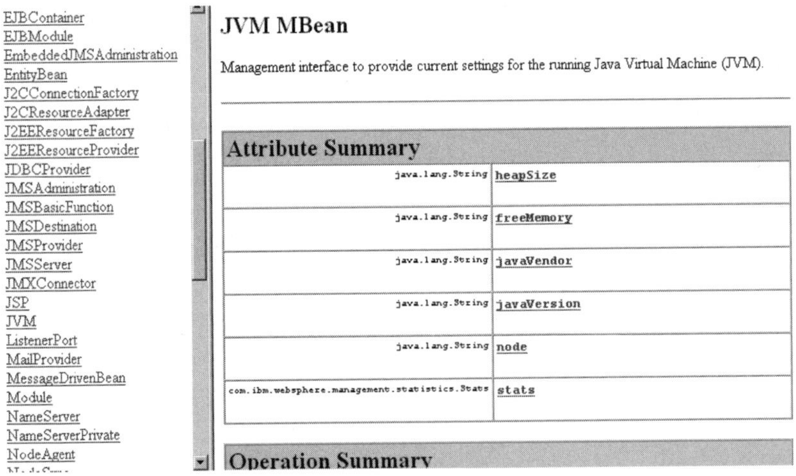

Figure B.2
WebSphere JVM MBean documentation.

WebSphere Version 5 Configuration Models

This Appendix provides details of each of the WebSphere configuration model classes and their attributes. This information is essential when automating the process of configuring components of WebSphere Version 5. Full documentation of all of the WebSphere configuration objects is available in an html table that is installed with each copy of the WebSphere product. Instructions for accessing the configuration documentation shipped with WebSphere are included at the end of this Appendix.

OVERVIEW OF CONFIGURATION MODELS

The configuration model for WebSphere Application Server Version 5 is large and complex. When viewing the XML data in the various configuration files, you can discern relationships between the configuration objects. The illustrations and tables in this appendix attempt to provide an alternative visualization of the configuration models and their associations. Understanding these relationships between configuration objects is essential when writing `wsadmin` scripts or Java programs that perform configuration functions.

For instance, Figure C.1 shows the relationship between the top-level Server configuration object and the list of its services and component elements that can be seen in the *server.xml* configuration file.

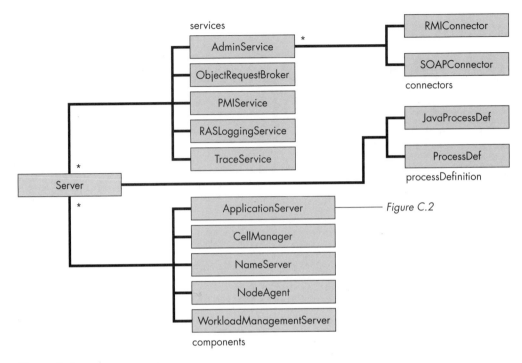

Figure C.1
Top-level Server configuration relationships.

Not all of the services and components that are shown in Figure C.1 are present in each *server.xml* file, but relationships between the top-level Server class and any of the contained configuration objects remain consistent for all server configuration files.

For instance, the following excerpt from the *server.xml* file shows the top-level Server configuration object containing three services: PMIService, AdminService, and TraceService; as well as two components: NameServer and ApplicationServer. A normal *server.xml* file contains several layers of nested configuration objects, but this modified illustration highlights how the structure in the XML matches the structure in Figure C.1.

```
<process:Server ... xmi:id="Server_1" name="server1">
  ...
  <services xmi:type="pmiservice:PMIService" xmi:id="PMIService_1"
enable="false" />
  <services xmi:type="adminservice:AdminService"
xmi:id="AdminService_1" enable="true" ...>
    ...
  </services>
  <services xmi:type="traceservice:TraceService"
xmi:id="TraceService_1" enable="true" ...>
```

```
   ...
</services>
   ...
<components xmi:type="namingserver:NameServer" xmi:id="NameServer_1">
   ...
</components>
<components xmi:type="applicationserver:ApplicationServer"
xmi:id="ApplicationServer_1" ...>
   ...
</components>
```

Each of the services and components that make up the list contained by the Server configuration object can itself contain internal configuration objects. One example is the ApplicationServer configuration component. As shown in Figure C.2, the ApplicationServer can contain a rich variety of services and components of its own.

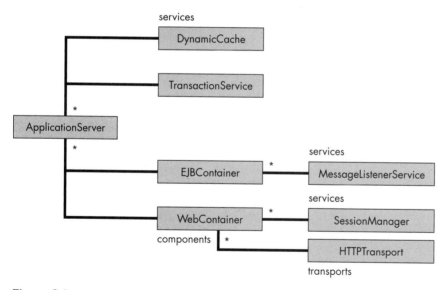

Figure C.2
ApplicationServer configuration relationships.

CONFIGURATION MODEL TABLES

The html tables that are included with WebSphere Version 5 show all of the properties associated with each configuration class. This complete documentation for each configuration class is installed and available with the product in a directory under the main install directory.

Under the main install directory for the product, there is a directory named web. And under that directory is another directory named configDocs. In the configDocs directory are several subdirectories, one for each configuration package in the model. There is also an *index.html* file that ties all of the individual configuration packages together in a top-level navigation tree. If you open the *index.html* file in your browser, you will see an top-level page similar to Figure C.3.

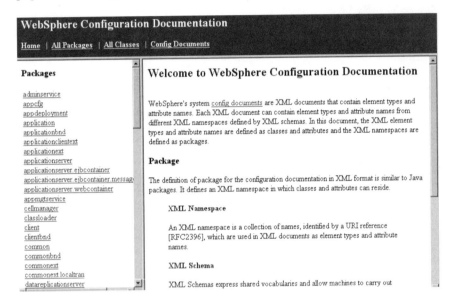

Figure C.3
WebSphere configuration tables index.

Clicking on any package name in the navigation list in the left-hand frame of the index page will take you to the page that contains the detailed documentation for that particular configuration package, as shown in Figure C.4.

For instance, if you look in the table for the TransactionService, you will see that it supports four properties:

- transactionLogDirectory
- totalTranLifetimeTimeout
- clientInactivityTimeout
- enableLoggingForHeuristicReporting

The semantics and valid values for each property are described in the table. You can use the diagrams to understand the object-level navigation through the configuration model and the tables provide the details of the configuration properties for the object once you navigate to

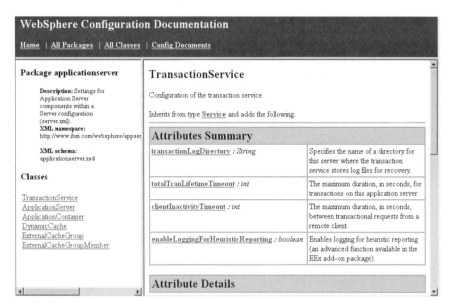

Figure C.4
WebSphere TransactionService configuration package documentation.

it. In the tables, properties with names that end with the special "at" (@) character imply that that property is actually a reference to some other configuration object within the configuration data. Properties with names that end with an asterisk (*) imply that the property is actually a list of other configuration objects.

Another area of configuration that is more complex than most others is the configuration data for J2EE resources. Figure C.5 shows the top-level configuration objects that can be found in the *resources.xml* file under any of the Cell, Node, or Server scopes. The term scope means the directory in the configuration tree that holds the *resources.xml* file.

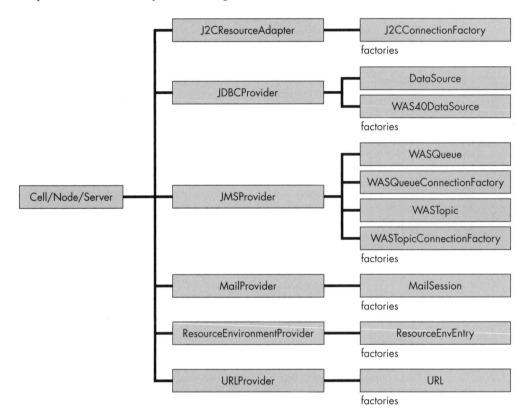

Figure C.5
Resource configuration relationships.

The Security configuration model can also be difficult to follow without a picture of the classes and their relationships. Figure C.6 illustrates the many security related configuration classes and their connections with one another.

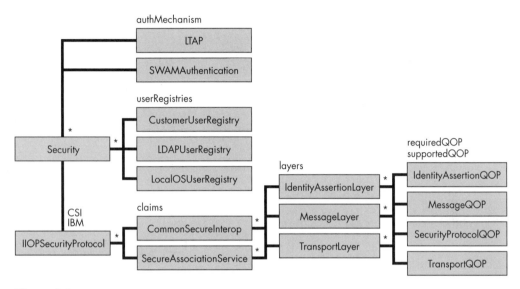

Figure C.6
Security configuration relationships.

Another view of the configuration tables that can be especially helpful is to start from the XML configuration file in the WebSphere repository and drill down from the root object of the configuration data in that file. You can access this view by clicking on the "Config Documents" link in the header of the html configuration index, as illustrated in Figure C.7.

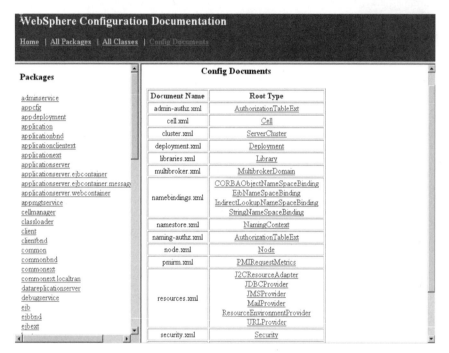

Figure C.7
Document oriented view of the WebSphere configuration tables.

Click on the "VirtualHost" link in the table of configuration documents in the right hand pane and you will be taken to the page for the root object of that configuration file. Figure C.8 illustrates the root object of the *virtualhost.xml* file.

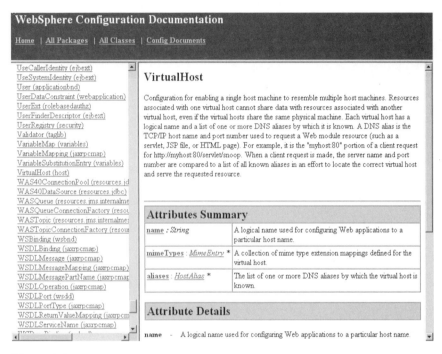

Figure C.8
Root object of the virtualhosts.xml configuration documentation.

CD-ROM Contents

This book includes a CD-ROM that contains the trial version of WebSphere Application Server Version 5.1 for Microsoft Windows operating systems. The trial version installation image does not include the IBM HTTP Server (IHS) nor does it include the Embedded Messaging Server for WebSphere 5.1. A trial version of the IHS Web server that matches the trial version of the application server can be downloaded from the IBM Web site. During installation of the trial version of the application server, you may see panels that refer to either the IHS Web server or the IBM Embedded Messaging. However, once you have completed the installation (following instructions in the next section), you will find that neither IHS nor the Embedded Messaging feature are actually installed. This is a limitation of this free trial version of the application server product.

The system requirements to support the trial version of WebSphere contained on the CD-ROM include:

- Windows 2000 Server SP3 or SP4, or Windows 2003
- Intel Pentium processor (or equivalent) at 500 MHz or faster, or AMD 64-bit Opteron (32-bit support only)
- Minimum 596 MB free disk space for installation (includes SDK)
- Minimum 256 MB physical memory; 512 MB recommended
- CD-ROM drive

INSTALLING THE TRIAL VERSION OF WEBSPHERE FROM THE CD-ROM

Begin the installation process by inserting the CD into your CD-ROM drive. The WebSphere Application Server product installation wizard should automatically run. The Java Virtual Machine will load and the Installation Wizard program welcome page will display as shown in Figure D.1.

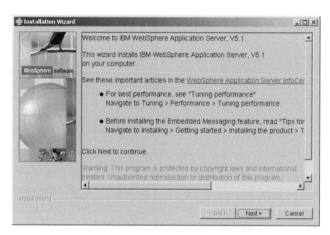

Figure D.1
WebSphere product installation wizard welcome page.

Click the "Next" button. The wizard will display a page where you have the choice of Full or Custom install features (Figure D.2). Custom install allows you to select just the features you want, as shown in Figure D.3. You can hold the mouse over the custom install feature selection checkbox in order to see an explanation of the feature in the description field at bottom of the custom install page.

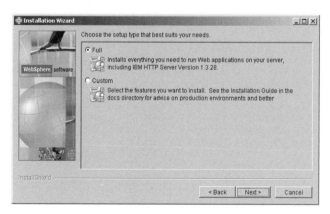

Figure D.2
Full or custom installation selection page.

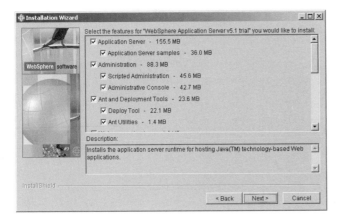

Figure D.3
WebSphere product custom installation page.

Assume that you select "Full" installation—click the "Next" button. The wizard proceeds to the panel for suggested directories to place product files (see Figure D.4). Note that only the "WebSphere Application Server v5.1 trial" directory will be used, since neither IBM HTTP Server nor Embedded Messaging Server are available from the trial install image. You can just take the suggested location, or overwrite, or Browse to select a different directory for the application server product installation. Click the "Next" button.

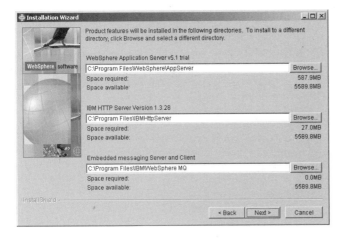

Figure D.4
WebSphere product install directory page.

The installation wizard goes to the page that allows you to define the name of the node and host to be used, as shown in Figure D.5.

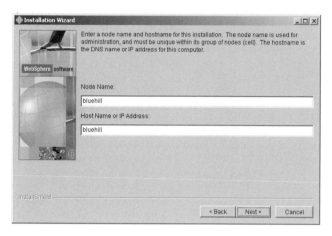

Figure D.5
WebSphere node and host name setting page.

The default value for both node and host name is the short IP hostname for the computer on which WebSphere is being installed. You can keep the suggested default, or modify either value. Click the "Next" button.

The wizard proceeds to the panel that allows you to register the application server as a Windows operating system service (Figure D.6). Note that even though the page also mentions the IHS Web server, this is not available on the trial CD so no Web server will be registered. An important limitation for the userID used to register the application server as an operating system service is that the user must have administrator authority on the computer system. Click the "Next" button.

Figure D.6
Register WebSphere Application Server as a Windows service.

Once past the page for registering as a Windows operating system service, the wizard goes to a page for final review and confirmation of features to be installed (as shown by Figure D.7).

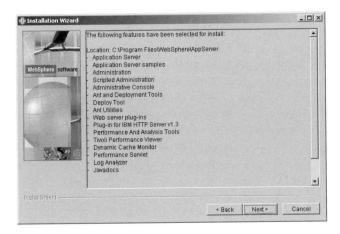

Figure D.7
Install Wizard confirmation page.

Click the "Next" button. The Install Wizard places files on the disk. Figure D.8 shows the page containing the progress indicator as the install process proceeds. Be very patient! Depending on the speed of your machine and available disk space, the installation for the trial version of WebSphere Version 5.1 can take several minutes.

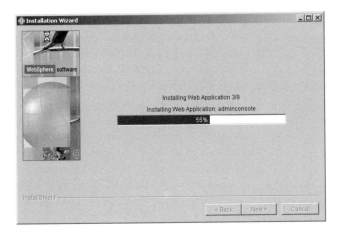

Figure D.8
Progress indicator as WebSphere install wizard runs.

After the Install Wizard is complete, the First Steps Wizard will launch. Figure D.9 shows the First Steps Wizard. You can do several things from this wizard, including launch the application server or access the online product information center.

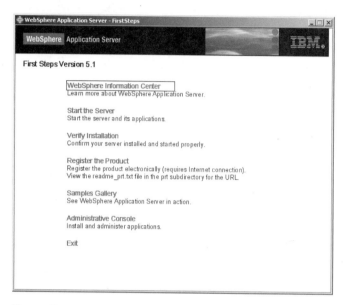

Figure D.9
WebSphere First Steps wizard.

You are done, you can remove the CD-ROM and proceed to use the trial version of Web-Sphere 5.1.

Index _____

References to tables are indicated with a *t*; references to figures are indicated with an *f*; and references to code listings are indicated with a *c*.

A

addNode program, 5, 36–39
AdminApp, 111–112
    commands, 112t–113t
    edit applications, 113, 118–119
    install applications, 113–114
        options, 114t–118t
    uninstall applications, 121
    update applications, 113, 119–121
AdminClient interface, 238–239
    administrative client program (build/run),
        269–270
AdminConfig, 97–98
    commands, 98t–100t
    create configuration objects step, 105–110
    identify configuration type and attributes step,
        100, 101–102
    query configuration objects step, 100, 103–105
    save configuration step, 111
AdminControl, 121
    commands, 122t–123t
    list attributes/operations of running MBeans
        step, 123, 125
    live running objects, 121, 291–295
    modify attributes on running MBeans step, 123,
        128–129
    perform operations on running MBeans step,
        123, 125–128
    query running MBeans step, 123–125
Administration
    common scenarios, 228
        install/start application on new cluster, 229,
            229c–234c

        install/start application on new server, 226,
            226c–229c
    documentation, 271
    programming interfaces, 235. *See also* Application
        tion management; Configuration man-
        agement; JMX; Operational
        management
    sample tasks (Web site), 270
    Version 4 vs. Version 5, 5–6, 6t
Administration tools, 6–7. *See also* Administrative
    Console; z/OS additional administrative
    features
    Command-line tools, 7
    Java Programming API (administrative program-
        ming interface), 10–11
    Scripting tool, 9–10, 87. *See also* wsadmin tool
Administrative commands, 33–34, 33t. *See also* Other
    commands
    backup/restore commands, 41
        backup configuration, 41–42
        restore configuration, 42
    network deployment commands, 36
        CleanupNode, 40
        defederation, 39–40
        federation, 37–39
        SyncNode, 40–41
    server management commands
        server status, 36
        starting servers, 34–35
        stopping servers, 35–36
Administrative Console, 7–9, 8f, 29, 50f
    accessing, 56–57
        frame areas, 56–57, 57f
    design objectives, 49

313

environment, 49
installation, 50–51, 51f
scale objectives, 50
security objectives, 49–50
settings, 57
   accessibility mode, 61
   configuration/operations management sep-
      aration, 62
   filter criteria entry panel, 59, 59f
   global preferences, 57–58, 58f
   preferences, 58–59, 59f
   role-based task filtering, 62
   scope, 59–61, 60f, 61f
tasks (common), 62
   home, 65
   login, 63–65, 63f, 64f
   logout, 68
   save, 66–67, 66f, 67f
   security cookie timeouts, 68
   session timeouts, 68
Administrative Console problem determination, 82
   status tray, 83, 83f
   troubleshooting tasks, 84
      configuration problems, 85–86
      logs/trace, 84–85, 85f
      unavailable server status, 84
Administrative Console task reference, 69
   manage applications; Enterprise Applications,
      74–75
   manage resources, 75–76
   manage security; global security, 77–78, 77f
   manage servers, 69
      Application Servers create/delete/edit,
         69–72, 69f, 71f, 72f
      clusters (Network Deployment), 73–74,
         73f, 74f
   manage system administration, 80
      Cell task, 80
      Console Groups task, 82
      Console Users task, 82
      Deployment Manager task, 80–81
      Node Agent, 81–82
      Nodes task, 81, 81f
   other environment elements (Network Deploy-
      ment), 78
      shared libraries (jars), 79–80
      virtual hosts, 79
      Web server plug-ins updates, 79
      WebSphere variables, 79
tasks, 51, 52t–56t

Administrative scripting. *See* wsadmin tool
Administrative scripting task reference, 129–130.
    See also Online interactive help
   manage application servers. *See also* Configura-
      tion coding case examples (Adminis-
      trative scripting/application servers)
      create/delete application server definition,
         131
      listing application servers, 130
      start/stop application servers, 130–131
      view/modify application server run time,
         150–152
   manage clusters (Network Deployment), 155
      create new cluster definition, 156–157
      delete cluster definition, 157
      immediate stop cluster, 156
      list clusters, 155
      start/ripple start cluster, 156
   manage Enterprise applications, 157. *See also*
      Configuration coding case examples
      (Administrative scripting/applica-
      tions)
      configuration modification, 163
      export application, 163
      export DDL, 163
      install application/examples, 159,
         159c–161c
      list of installed applications, 157
      start/stop application, 158–159
      update application/examples, 162, 162c
   manage JMS servers (Network Deployment)
      list JMS servers, 152
      modify JMS server configuration, 153–154
      modify JMS server run time, 155
      start/stop JMS servers, 153
   manage other environment elements, 199
      internal replication domains, 202,
         202c–205c
      naming/CORBA naming service groups,
         209, 210c–211c
      naming/CORBA naming service users,
         207, 207c–209c
      naming/namespace binding, 205, 205c–207c
      shared libraries, 201, 202c
      virtual host, 199, 199c–200c
      Web server plug-in, 199
      WebSphere variables, 200, 200c–201c
   manage resources, 168
      generic JMS providers, 170, 170c–171c
      JDBC providers, 168–169, 169c–170c

mail providers, 176, 176c–178f

resource adapters, 181, 181c–182c

resource environment providers, 178, 178c–179c

URL providers, 180, 180c–181c

WebSphere JMS providers, 171–172, 172c–174c

WebSphere MQ JMS providers, 174, 174f–176f

manage security. *See* Security management (Administrative scripting task reference)

manage system administration, 211. *See also* Nodes/tasks (Administrative scripting)

cell, 211, 212c

deployment manager, 212

manage system administration/troubleshooting, 217

configuration problems, 220

logs/traces, 217–220

PMI request metrics, 221

Agent, 14

Ant, 45

usage automating WebSphere commands, 45–47

AppDeploymentController, 261

task attributes, 258t

task names, 258t–261t

Application Assembly Tool, 256

Application management

application management support, 263

AppManagementProxy, 263–264, 264f

editing applications, 268

installing applications, 265–266, 265t, 267f

redeploying (updating) configurations, 269

session sharing, 265

starting/stopping applications, 269

uninstalling applications, 267

application preparation, 256–257, 256f

create AppDeploymentController, 256

manipulate task data, 262

obtain AppDeployment Task Instances, 257, 258t–261t, 261

save EAR file/obtain install options, 263

Application Servers, 1, 69. *See also* Administration; Base Application Server; Network Deployment

architecture, 13

basic packages, 2

configuration repository, 26

create/delete definition via Administrative scripting, 131

create/delete/edit via Administrative console, 69–72, 69f, 71f, 72f

list, 130

modify configuration via Administrative scripting, 131. *See also* Configuration coding case examples (Administrative scripting)

start/stop, 130–131

Attribute lists, 250

collection attributes, 250–252

complex attributes, 250

reference attributes, 252

simple attributes, 250

`attributes` command, 101–102, 125

Automatic Synchronization checkbox, 82

B

`backupConfig` command, 41–42

Base Application Server administration, 13

administrative security, 18

application deployment, 17

main tasks, 81f

Application Server internals, 14, 15f

configuration vs. run-time control, 16

z/OS environment considerations, 15

configuration, 16–17

run-time control, 17

Base Application Server Package, 2–3, 3f

Administrative Console, 8

BSF (Bean Scripting Framework), 89

C

Cell, 3, 80

directory/subdirectory, 26–29

management (Administrative scripting), 211

configuration coding example, 212c

and resource management, 75–76

structure, 19–20, 19f

building a cell, 20

Classloader policy/mode, coding examples, 164

`CleanupNode` (Network Deployment), 40

Clusters, 155

Cluster, 5, 73–74

management of. *See* Administrative scripting task reference

Commands. *See* Administrative commands; Other commands

`completeObjectName` command, 124–125

ConfigService. *See* Configuration management
Configuration management, configuration objects, 244–245
Configuration. *See also* AdminConfig; Configuration management; Configuration models
changes, 66–67
and AdminApp, 163
problems, 85–86, 220–221
repository, 26, 59
directory structure, 26–29
document sample, 31–32
files/content/structure, 29, 29t–31t
vs. run-time management, 16
scope, 59–61, 60f, 61f
synchronization, 24–25, 24f
validation, 226
Configuration coding case examples (Administrative scripting/application), 163
classloader mode, 163
classloader policy, 164
connector modules, 168
EJB modules, 166, 166c–167c
libraries, 165, 165c–166c
map modules to application servers, 166
session management, 164, 164c–165c
starting weight, 163
target mappings, 165
Web modules, 167
Configuration coding case examples (Administrative scripting/application servers)
configure administration service, 143c–144c
configure classloader, 149–150
configure custom properties, 142c–143c
configure custom service, 145c–146c
configure debugging service, 145c
configure dynamic cache, 138c–139c
configure EJB container, 137c–138c
configure end points, 148–149
configure HTTP transport for Web container, 133c–134c
configure message listener service, 140c–141c
configure Object Request Broker service, 141c–142c
configure performance monitoring service, 147c–148c
configure process definition, 146c–147c
configure session manager for Web container, 134c–137c
configure thread pool properties for Web container, 132c–133c

configure trace service, 144c
configure transaction properties, 132c
Configuration management, 244
configuration objects
identification, 247–248
location, 248–249
configuration objects/usage, 249
creating, 252–255
deleting, 255
modifying, 249–250
using attribute lists, 250–252
configuration service interfaces (ConfigService), 245–247, 246f
deployment options, 269
grouping (session), 246
session sharing, 265
vs. operations management, 62
Configuration models, 297
ApplicationServer configuration, 299
table documentation, 299, 304–305
J2EE resources/configuration data, 302
main install directory, 300–301
Security configuration model, 303
top-level server configuration relationships, 298–299
Configurator layer of privilege (administrative security), 18
Connectors, 14, 21–22. *See also* RMI/IIOP (JMX connector); SOAP/HTTP(S) (JMX connector)
case example, 168
coding example, 168
Console. *See* Administrative Console
Console Groups, 82
create/createUsingTemplate commands, 105
examples, 105–106
generic attributes, 109–111
nested attributes, 106–107
nested list attributes, 107–109
reference attributes, 109
simple attributes, 106
createConfigData method, 252–254

D

Deployment Manager
configuration, 212
node and document storage, 26
program, 4
run time, 212
task and DMgr management agent, 80–81

Document storage, 26
Documentation (WebSphere), 271. *See also* Configuration models/table documentation
 configuration objects, 297
 individual MBean documentation, 295–296

E

EAR file, 17, 18f, 25–26, 256f
 directory structure, 266t
EARExpander command, 42–43
edit/editInteractive commands, 118, 163
EJB modules, coding example, 166, 166c–167c
Enterprise Applications, 74–75
Event Notifications
 handling, 243
 registering, 242–243

F

File Synchronization subtask, 82
File transfer service, 22, 23f
Full Administrator layer of privilege (administrative
 security), 18

G

getAttribute/getAttributes commands,
 128–129, 249–250
getid command, 103–104

H

handleNotification method, 243–244
Help. *See* Online interactive help
Home, 65, 65f

I

install/installInteractive commands, 113
Instrumentation, 14
Internal replication domains, 202, 202c–205c
invoke command, 125–128

J

Jars (libraries) shared, 79–80
JCA (J2EE Connector Architecture) resource adapters, 16

JDBC (Java DataBase Connectivity) datasources, 16
 configuration coding example, 168–169,
  169c–170c
 and provider creation, 254–255
JMS (Java Message Service) queues, 16
JMS provider
 generic configuration coding example, 170,
  170c–171c
 WebSphere configuration coding example,
  171–172, 172c–174c
 WebSphere MQ configuration coding example,
  174, 174c–176c
JMS servers, management of. *See* Administrative
 scripting task reference
JMX, 235–236
 additional information sources, 270
 architecture, 236f
 layers of function, 14, 235–236
  and distributed events/notification, 22
  JMX connectors, 21–22
 in WebSphere, 236–237, 237f
JNDI name, 75–76
Jython syntax, Scripting tool support of, 9, 88

L

Libraries (jars)
 /shared, 79–80, 201–202
 coding example, 165, 165c–166c
list command, 104
Login, 63–65, 63f, 64f
Logout, 68
Logs/trace, 84–85, 85f, 217, 217c–220c, 225–226

M

Mail provider/mail session, configuration coding example, 176, 176c–177c
MBean (Managed Bean) interface, 14, 235, 241
 accessing, 239–241
 commands for help, 224
 documentation, 295–296
 getting/setting attributes, 241–242
 invoking operations, 242
 MBean server, 236
 ObjectName, 14, 22
 working with (steps), 123. *See also* AdminControl; Run time MBeans (Version 5)
message command, 224–225
Monitor layer of privilege (administrative security), 18

N

Network Deployment administration, 18–19
  administrative agents, 20–21
  application deployment, 267f
  cell structure, 19–20, 19f
    building a cell, 20
  distributed administrative services, 21
    application installation/distribution, 25–26
    configuration synchronization, 24–25, 24f
    distributed JMX events, 22
    file transfer service, 22, 23f
    JMX connectors, 21–22
    process discovery, 21, 21f
    request routing, 22
Network Deployment Package, 2, 3–5, 4f. *See also*
    Deployment Manager program
    Administrative Console, 8
Node agents, 20, 81–82
  node agent functions, 20–21
  and NodeSync logic, 24–25, 24f
  tasks (Administrative scripting), 215
    modify configuration, 216–217
    restart, 215–216
    stop, 215
Nodes, 3, 19–20. *See also* Administrative commands/
    network deployment commands
  node defederation process, 39–40
  node federation process, 36–39
  relationships (example), 254f
  subdirectories, 27–29
  task, 81, 81f
  tasks (Administrative scripting), 212
    list, 212
    modify configuration, 213–215
    remove, 213
    stop, 213
    sychronize/full synchronize, 213

O

ObjectName
  and accessing MBeans, 239–241
  and ConfigService, 247–248
    key properties, 248t
  key property names, 239t
  and request routing, 22
  string, 123–124
  template, 124
  with wildcard key properties, 240f

Online interactive help, 221
  commands for help on running MBeans, 224
  examples, 222–223
  Help scripting object, 223
  and message command, 224–225
Operational Management
  accessing MBeans, 239–241
  AdminClient interface, 238–239
  using event notifications, 242–244
  using MBeans, 241–242
operations command, 125
Operations model integration (z/OS), 276–281
Operator layer of privilege (administrative security), 18
Other commands, 42. *See also* Administrative com-
    mands
  adding WebSphere instances, 43–45
  EAKExpander, 42–43
  WebSphere commands automation via Ant,
    45–47

P

Process discovery, 21
  flow, 21f
Process model integration (z/OS), 273–276

Q

QueryNames command, 123–124

R

redeployApplication API, 269
removeNode, 39–40
Resource adaptors, coding example, 181, 181c–182c
Resource environment provider/entry, coding exam-
    ple, 178, 178c–179c
restoreConfig command, 42
RMI/IIOP (JMX connector), 14, 20–21
Run-time MBeans (Version 5), 291–295
Run-time vs. configuration management, 16

S

Security cookie timeouts, 68
Security issues. *See also* Security management (Ad-
    ministrative scripting task reference); z/OS
    additional administrative features/security
    model integration

administrative security, 18
    layers of privilege, 18, 62
and console design, 49–50
Global Security configuration task, 77–78, 77f
security settings storage, 16
Security management (Administrative scripting task reference), 182
authentication protocol
    CSIv2
        inbound authentication, 192, 192c–194c
        inbound transport, 195, 195c–196c
        outbound authentication, 194, 194c–195c
        outbound transport, 196, 196c–197c
    SAS
        inbound transport, 197, 197c–198c
        outbound transport, 198, 198c
configuring SSL, 183, 183c–185c
global security configuration coding example, 182, 182c–183c
J2C authentication data, 191, 191c–192c
JAAS; application logins, 189, 190c–191c
LTPA authentication mechanism/coding example, 185, 185c–187c
user registry
    custom, 189
    LDAP, 187–188, 188c–189c
    local OS, 187
Servers, 69. *See also* Application Servers
    creating, 252–254, 254f
Session management, 164, 164c–165c
    session object, 246
    session timeouts, 68
setAttribute/setAttributes commands, 128–129, 251
SOAP/HTTP(S) (JMX connector), 14, 21–22
Starting weight, 163–164
startServer/startNode/startManager/commands, 34–35
Status tray, 83, 83f
stopServer/stopNode/stopManager/commands, 35–36
syncNode, 40–41

T

Target mappings, 165
Tcl syntax, Scripting tool support of, 9

Trace/logs, 84–85, 85f, 225–226
Troubleshooting. *See also* wsadmin/problem determination
    CleanupNode (Network Deployment), 40
    syncNode, 40–41
    tasks, 84
        configuration problems, 85–86
        logs/traces, 84–85, 85f
        unavailable server status, 84
    via Administrative Console, 82–83
    via Administrative scripting, 217–221
types command, 101

U

uninstall command, 121
URL providers, coding example, 180, 180c–181c

V

Virtual Hosts, 79, 199–200

W

Web modules, coding example, 167, 167c
Web service plug-ins, 79, 199
WebSphere Application Server. *See* Application Server
WebSphere instances, 43–45
WebSphere variables, 79, 200–201
Workload Management (WLM) model integration (z/OS), 281–283
wsadmin tool, 7, 87–88. *See also* Administration/common scenarios; Administrative scripting task reference
    applications management. *See* AdminApp
    batch mode, 10
    command mode, 10
    configuration management. *See* AdminConfig
    interactive mode, 9
    invoking, 89
    live run-time components management. *See* AdminControl
    options, 89–91
        syntax examples, 91–92
    problem determination
        configuration validation, 226
        run-time long, 225–226
        trace log, 225

properties, 92–93, 93t–95t
    sample file, 95c–97c
usage, 10
`wsinadmin AdminApp` command, 26
`wsinstance` command, 43–45

Z

z/OS additional administrative features, 273
    operations model integration, 276–280
        control process JCL (BBO5ACR), 280
        servant process JCL, 280
        STOP BBOS001, 281

`STOP` command, 280–281
process model integration, 273–276
security model integration, 283
    global security features, 283–284
    ICSF authentication mechanism, 288
    JSSE Ciphers, 286
    local OS, 289
    SAF key ring, 287–288
    SSL repertoires, 284–285, 286–287
    zSAS configuration, 289–290
Workload Management (WLM) model integration, 281–283

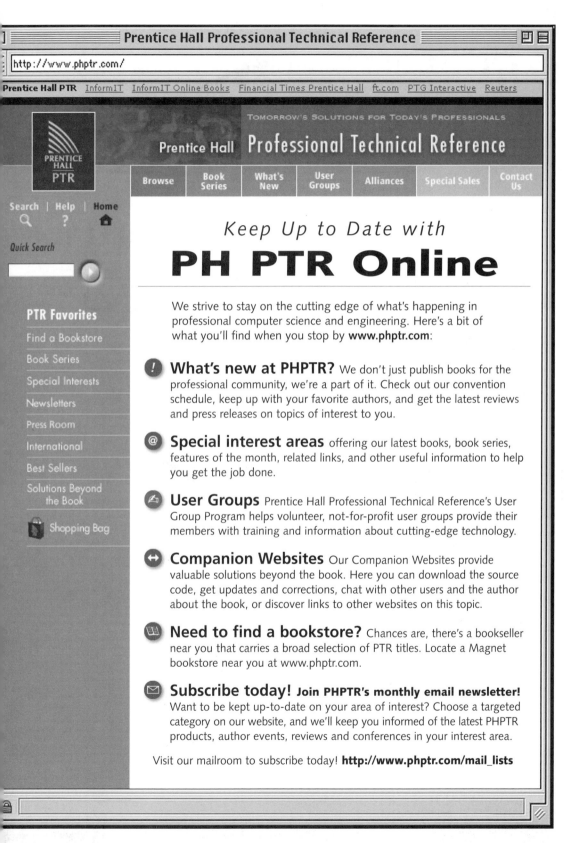

Prentice Hall Professional Technical Reference

http://www.phptr.com/

Prentice Hall PTR   InformIT   InformIT Online Books   Financial Times Prentice Hall   ft.com   PTG Interactive   Reuters

PRENTICE HALL PTR

TOMORROW'S SOLUTIONS FOR TODAY'S PROFESSIONALS

Prentice Hall **Professional Technical Reference**

Browse | Book Series | What's New | User Groups | Alliances | Special Sales | Contact Us

Search | Help | Home

Quick Search

PTR Favorites

Find a Bookstore

Book Series

Special Interests

Newsletters

Press Room

International

Best Sellers

Solutions Beyond the Book

Shopping Bag

Keep Up to Date with

PH PTR Online

We strive to stay on the cutting edge of what's happening in professional computer science and engineering. Here's a bit of what you'll find when you stop by **www.phptr.com**:

What's new at PHPTR? We don't just publish books for the professional community, we're a part of it. Check out our convention schedule, keep up with your favorite authors, and get the latest reviews and press releases on topics of interest to you.

Special interest areas offering our latest books, book series, features of the month, related links, and other useful information to help you get the job done.

User Groups Prentice Hall Professional Technical Reference's User Group Program helps volunteer, not-for-profit user groups provide their members with training and information about cutting-edge technology.

Companion Websites Our Companion Websites provide valuable solutions beyond the book. Here you can download the source code, get updates and corrections, chat with other users and the author about the book, or discover links to other websites on this topic.

Need to find a bookstore? Chances are, there's a bookseller near you that carries a broad selection of PTR titles. Locate a Magnet bookstore near you at www.phptr.com.

Subscribe today! Join PHPTR's monthly email newsletter! Want to be kept up-to-date on your area of interest? Choose a targeted category on our website, and we'll keep you informed of the latest PHPTR products, author events, reviews and conferences in your interest area.

Visit our mailroom to subscribe today! **http://www.phptr.com/mail_lists**

CD-ROM Warranty

Prentice Hall PTR warrants the enclosed CD-ROM to be free of defects in materials and faulty workmanship under normal use for a period of ninety days after purchase (when purchased new). If a defect is discovered in the CD-ROM during this warranty period, a replacement CD-ROM can be obtained at no charge by sending the defective CD-ROM, postage prepaid, with proof of purchase to:

Disc Exchange
Pearson Technology Group
75 Arlington Street, Suite 300
Boston, MA 02116
Email: AWPro@aw.com

Prentice Hall PTR makes no warranty or representation, either expressed or implied, with respect to this software, its quality, performance, merchantability, or fitness for a particular purpose. In no event will Addison-Wesley, its distributors, or dealers be liable for direct, indirect, special, incidental, or consequential damages arising out of the use or inability to use the software. The exclusion of implied warranties is not permitted in some states. Therefore, the above exclusion may not apply to you. This warranty provides you with specific legal rights. There may be other rights that you may have that vary from state to state. The contents of this CD-ROM are intended for personal use only.